Ithamar Theodor is Associate Professor of Hindu Studies at Zefat Academic College, Safed, Israel, and is concurrently Lecturer in Hindu-Jewish Studies at the University of Haifa. He is a graduate of the University of Oxford, a Life Member of Clare Hall in the University of Cambridge and has been an Adjunct Assistant Professor at the Chinese University of Hong Kong. His first book *Exploring the Bhagavad Gita: Philosophy, Structure and Meaning* (2010) was a *Choice* Outstanding Academic Title for 2011 and winner in 2013 of the Dharma Academy of North America (DANAM) Book Award for Excellence in Indic Studies.

'The influence of the *Bhagavata Purana* on what has come to be known as Hinduism is paralleled only by the epic *Ramayana*. Yet it is, at first glance, a thematically complicated and stylistically unusual text. Building on his work analyzing the narrative structure of the *Bhagavad Gita*, Ithamar Theodor expertly argues that the combining of all the elements contained in the *Bhagavata* was a conscious harmonizing of two distinct orthodox scholastic traditions: the philosophical one stemming from the *Upanishads*, and the literary aesthetical one drawing from the *rasa* theory of *kavya* poetics. Theodor demonstrates how this confluence resulted in a theological masterpiece – not just stylistically in terms of harmonizing these various elements, but because of the unique theological motive of the text. He argues that one of the main agendas of the *Bhagavata* is to contrast impersonal liberation with personal liberation. With great erudition and an intimate knowledge of his material, Theodor expertly elucidates how each of the two intellectual streams noted above feed into one of these two possibilities respectively, and how the *Bhagavata* both contrasts and harmonizes these ultimate but distinct forms of liberation. This is a fascinating and groundbreaking work.'

– *Edwin Bryant, Professor of Hindu Religion and Philosophy, Rutgers University*

'The *Bhagavata Purana*, composed in eloquent Sanskrit about a thousand years ago, has subsequently become one of the principal sources of inspiration for Hindu traditions of devotion to Krishna as Supreme Being. In his carefully researched work, Ithamar Theodor takes us along a new path of interpretation, arguing systematically for an aesthetic understanding of the text as key, and showing in the process how apparent incompatibilities of its teaching – for example of both an impersonal and personal view of the Supreme Being – can be reconciled by this approach. In future, no meaningful comment about or study of the *Bhagavata Purana* can afford to neglect the illuminating argument of this book.'

– *Julius Lipner, FBA, Professor Emeritus of Hinduism and the Comparative Study of Religion, University of Cambridge*

THE 'FIFTH VEDA' OF HINDUISM

Poetry, Philosophy and Devotion in the Bhāgavata Purāṇa

ITHAMAR THEODOR

BLOOMSBURY ACADEMIC
LONDON • NEW YORK • OXFORD • NEW DELHI • SYDNEY

To my dear and loving parents
Rachel and Emanuel Theodor

BLOOMSBURY ACADEMIC
Bloomsbury Publishing Plc
50 Bedford Square, London, WC1B 3DP, UK
1385 Broadway, New York, NY 10018, USA

BLOOMSBURY, BLOOMSBURY ACADEMIC and the Diana
logo are trademarks of Bloomsbury Publishing Plc

First published in Great Britain by I.B. Tauris 2016
Paperback edition published by Bloomsbury Academic 2020

A catalogue record for this book is available from the British Library.

A catalog record for this book is available from the Library of Congress.

ISBN: HB: 978-1-7845-3199-7
PB: 978-0-7556-2731-8
ePDF: 978-0-8577-2574-5
eBook: 978-0-8577-3925-4

Series: Library of Modern Religion 49

Typeset by Garamond Three by OKS Prepress Services, Chennai, India

To find out more about our authors and books visit
www.bloomsbury.com and sign up for our newsletters.

CONTENTS

LIST OF TABLES

PREFACE

The *Bhāgavata Purāṇa* (*BhP*) is a somewhat mysterious treatise that has long puzzled me. It is *purāṇic* or epic in style, yet it has a unique character that can touch the heart of the reader in a way no other literature that I know of does. It certainly adheres to the *purāṇic*, *Vedāntic* and *Upaniṣadic* genres, but it has another, more personal, lyrical, perhaps poetic feature, which is somewhat difficult to identify. It seems as if this great *purāṇa* tries to say something beyond its direct contents, to further a change of heart which wouldn't necessarily be considered a religious conversion in the Judeo-Christian sense of the word, of sinners repenting and relinquishing their former non-religious or immoral way of life. Neither is this an expression of a *Vedāntic* enlightenment in the sense of realizing the inherent and all-pervading spirituality underlying one's entire existence. To my mind, reading, or rather hearing, the *BhP* is a kind of dramatic experience of a universal story, encompassing the entire realm of existence, but at the same time careful to maintain its dramatic framework. It seems that the *BhP* expresses its great *mahāvākya* already in its very first opening line, which reads *oṁ namo bhāgavate vāsudevāya*, translated as 'I offer my obeisance unto Śrī Kṛṣṇa, son of Vasudeva, who is the Supreme Person'. The entire *purāṇa* represents an attempt to echo, expand and comment on this statement, or perhaps to express just this very personal truth in a variety of philosophical and poetic ways. This work is an attempt to touch upon the *BhP*'s subtle, personal and poetic nature by highlighting its special structure combining the *Vedāntic* and poetic *rasa* traditions. Here is a verse that points to this unique combination (*BhP* 12.13.15):

sarva-vedānta-sāram hi śrī-bhāgavatam iṣyate
tad-rasāmṛta-tṛptasya nānyatra syād ratiḥ kvacit

> The *Bhāgavata Purāṇa* is considered the essence of the entire *Vedānta* tradition. As such, for one who is satisfied by tasting its nectar-like *rasa*, there does not exist any other delight elsewhere.

I wish to conclude the Preface by highlighting the importance of studying the *Bhāgavata Purāṇa*. As philosophy and theology may need to further develop a language fully appropriate to deal with the personal encounter between the human and the divine, I hope that this study will help readers understand how a particular religious tradition attempted to overcome this seemingly insurmountable gap, through gradual personal encounters with the divine, and how it engaged the best philosophical materials available at the time for this purpose. As I hope that this work will contribute to the study of comparative theology, I would like to follow R.C. Zaehner's vision:

> R.C. Zaehner thought that the study of comparative religion can aim at creating a symphony of faiths. This image accounts for the distinctness and individual value of each religious tradition but at the same time it can be made to tune in with the intended symphony. (Matilal, *Logical and Ethical Issues of Religious Belief*, pp. x–xi.)

I sincerely hope that this work will contribute, even in a minor way, towards the noble goal of creating a symphony of faiths as well as a symphony of philosophies of religion.

Ithamar Theodor, Zefat,
30 November 2014

ABBREVIATIONS

BRS	*Bhaktirasāmṛtasindhu*
BS	*Brahma Sūtra*
Bg	*Bhagavad Gītā*
BhP	*Bhāgavata Purāṇa*
S-ka	*Sarasvatī-kaṇṭhābharaṇa*
Śṛ-pra	*Śṛṅgāra-prakāśa*
ŚBh	*Śrī Bhaṣya*
ŚvUp	*Śvetāśvatara Upaniṣad*
TVM	*Tiruvāymoli*
VS	*Vedānta Sūtra*
VP	*Viṣṇu Purāṇa*

ACKNOWLEDGEMENTS

It is a great pleasure to acknowledge and thank the numerous people who have helped me in bringing this research work towards completion. It was Klaus Klostermaier with whom I had articulated the initial ideas of this work at the Theology Faculty, University of Oxford, while Keith Ward served as a constant source of inspiration through ongoing dialogue. Frank Clooney contributed much and so did Sanjukta Gupta, and the late M. Nrisimhacary and Josef O'Connel. Martin Francis and Jim Benson, both from Wolfson College, Shaunaka Rishi and Howard Reznik – all were a constant source of encouragement and support, and so were my dear friends Gil and Shira Daryn. Some of David Shulman's ideas are reflected here too, and thanks go to Oded Balaban for a fruitful exchange of ideas. Very special thanks are due to Julius Lipner who invited me to spend a year as a Visiting Fellow at Clare Hall and the Divinity Faculty, University of Cambridge, to bring this work to completion.

Many thanks are due to Matthew Kessell for Sanskrit editing and to Alex Wright, Sophie Campbell and the I.B.Tauris editorial team, who all helped take this book through the production process. Special thanks are due to my wife Michal and my three daughters, Inbal-Jahnavi, Nili-Nila Madhava and Kamah-Kamalini, who lovingly bore the weight of writing this work. Last but not least, let me thank my parents, Rachel and Emanuel Theodor, who have helped me tremendously in various ways in my academic work over many years. This book is dedicated to them.

INTRODUCTION

The *Bhāgavata Purāṇa* is a Sanskrit *purāṇa*,[1] considered to be one of the most sacred texts for some of the major *Vaiṣṇava* denominations. It contains 335 chapters, is approximately 14,100 to 14,400 verses long[2] and propounds the divinity of Kṛṣṇa, a theme expressed in a rather personal manner. The *Bhāgavata Purāṇa* combines *Vedāntic* philosophy, dramatic and aesthetic elements and personal expressions in a unique manner, so much so that it is considered to be one of the foremost Hindu scriptures. In general, the *purāṇas* are considered authoritative within Hinduism and, as such, *Vaiṣṇavas* would quote the *Viṣṇu Purāṇa* and the *Bhāgavata Purāṇa* side by side with the *Upaniṣads* as equal in authority.[3] The *BhP* holds a unique position among the *purāṇas*, and is considered by many to be the most important. Its influence as a religious book has been phenomenal, comparable only to the epics – the *Rāmāyaṇa* and the *Mahābhārata*.[4] The *BhP* is rich with cosmogonic narratives, and these are unique in that they have more of a philosophical character than other *purāṇas*. Indeed, the *BhP*'s cosmogonic narratives are mostly like those of the *Viṣṇu Purāṇa*, with slight differences, in that its cosmogony is characterized by a *Vedāntic* flavour rather than the *Sāṅkhya* influence that generally prevails the *purāṇas*.[5] Perhaps a different way of stating this would be that there are minor differences of evolutionary sequence between the *Sāṅkhya* of the *Bhāgavata* and the classical *Sāṅkhya* of Īśvarakṛṣṇa. As such, the *BhP* presents a third ontological entity as the ultimate cause of both the *puruṣa* (souls) and *prakṛti* (matter) and of their union. This is *Īśvara*, God, and the text identifies this Supreme Being to be Kṛṣṇa.[6] Although there is little doubt as to the *BhP*'s dominant

Vedāntic character, its *Vedānta* is expressed in a unique style, which more closely associates it with *Kāvya*[7] than with the general *purāṇic* genre. Moreover, its aesthetic nature is highlighted also by its striking unity, which suggests a careful and pedantic composition, a feature shared by Sanskrit poetry. In many ways the *BhP* seems closer to *kāvya* than to *purāṇa*, and the striking unity of the text together with its unusual style would suggest a single author or, at most, a very small group of poets working together at a single historical time and place.[8] Apparently, the final redactor of the *BhP* was not only a philosopher or theologian, but an epic poet; there are entire sections of the text that exhibit the various characteristics of exquisite *kāvya* poetry. Overall, the *BhP*'s tenth book ranks as an outstanding product of Sanskrit literature, a fact that has yet to receive the scholarly attention it merits.[9] Not only does the *BhP*'s unique literary genre combine *Vedānta* and *Kāvya*, but it is also characterized by a notable dramatic character. Partly this has to do with the dramatic settings within which the frame story is taking place. Accordingly, not only is the *BhP* the last message King Parīkṣit hears before his death, but listening to this message attentively is his last hope to achieve salvation. As such, most of the text is narrated by the sage Śuka to King Parīkṣit as the latter sits by the Ganges and prepares for his fateful death by snakebite. This dramatic framework may suggest that the *BhP* has somewhat different emphases and goals than those of other *purāṇas*. The audience is literally situated between life and death, and the ultimate seriousness of the narrator's message is thereby powerfully heightened.[10]

King Parīkṣit's hearing of the *BhP* is not only an expression of his own devotion or *bhakti*, but also of his faith in *bhakti* as a liberating process. Indeed, *bhakti* is a major feature of the *BhP*, so much so that it is sometimes considered a gospel of devotion; moreover, the emotional constituent of *bhakti* is complex and includes feelings of adoration, love and the dependence of the devotee on his deity. In a sense, the *BhP* preaches the highest form of *bhakti*, in that it does not seek the fulfilment of desires and is unconditional.[11] As opposed to *bhakti*, which seeks fruitfulness and as such is *sakāma*, it seems that the *BhP*'s *bhakti* does not seek the fulfilment of desires (*niṣkāma*), and even tends to devaluate the *Upaniṣadic* ideal of *mokṣa*.[12] The *BhP* proclaims *bhakti* to be the 'highest religion'.[13] Devaluing the idea of *mokṣa* in favour of *bhakti* suggests a theistic form of *Vedānta*. This is further reinforced by some scholars who not only highlight the significant place *bhakti* occupies within the *BhP*, but go as far as to argue that devotion is the *BhP*'s single most important feature. Hopkins, for example, considers the single most important feature of the *Bhāgavata* to be its emphasis on *bhakti*, or devotion directed to Viṣṇu and his various incarnations, giving the *BhP* its purpose and consistency.[14] This mode of devotion may be considered exclusive and total. In the *BhP*, as in the *Ālvārs*, it is a passionate devotion of one's whole self in complete surrender to the Supreme Lord, a total way of life that is not one way among many but the only way to true salvation.[15] Still, beside the *BhP*'s 'passionate' devotion it presents also more *yogic* and sober modes of devotion, such as those presented in the *Bhāgavad gītā*, and these various modes complement each other.

In general, there is a traditional differentiation between devotion and knowledge within *Vaiṣṇavism*. Devotion or *bhakti* held a major place already in the *Bhagavad Gītā* and other earlier works, and it was accepted as one of the ways to salvation along with *karma* and *jñāna*.[16] Whereas the path of *jñāna* laid emphasis on cognitive endeavour as the means to *mokṣa*, the path of *karma* laid emphasis on a performative endeavour for that same purpose. Accordingly, *karma* and *jñāna* can be distinguished as practical and philosophical. The roots of this dichotomy are ancient. Since early times, Brahminical orthodoxy had two major emphases: *Vedic* knowledge (*jñāna*) and proper action (*karma*). These two emphases, one philosophical and the other practical, were preserved in the later Hindu tradition in the systems of *Vedānta* philosophy based on the *Upaniṣads* and in the *Smārta* concern for Brahminical *dharma*.[17] The deliberation between the path of action and the path of knowledge appears already as early as the *Bhagavad Gītā*, wherein the question arises: Which is the better path for the attainment of the highest good?

> 1 Arjuna said: O Janārdana, if you consider enlightenment to be
> better than action, why then do you enjoin me to perform this
> terrible act? 2 Your equivocating words confuse my mind. I beg
> you, make me certain of one thing, by which I may attain the best.
> 3 The blessed Lord said: I have propounded since the days of yore,
> O Blameless Arjuna, that in this world there are two paths: for
> those who uphold reasoning, it is the path of *jñāna* or intellectual

yoga, whereas for those who uphold action, it is the path of *karma yoga*, or *yoga* of activity.[18]

It may well be that the path of *karma yoga* mentioned above refers to a devotional type of action, wherein the *bhakta* or devotee considers his work to be service to the Supreme and, as such, presents servitude or *dāsya*. Being one of the three textual foundations of *Vedānta*,[19] the *Bhagavad Gītā* naturally accepts the ideal of *mokṣa* or the attainment of *Brahman* as the highest goal, to be achieved either by *karma* or by *jñāna*. Still, in general, it is the *jñāna-kāṇḍa* portion of *śruti* that aims at and culminates with knowledge of *Brahman*. *Jñāna-Kāṇḍa* is not interested in things of this earth, nor in heaven. It wants insight into, and communion with, a reality that is non-sensual and non-transient: *Brahman*.[20] The term *Brahman* can be understood in two major ways: as impersonal or as personal. Indeed, the two trends of thought, the impersonal and personal, are an ongoing feature of the religious history of India. Although originally two aspects of the same concept, they developed later as two competing ideologies. As such, the religious history of India is marked by the conflict and the interaction of two major trends: to conceive of the absolute, either in terms of a somewhat mystical state of being or as the Supreme Person. The difference is not one of origin, for both trends have their roots in the *Vedas*. In other words, that which at a later stage emerged as two different ideological positions appears in the *Vedas* as two aspects of one concept.[21] It may well be that the dichotomy of devotion and knowledge has its source already in the *Vedas* through these two concepts of the absolute. As the *BhP* contains clear traces of knowledge or *jñāna*, the question arises: What is the significance of knowledge in the *BhP*, and how does it, if at all, relate to devotion?

The relation between knowledge and devotion in the *BhP* could also be seen through the process of Sanskritization of the new *bhakti* religion and the popular Kṛṣṇa legends. The newly emerging *bhakti* movement was in need of legitimization and orthodox acceptance, and thus associated itself with the *Upaniṣadic* literature, otherwise known as the *jñāna kāṇḍa* portion of the *Veda*. In general, Sanskritization refers to a process in Indian civilization in which a person or a group consciously relates to an accepted notion of true and ancient ideology and conduct.[22] The Sanskritization of the *BhP* was, however, unique in its usage of an archaic language that already in the fifth century BCE stood 'in need of a glossary'.[23] It is therefore a unique phenomenon that far later in the history of literature, when Sanskrit letters were in fact on the decline, a text purporting to belong to the *Purāṇic* tradition consciously attempted to archaize its language.[24] This open endeavour to Sanskritize and archaize the *BhP* raises the question: Why was the *BhP* Sanskritized? Put differently, why did the author or authors responsible for the final version of the *Bhāgavata* want the book to sound *Vedic*? The question is even more challenging because the *Purāṇa* has a somewhat ambivalent attitude toward *Vedic* orthodoxy. On numerous occasions the empty and conceited formalism of the *Vaidikas* is unfavourably contrasted with the simple and sincere devotions of the *bhakta*.[25] It may well be that the newly established *bhakti* movement was in need of obtaining a legitimate and orthodox position, for in spite of the history of *bhakti*, the southern *bhakti* movement was something new (not necessarily per se, but for the first time a consistent effort was being made to place it in the Brahminical tradition). In the work of Nāthamuni, Yāmuna and Rāmānuja a consistent effort to promote the Sanskritization of the *bhakti* religion can be observed. The *bhakta*'s worshipful deity is equated with the supreme principle of the *Upaniṣads*: the adoring contemplation of the deity in his heaven by the worshipper is equivalent to *mokṣa*. The acts of worship and veneration are on a par with the rites prescribed by scripture and tradition. Similarly, in the archaic emphasis of the *BhP* we find an attempt at Sanskritization of the popular Kṛṣṇa legend. Kṛṣṇa is no longer merely a little boy who is also a lover, set in the rustic scene of pastures, cows, cattle tenders and their wives. *Purāṇic* rather than epic, let alone *Vedic*, in provenance, it now speaks, or at least tries to speak, in the solemn language of the *Vedic* seer.[26] As such, the young and popular *bhakti* movement associated itself with the ancient and respectable *Upaniṣadic* tradition. The union of both traditions bore an impressive fruit: the *Bhāgavata Purāṇa*.[27]

We may now ask: Does the *Upaniṣadic* knowledge pervading the *BhP* occupy no other place than that of legitimizing its simple and total devotion? Is it possible that such a complex, sophisticated and theologically significant text would, on the one hand, treat the orthodox sources with such a profound level of scholarship, by writing the entire text in a *Vedic*-archaic style, and then present its main thesis of total devotion in a rather simplistic, naive and legendry style? Do the

Upaniṣadic sources make any contribution to the *BhP*'s philosophical thesis and theme of *bhakti*, or are they implicitly referred to merely for the purpose of legitimizing the new emotional tradition? Does the *BhP*'s poetic style indicate the amalgamation of an orthodox aesthetic theory, and is it possible that this orthodox aesthetic tradition merged with the orthodox philosophical tradition, thus furthering the formation of a new concept of *bhakti* within the *BhP*? Is it possible that in its passion for *Vedism*, the *BhP* absorbed not only an archaic language style but an archaic ideology? If the *BhP* has indeed absorbed this archaic ideology, could it be that it takes the two aspects of the supreme, the personal and the impersonal, as two aspects of one idea, co-existing in harmony, as opposed to perceiving the two as distinct and conflicting ideologies – a concept which apparently developed only much later? It is my conviction that in absorbing *Vedic* elements, the *BhP* absorbed not only an archaic Sanskrit style and *Upaniṣadic* discourses but another, second, orthodox Brahaminical tradition, which is the *rasa*-aesthetic school originating in Bharata. As the *Upaniṣadic* tradition underlies the *jñāna* portions of the *BhP*, the aesthetic tradition underlies the *BhP*'s *bhakti* portions.

Moreover, I argue, the meeting of these two great traditions in the *BhP* was coherent and harmonic and, as such, a theological masterpiece was created wherein one supports the other. In this, the *BhP* returns to *Vedic* sources not only linguistically, but ideologically or theologically as well. When read as a meeting place of these two great orthodox traditions, the *Vedic-Upaniṣadic* and the aesthetic, the *BhP*'s structure as a coherent theological treatise comes to light. It appears to be a theological magnum opus taking as its point of departure the *Upaniṣadic mokṣa*, and gradually leading its devoted reader further into the realm of total, personal self-surrender and passionate devotion. Once read in this way, the *BhP* is seen to have a unified theological structure, distancing it from the realm of apologetics, legends and mythology, and warranting its unique position as one of India's greatest theological treatises expressing a new literary genre of aesthetic *Vedānta*. Uncovering the underlying assumptions of the 'aesthetic self of the *BhP*', it seems that *jñāna* leads one all the way to the realization of Impersonal *Brahman*, and indeed, Impersonal *Brahman* is the highest philosophical achievement and ultimate abstraction possibly perceived by the intelligence, or attained by the process of rationalization. However, seen from the aesthetic point of view, the same state of Impersonal *Brahman* realization becomes divinity in a state that evokes *śānta rasa*. From this point of realization, the *BhP* develops the aesthetic theme further and further and offers various notions of divinity, from those evoking *śānta rasa* up to those evoking *śṛṅgāra rasa*. Thus the *BhP* relies on *jñāna* to establish the greatness of *Brahman* realization, and relies on aesthetics to lead one further into the personal realm of divinity. Therefore the two concepts of the absolute – the impersonal and personal – dwell in harmony within the *BhP*, each having their role to play, and both essential to the articulation of the *BhP*'s theme. Both express the greatness of the absolute in their own way. Seen philosophically, the realization of Impersonal *Brahman* is the highest position, and seen aesthetically, experiencing intense romantic emotions towards the divine 'in person' is the highest emotional state possible. Thus the *BhP* reconciles that which 'at a later stage[28] emerged as two different ideological positions'[29] and returns to the archaic *Vedic* state of affairs where the two seemingly different ideological positions 'appear in the *Vedas* as two aspects of one conception'.[30]

Analysis of the *BhP*'s structure highlights its construction of divine personhood, and so this work could also be taken as a study of this principle in the *BhP*. As the notion of personhood is central to my work, we may look at it more closely. The discourse of personhood has not only religious, but philosophical and specifically ontological aspects as well. In other words, the impersonalist believes that underlying the whole of reality there exists an impersonal principle. Conversely, the personalist believes that it is ultimately a person who underlies reality. Erazim Kohak raises a related question: 'Is the Person or is matter in motion the root metaphor of thought and practice? That answered, all else follows.'[31] This question seems to have deep existential implications. Accordingly, everyone has some idea of the root metaphor of thought and practice, whether it is personal or impersonal, and one's whole worldview may derive from that. My work deconstructs the *BhP* into its two conceptual foundations, and by doing so takes an impersonal approach. In other words, it assumes that personhood in the *BhP* is constructed by a combination of the two components of philosophy and aesthetics. However, had I taken a personal approach, assuming that a person is the 'root metaphor of thought and practice', I would have considered philosophy and aesthetics not to construct personhood but to be its derivatives. In other words, a truly personal approach considering the person to be the 'root metaphor of thought and practice' would assume that the impersonal ideas (i.e. the two orthodox *Brahaminical* doctrines underlying the *BhP*) emerge or emanate from a person. In light of the above, I plan to deconstruct the *BhP* into its two underlying paradigms – the philosophical and the aesthetic – and offer an assessment of each. Based on that, I aim to demonstrate how the *BhP*'s notion of divine personhood is constructed, as representing various mixtures of these two modes of perception and expression.

CHAPTER 1

ASSOCIATING THE *BHĀGAVATA PURĀṆA* WITH *RASA* THEORY

Personhood in the Hindu Context

The following section is engaged with personhood. It first looks into various notions of personhood, then suggests another notion of aesthetic personhood that will be discussed in this work, and finally offers an articulation of the *BhP*'s notion of personhood. This section opens the door for a syncretic or harmonious understanding of the four notions of Hindu personhood discussed.

Attempting to articulate notions of personhood within Hinduism, one faces a translation problem, as the term 'person' is a somewhat Western imposition on Indian culture. The uncertain status of the notion of person in India is conditioned by the fact that it is foreign to the Sanskrit tradition and has no adequate rendering in any of the Sanskritic languages. When dealing with either the human being or the deity, Indian philosophy always worked with other concepts, which rarely imported the holistic signification of person.[1] As the term person has no adequate rendering in any of the Sanskritic languages, various terms such as *ātman*, *puruṣa*, *jīva*, *īśvara*, *bhagavān*, *avatāra* and *mūrti* are used to denote both human and divine persons within various contexts.

The term 'person' has a long history, dating back to the Greco-Roman period, where it was used to denote the stage masks of the actors.[2] It came to signify a dramatic hero, and hence became applicable by the Stoics to every human being, as all are endowed by God to play on the world stage. Roman law defined the citizens as persons, and as opposed to slaves they had legal rights and duties. Boethius[3] coined a basic definition of the person, emphasizing rationality as a major quality characterizing personhood, and the Christian tradition adopted the term to designate the Trinity. As it viewed all men as brothers, it considered all to be persons, whether free citizens, slaves or foreigners. In the medieval period the term person was considered to belong to the realm of responsible action and to refer to an intellectual and morally free subject. Consequently, Aquinas refined Boethius' definition finally to declare that 'person' means an integral and unitary self-subsistent subject characterized by intellectual consciousness, moral freedom and all properties ensuing from these defining traits. Prominent among these properties were privacy, ownership of natural rights, moral responsibility, being a source of value in one's own right and the capacity to initiate interpersonal relationships. The definition was such that it could with due precision apply analogically to the divine as well as to human persons.[4] This usage remained for hundreds of years, but was later restricted to mean 'human individuals', whereas its application to the divine was taken as merely anthropomorphic. The translators of Sanskrit works in the late nineteenth century translated the terms *nirguṇa* and *saguṇa brahman* as impersonal and personal *Brahman*. Other terminology used by them was to refer to *nirguṇa brahman* as the Absolute, and to *saguṇa brahman* or *īśvara* as God. Underlying this obscure usage of terms was the assumption that the Hindu personal notions were not absolute.

Against this background it becomes understandable that the question of personhood in Indian thought has become far too complex and obscure to be dealt with beyond the constraints of modern humanism. Yet the materials for an Indian recognition of the person are present in some theology and anthropology of the Indian tradition.[5] Having briefly touched upon the complexity of the usage of this term in the Indian context, we may now turn to articulate three such notions intrinsic to the Hindu orthodox tradition. These are the worldly self of *Mīmāṁsā*, the solitary self of *Sāṅkhya*, and the transcendental self of *Vedānta*.

In articulating 'the Worldly Self of *Mīmāṁsā*', the broader social context may be considered. In general, the *Vedic* society was world-affirming and sacrifices occupied a central place in its daily affairs. The individual enjoyed full dignity in so far as he was a *yajamāna.*[6] Not only did the sacrifice define the human person as a sacrificer, but it consolidated the four-class social division as well. The Brahmins were the priests enacting the sacrifice, and the members of the other three *varṇas* or social categories each had their role to play in the sacrificial activity. The *Mīmāṁsā* was humanistic and active and the early *Mīmāṁsā* did not consider the Supreme Person or *mokṣa* to be very important subject matters.[7] As a realistic school, the *Mīmāṁsā*'s main interest was mainly practical rather than speculative, as it enquired into the nature and means of *Dharma*.[8] The fundamental philosophical basis is Jaimini's *Mīmāṁsā Sūtras*[9] and the major commentators are *Śabara*,[10] *Kumārila Bhaṭṭa* and *Prabhākara*.[11] Jaimini admits the reality of the *Vedic* deities to whom the sacrifices were offered. As far as the Supreme Person, he neither argues for his existence nor denies him, but mainly ignores him.

The *Mīmāṁsā* perceived human life as a life of action and thus life was expressed through action. However, action was not just any action but that under the *Vedic* injunctions. The *Veda* itself was taken to be *apauruṣeya*, that is not composed by any person, not even by a Supreme Person, who was taken to be superfluous in the presence of the eternal *Veda*. The *Mīmāṁsā* is pluralistic, and as far as its *Vedic* textual affiliation, it deals with the first two categories of *Vedic* texts, namely the *Saṁhitās* and the *Brāhmaṇas*.[12] The *Mīmāṁsā* is the 'most orthodox of all the orthodox systems',[13] and accepted by all other schools as authoritative with regards to the individual's relations to society, forefathers, teachers and gods. The framework underlying proper human action as well as his relations with society and the world was *dharma*, and thus the *Mīmāṁsā Sūtra* of Jaiminī commences as follows: 'Next, therefore, comes the enquiry into *dharma. Dharma* is that which is indicated by means of the *Veda* as conducive to the highest good.'[14] In the *Mīmāṁsā* system, there is a connection between the act and its result or fruit. As such, an act performed at present will yield a future result, while in the meantime it takes the form of *apūrva*,[15] which may be taken as an imperceptible antecedent of the fruit or an after-state of the act itself. Liberation for *Mīmāṁsā* refers mainly to life in heaven, although later thinkers did take *dharma* to be leading to *mokṣa*. *Prabhākara* defined liberation as 'the absolute cessation of the body caused by the disappearance of all *dharma* and *adharma*', and for *Kumārila Bhaṭṭa* it is the state of the self free from pain.[16]

The *Mīmāṁsā* accepts the existence of the soul, distinct from the mind, body and senses. The soul is the essence of human personality and there is a plurality of souls; it is the agent in each action and experience, and the resting place of *apurva*. Being eternal, it allows the reaping of a deed's fruits in a future life. Still, *Mīmāṁsā* doesn't aim to deconstruct the human person, and the physical body is no object of contempt, as it is an important instrument in pursuing *dharma*. Moreover, it approves of human volition as a positive force, motivating one to *pravṛtti*, or action according to *dharma*. The *Mīmāṁsā* thus represents a holistic human approach, and with its realistic grandstanding and its humanistic and activist ethics, it places the human being at the centre of the universe, while being deeply committed to human welfare.[17] The centrality of human welfare serves as an impetus for the human being to control the world in order to fulfil his desires, and the instrument for achieving this is the *Vedic* sacrifice, which, in a sense, becomes the external manifestation of desire. Yet sacrifice is a necessary manifestation and so action has to be performed. Only then are the gods pleased, is proper enjoyment obtained for them and do natural forces and the world yield to human wishes.[18] Later commentators differ in their relation to the fulfilment of desires. Whereas Kumārila holds that one should adhere to *dharma* as that would lead to happiness and exterminate sorrow, Prabhākara maintains that *dharma* should be followed for its own sake, without regarding possible gains or consequences. In summary, the notion of personhood in *Mīmāṁsā* is humanistic, realistic, active and defined by adherence to *dharma.* Self-fulfilment is defined in terms of sacrifice, and it can be measured in terms of worldly success – in this life as well as in the next.

In articulating the 'Solitary Self of *Sāṅkhya*', the metaphysics of the *Sāṅkhya* system may be considered. *Sāṅkhya* is notable for its theory of evolution and its reduction of all that exists to the two fundamental categories of *puruṣa*[19] and *prakṛti.*[20] *Prakṛti* is composed of three constituents called *guṇas*, and is in a potential and neutral state which is activated and actualized by the *puruṣa*. The evolution of the unconscious *prakṛti* can take place only through the presence of the conscious *puruṣa*. As such, the presence of the *puruṣa* excites the activity of *prakṛti* (thus upsetting the equilibrium of the *guṇas* in *prakṛti*) and passively starts the evolutionary process. The union of the *puruṣa* and the *prakṛti* is compared to a lame man of good vision mounted on the shoulders of a blind man of sure foot.[21] The *prakṛti* first evolves into the *mahat*[22] and from it evolves *buddhi*.[23] The *ahaṅkāra*[24] is the principle of individuation, and from its *sattva guṇa*[25] arise the *manas*,[26] the five organs of perception[27] and the five organs of action.[28] From the *ahaṅkāra*'s *tamo guṇa*[29] arise the five fine or subtle elements[30] known as *tanmātras*, and from these arise the five gross elements[31] known as the *mahābhūtas*. The *rajo guṇa*[32] acts as an energizer to support this evolution, and thus creation represents the unfolding of the phenomenal world from the original *prakṛti*, whereas dissolution is the world's absorption back into *prakṛti*.

The individual is not the body, either gross[33] or subtle,[34] rather the eternal conscious self, the pure spirit who is the *puruṣa*. The subtle and gross body is the instrument of consciousness but is unconscious in itself. The subtle body is composed of *buddhi*, *ahaṅkāra* and *manas*, and these three combined comprise the inner organ[35] that accounts for the various types of subjective and psychic experiences.[36] At the time of death the gross body alone is relinquished whereas the subtle-psychological body accompanies the *puruṣa* to the next body, and only at the stage of final aloofness is the subtle body entirely given up. As there are many such conscious selves, both in the state of bondage as well as in the liberated state, and as there is a fundamental distinction between the conscious *puruṣa* and unconscious *prakṛti*, *Sāṅkhya* is both pluralistic and dualistic. As opposed to the *puruṣa*, which may be designated as the 'essential self', the term 'empirical self' may be applied to the human being. In that human condition, the *puruṣa* identifies with its gross and subtle bodies and is deluded to perceive itself to be thinking, feeling and acting, when actually it is only the *guṇas* who are activating the human being. In general, the term *guṇa* has three meanings, namely 'quality', 'rope' and 'not primary'. The *guṇas*, however, are substances and not mere qualities. This is because in *Sāṅkhya* philosophy there is no separate existence of qualities. It holds that each and every unit of quality is but a unit of substance.[37] The *guṇas* are thus subtle entities, which characterize every phenomenon, gross or subtle, comprise *prakṛti* and bind the *puruṣa*. In the stage of bondage, the *puruṣa* agitates *prakṛti* and thus the *guṇas* are set in motion, whereas in the stage of salvation the *puruṣa* achieves *kaivalya*, which is a state of aloofness and distinction from *prakṛti*. The state of embodiment is only apparent as the experience of repeated births is a mere false impression created by matter obscuring the *puruṣa*'s purity.

Non-theistic *Sāṅkhya* resembles Jainism but is more radical in its conception of the individual spirit. The latter, called *puruṣa* (human person) or *jña* (knower), is never really but only apparently embodied. Hence, it is never really affected by matter nor tainted in any way by activity, which is the exclusive province of unconscious matter (*pradhāna* or *prakṛti*). Its illusory feeling of repeated embodiments in the sorrowful round of births is due to its own reflection in the mirror-like density of matter. It is a mere fallacy that the *Sāṅkhya* teaching suffices to dispel, apart from any asceticism, by the finality of its demonstration of every *puruṣa*'s purity. Whenever this truth is grasped by one's consciousness,[38] the *puruṣa* at once recovers the untroubled awareness of his isolation (*kaivalya*) and becomes pure, unrelated and serene.[39] It seems that *Sāṅkhya* resembles *Vedānta* at least to some extent, in so far as it aspires to dispel the illusory feeling of repeated embodiments in the sorrowful round of births. Tradition ascribes the authorship of the *Sāṅkhya* system to Kapila,[40] and the earliest text on *Sāṅkhya* philosophy is the *Sāṅkhya-kārikā* of *Īśvarakṛṣṇa*,[41] which begins as follows: 'From torment by three-fold misery arises the inquiry into the means of terminating it.'[42]

Although the classical *Sāṅkhya* of *Īśvarakṛṣṇa* appears to be non-theistic or even atheistic,[43] it may well be that older *Sāṅkhya* strains in the Epic and *Upaniṣadic* literature support a theistic doctrine, and these theistic strains continued throughout the *Purāṇic* tradition, as well as in the *Bhagavad Gītā.*[44] However, though *Sāṅkhya* can at times support a theistic system, the notion of a Supreme Person is a non-essential component, the essential components being the total distinction between *puruṣa* and *prakṛti*, their union from which the world evolves and their separation at the perfectional stage. The *Yoga* system is quite close to the *Sāṅkhya* system in its metaphysics, but is distinct in that it includes not only theory but also a practical side which is a method meant for the liberation of the *puruṣa* from *prakṛti*. The method is based upon eight transformational stages and resembles a ladder by which one may raise one's self step by step. The transformation is an internal one and represents involution, that is, a process by which the *puruṣa* gradually separates itself from *prakṛti* until it reaches aloofness or complete isolation. In summary, the *Sāṅkhya* system defines personhood in terms of isolation. The more one is able to recover one's self from the covering of *prakṛti*, the more fulfilled a person one is. The more progress one is able to make, both theoretically and practically in the isolation process, the higher level of personhood is expressed. Complete isolation or *kaivalya* represents the stage of perfection.

In articulating the 'Transcendental Self of *Vedānta*', the *Vedānta* philosophy should be considered. It is derived from the *jñāna kāṇḍa* portion of the *Vedas*, represented by the *Upaniṣads*, and its three main teachers are Śaṅkara (788–820 CE), Rāmānuja (1017–1137) and Madhva (1238–1317). Later notable teachers are Nimbārka (mid-fourteenth century), Vallabha (1479–1531) and Caitanya (1486–1533). The self in *Vedāntin* thought is called *ātman*, is taken to be transcendental to the world, to exist eternally and to be conscious and blissful.[45] *Ātman* is non-dual with *Brahman*, which is the highest being and is a non-empirical, non-objective and wholly other reality. Whereas the world depends on *Brahman*, *Brahman* depends on nothing else. In the worldly state of existence, *ātman* is covered by ignorance[46] and the removal of this ignorance is called self-realization, a process by which the *ātman* learns to see or perceive itself as it really is. Self-realization leads to *mokṣa*, a stage where the *ātman* attains freedom or liberation from the bonds of *saṁsāra*. The personal God of *Vedānta* is called *īśvara*, and he is the creator and governor of the world. These foundations of *Vedānta* are interpreted somewhat differently by the various schools already mentioned.

Śaṅkara's school – *Advaita Vedānta* – propounds pure or absolute non-dualism; although the world in his system is not *abhāva* (non-existent) or *śūnya* (void), it is not ultimately real. Under ignorance, the self perceives itself to be different from *Brahman* and, following that, it perceives the phenomenal world as real. When ignorance is removed by knowledge, the self realizes its oneness with *Brahman* and experiences its true nature. The highest representation of the absolute perceived by logical categories is *īśvara*, sometimes translated as 'God' or a 'personal God'; taken to be *saguṇa Brahman*, or *Brahman* with qualities, and is a lower form of *nirguṇa Brahman*, or *Brahman* without qualities. Acts of devotion to *īśvara* are conducive to self-realization, although to achieve self-realization one would have to transcend even that form of *Brahman* and realize *nirguṇa Brahman*. The stage of *mokṣa* is not the dissolution of the world, but the displacement of a false outlook (*avidyā*) by the right outlook of wisdom (*vidyā*).[47]

Rāmānuja's school – *Viśiṣṭādvaita* – propounds the non-dualism of the qualified. In his system, God,[48] the selves and the world exist, whereas matter and the selves are dependent on God. They all form a unity in which matter and the selves exist as the body of *Brahman*. The individual self is essentially different from *Brahman* although it has no purpose to serve apart from his service to *Brahman*. Rāmānuja takes the world to be real, although dependent, admits the inalienable individuality of the selves and holds that the Supreme *Brahman* is personal. For him, there can be no such thing as undifferentiated *Brahman*.[49] For Rāmānuja, the Supreme Person is Viṣṇu Nārāyaṇa, and salvation is not the disappearance of the self merging with *Brahman* but its release from its limiting barriers. The self's dependence upon the Supreme Person continues in the released state, but whereas in the conditioned state it is dominated by its non-essential nature, at the state of release its essential nature is manifested, and thus it can continue to worship and revere the Supreme Person free from passion and ignorance.

Mādhva's school – *Dvaita* – propounds dualism, represented by five fundamental differences or distinctions: 1. between the Supreme Person and the individual self; 2. between the Supreme Person and matter; 3. between one individual self and another; 4. between the individual self and matter; and 5. between one individual substance and another. The Supreme Person, the selves and the world exist permanently, but the selves and the world are subordinate to the Supreme Person and dependent upon him. *Brahman* is identified with the Supreme Person who is Viṣṇu-Kṛṣṇa. He directs the world, is endowed with a supernatural body and is transcendent to the world as well as immanent. Selves are souls that are finite centres of consciousness, each with a unique essence of its own. As such, one finite centre of experience cannot possess as its own immediate experience the experience of another, and this non-transferable immediacy of experience distinguishes one self from another. The self is defined as having a dynamic personality endowed with the triple properties of will, cognition and activity; individuality is based on the uniqueness of personality which is a blending of consciousness, experience and works, in proportion to its intrinsic stature, and is the core of all human hedonistic, ethical and spiritual activities.[50] The state of *mokṣa* has not only a negative aspect, but a positive one as well, characterized by an intrinsic bliss of selfhood, and thus can the released souls enjoy themselves with their own spiritual bodies composed of *sat*, *cit* and *ānanda*.[51]

The *Vedāntic* notion of personhood is, therefore, based upon the process of self-realization, given the various interpretations of this term by the different schools. The more self-realized a person is, the more their personhood is manifested and expressed. Although the understanding of these three notions of personhood (the worldly self of

Mīmāṁsā, the solitary self of *Sāṅkhya* and the transcendental self of *Vedānta*) is essential to the understanding of personhood in the *BhP*, it is still not sufficient. I believe that a fourth notion of personhood has to be articulated for a better understanding of the *BhP*, and this notion may be referred to as the 'Aesthetic Self of the *BhP*'. According to this notion, personhood is defined through an aesthetic sensitivity and an emotional depth and, as such, the deeper one's aesthetic sensitivity and emotional experience of the supreme are, the more one is able to express one's personhood. The understanding of this notion is key to a better understanding of the *BhP*. For the purpose of understanding it, this work will uncover its underlying assumptions, and specifically, the relations between knowledge and aesthetics.

Having offered a brief discussion of personhood in the Hindu tradition, we may now proceed and attempt to shed some light over the question: What is the *BhP*'s idea of a person? We shall commence by referring to Zaehner on the nature of God in the *BhP*:

> God is in love with the soul, and the soul with God. In this divine love affair God is necessarily the male, the soul the female: God takes the initiative and the soul must passively wait for the divine embrace. The Kṛṣṇa of the *Bhāgavata Purāṇa* is a very different person from the rather austere Kṛṣṇa of the *Gītā*; he is not a teacher, but a lover, the handsome and wayward shepherd-boy who beguiles the soul with the sweet strains of his flute.[52]

Zaehner's emphasis lies in God, who is not only a person, but a person who loves as well. The idea of God as a loving person is closely associated with the term *Bhagavān*, in regard to which Sheridan writes:

> We have thus seen that one of the chief themes of the *Bhāgavata* is that Kṛṣṇa is the primary bearer of the title '*Bhagavān*', that he is the Supreme Being. This identification can be seen in the many passages where the *Bhāgavata* identifies Kṛṣṇa with Viṣṇu-Nārāyaṇa. Its approach is to show that Kṛṣṇa is Viṣṇu's equal or his superior, thereby replacing him as the highest identity of God.[53]

Sheridan's emphasis lies in Kṛṣṇa as *Bhagavān*, identical or superior to Viṣṇu-Nārāyaṇa. The question is: How can we progress from this point towards the definition of the term 'person', which seems to underlie the *BhP*? Let us progress step by step:

1. We know that the personal God is one of the main topics of the *BhP* and, by definition, that he is a person.[54]
2. There are other persons depicted in the *BhP* such as gods (Brahmā, Indra) and humans (Arjuna, the *gopīs*).
3. Leaving aside for now the question regarding the difference between the divine and the human person, it can be said that in the *BhP*, the divine person is the person who could most easily be studied, as he is depicted most clearly and in a variety of ways throughout the entire text.
4. Therefore, we propose to draw the definition of 'the person' from the descriptions of the Supreme Person found in abundance in the *BhP* – the rationale being that there is at least one person described throughout the whole text, on whose personhood there is wide agreement.
5. Having extracted basic information as to the qualities of this one great person, who seems to constitute one of the *BhP*'s main themes,[55] we may later engage with the question: Can this information help us in understanding the way in which the *BhP* views the human person?

Let us gather some information regarding this person:

1. Kṛṣṇa exists and as such he possess the quality of 'Being'.[56]
2. He is conscious of events external to him: he talks to others, he appears in *avatāra* forms to save the world, he fights, and he tempts the *gopīs*. Therefore he has the quality of being 'Conscious'.[57]
3. He is 'Rational', and as such he speaks the philosophical treatise known as the *Uddhava gītā*, which is quite similar to the *Bhagavad Gītā*.[58]
4. He is always 'Specific', although the specifications continually change; thus he has a specific name (such as Kṛṣṇa, Vāsudeva or Govinda), he always has a specific form (such as the son of Devakī or a half man-half lion) and so forth.
5. He has a specific 'Individual' character, that is as moral as Rāma or fierce as Nṛsiṁhadeva,[59] and therefore has a sense of 'Individuality'.

6. He 'Desires', has intentions and purposes, and thus he appears to relieve the burden of the world. He desires to protect his devotees and desires to dance with the *gopīs*.[60]
7. He is an 'Enjoyer' and seems to like enjoying.[61]
8. He exchanges and 'Reciprocates Relationships' with other persons, as he saves his devotees such as Uttarā, and kills his enemies such as Pūtanā.[62]
9. He is 'Creative', as he creates the world, and does so in creative ways, such as appearing in various *avatāra* forms.[63]

It seems that this information would suffice to present a preliminary definition of the term person as it underlies the *BhP*: 'A specific individual, conscious and rational being, whose nature is enjoyment, desires, creativity and reciprocal relationships with other similar beings.' Having offered a brief discussion of personhood in the Hindu context, and having articulated the *BhP*'s underlying definition of 'the person', we may now proceed to offer a holistic, harmonized or syncretic view, according to which the various notions of personhood within the *BhP* are intertwining harmonically with each other.

The *BhP*'s time of compilation was dominated by the dynamics of a polemical view. By the eighth and ninth centuries a crucial development had occurred that paradoxically both salvaged and destroyed the old *Sāṅkhya* philosophy, namely the emergence of *Advaita Vedānta* in the work of Śaṅkara and his successors. That is to say, while polemically regretting the errors of the older tradition, the newly emerging tradition assumed many of the essential features of the conceptual structure of the former tradition.[64] As the two systems were rather similar in many aspects, it seems that Śaṅkara may have needed the campaign against *Sāṅkhya* to establish his own position. Commenting on Bādarāyaṇa's *sūtras*, he was specifically disturbed about the dualistic nature of *Sāṅkhya*, and its pride in independent reasoning, and could not tolerate the *Sāṅkhya* notion of an independent material (*pradhāna* or *prakṛti*) apart from consciousness (*puruṣa*). It was even more difficult for him to accept the crucial role of inference apart from scriptural authority that the *Sāṅkhya* notion of materiality permitted.[65] Śaṅkara's attack on the *Sāṅkhya* system provides an insight into the polemical atmosphere of his period. However, we have already pointed out the *BhP*'s deliberate attempt to associate itself with archaic ideology,[66] and it is therefore not surprising that it takes an archaic, conservative, non-polemic and holistic approach in its articulation of personhood, too. In attempting to further articulate the complementary dynamics of personhood in the *BhP*, I wish to first relate it to an earlier and closely related text, the *Bhagavad Gītā*, which naturally reflects upon the *BhP*.

The *Bg* represents a somewhat conservative approach, which sees the various paths as basically propounding one single way, that is the way to *mokṣa*. As such, the different paths of *karma-yoga*, *jñāna-yoga* and *bhakti-yoga* are seen as three emphases of one single way, meant for followers of different temperaments.[67] It may well be that the archaic approach was more holistic, whereas the polemical approach, in which the followers of various sects competed with each other over ideological supremacy, was to appear only later, specifically during the second half of the first millennium CE. According to this approach, *Sāṅkhya* and *Yoga*, *Mīmāṁsā* and *Vedānta*, *Vaiśeṣika* and *Nyāya* are the six classical systems or philosophies, or more literally 'points of view', and are regarded as the six aspects of a single orthodox tradition. Although apparently and even overtly contradictory, these are understood to be complementary projections of the one truth on various planes of consciousness, valid intuitions from differing points of view.[68] This holistic view can be found in some traditional sources, such as, for example, Vijñāna Bhikṣu, who was a sixteenth-century Bengali *yogī* and philosopher, and who thought that the *Sāṅkhya* and *Yoga* philosophies are intimately connected with *Vedānta* and are referred to in the *Upaniṣads*. According to this view, certain topics, for example the problem of experimental knowledge, are not described in *Vedānta*, but rather are to be supplemented from the *Sāṅkhya* and *Yoga*. If there is any seeming antagonism between the two, these also have to be explained so that the opposition may be reconciled. Bhikṣu takes this attitude not only towards *Sāṅkhya-Yoga* but also towards *Nyāya-Vaiśeṣika* and the *Pañcarātra*. According to him all these systems have their basis in the *Vedas* and the *Upaniṣads* and have therefore an internal affinity which is not to be found in the *Buddhists*, which are therefore the only real opponents. Thus he attempts to reconcile all the *āstika* systems of philosophy as more or less supplementary to one another or at least as presenting differences which can be reconciled if they are looked at from proper angles of vision.[69] We wish to apply this approach to the interpretation of the *BhP*, too, in regard to the subject matter of personhood: although we have articulated three different notions of personhood, and are now articulating a fourth one, we nevertheless propose to see all four as internal elements coexisting harmoniously with each other within the general framework of personhood in the *BhP*. We believe that the notion of personhood with which the *BhP* begins is comprised mainly of the first three and, as the text develops, the fourth element, that is the aesthetic one, becomes more notably emphasized.

Deconstructing the *Bhāgavata Purāṇa* into its Literary and Ideological Components

This section first highlights the *BhP*'s nature as an *opus universale*, absorbing literary elements from both north and south, and raises the question of whether the *rasa* theory could also have been absorbed in the *BhP*'s construction. It then looks into the southern emotional religion and its poetic expressions, and into the northern religious poetics and concludes that it is likely that the *rasa* poetics have indeed been absorbed in the *BhP*'s literary and ideological ingredients. It then questions the usefulness of the term 'north' and 'south' and offers an alternative reading of the terms 'knowledge' and 'aesthetics'.

In deconstructing the *BhP*, it may be helpful to consider the period of its composition, which was extremely flexible and undefined. Hardy writes:

> The period under discussion, say sixth to tenth century AD, may generally be characterized as extremely flexible and undefined, which means that indigenous trends and various Northern stimuli left sufficient scope for a great variety of sociological, doctrinal and personal idiosyncrasies and innovations. This situation gave birth to superb and unique creations (examples of which I see in the *TVM*[70] and the *BhP*), but it is not surprising that after a century or so the ferment calmed down and more stable (and rigid) systems evolved. On the whole this was due to the consolidated influence of the *Vedānta* in the South, which gave rise to the formation of schools of thought like the *Advaita Vedānta* and *Viśiṣṭādvaita*, which enter into open antagonism with each other.[71]

Hardy considers the northern influence, represented by the *Vedānta*, to have a consolidating effect, whereas he considers the southern culture to have a more emotional and more aesthetic effect. He also considers the *BhP* to be an *opus universale* and writes:

> As we have already had ample opportunity to notice, the period from about the sixth to about the tenth century in the Tamil South is characterized by a very fertile and multifarious encounter between two cultures, the Tamil and Sanskritic Hindu. The *BhP* is an attempt to harmonize the various complexes involved in this encounter and to resolve the tensions it had given rise to. Simplifying issues considerably, we can say: Northern culture oriented itself by a social system (the brahmins as the foremost *varṇa*) and an ideology (the *Vedānta*, i.e. the systematization of the teaching of the *Upaniṣads*), while Southern culture was characterized by an emotional religion (of the *Āḷvārs*) and by great aesthetic sensibility (the old *caṅkam* poetry, and the *akattiṇai*). The *BhP* tries to integrate all four complexes, and it uses the symbol of the *Vedas* to achieve this, while adopting the *purāṇic* literary form. Thus, as authors have time and again pointed out, the *BhP* stands quite apart from other *purāṇas* – it is an *opus universale* attempting to encompass everything.[72]

Hardy points to the *BhP*'s attempt to syncretize northern and southern culture and ideology, and highlights its application of *Vedic* symbols for the purpose of integration. Moreover, he considers the *BhP* to be unique and to stand quite apart from other *purāṇas* by being an *opus universale*, that is attempting to encompass everything. Could it possibly be that in attempting to encompass everything, northern and southern, and by being of great aesthetic and poetic sensibility, it has assimilated the classical aesthetic tradition originating from *Bharata*, which is considered traditionally to have a *Vedic* origin, descending from the god Brahmā? Considering the *BhP*'s nature as an *opus universale*, and its passion for orthodox ingredients, it would have been surprising had this *not* happened. In other words, it may well be that the northern Sanskritic culture had made not only an ideological contribution, accompanied by a social system, but an aesthetic contribution, by which the *rasa* theory became one of the *BhP*'s building ingredients. However, before considering the deep theological implications of this idea, we shall look closer into the southern emotional religion.

The *Vaiṣṇava* devotional movement developed during the second half of the first millennium, and represented, as mentioned above, a mingling of the Tamil and *Vedic* cultures. As such, we may consider the elevation of the *Drāviḍa Veda* to the position of the Sanskrit *Veda* from two aspects. The first relates to the prestige of the *Drāviḍa Veda* with its increased usage by *Ācāryas* and the development of a system of Tamil *Vedic* texts parallel to those in Sanskrit, so that the latter tend to be forgotten in favour of the former. The second is the employment of the *Drāviḍa Veda* and allied texts in the religio-social set up of *Vaiṣṇavism* for all rituals, festivals and other observances in the daily life of followers of the faith, for which Sanskrit mantras were in vogue.[73] The two cultures deeply merged with each other, leading to a special southern devotional mood, which stressed the personal relationship between the devotee and the deity. *Āḷvārs* is the name by which 12 *Vaiṣṇava* religious poets of Tamil Nadu are known; the term *Āḷvār* in Tamil is interpreted as one 'immersed', here, in the context of love of God, and it is added to the names of the poets as in Poigai *Āḷvār* or Pey *Āḷvār*.[74]

The *Āḷvārs* were drawn from all classes of society and from both genders; the poetry of the Nāyanārs and Āḷvārs was strongly influenced by the stories of the gods in the epics and the *Purāṇas*, and they brought this to a popular level in their hymns and songs, transforming them by the quality of their devotion into a message of divine love. The message was highly emotional and intensely personal. It was their own relationship with the Supreme Person that they expressed, conveyed in terms of human feelings – love, friendship, despair and joy. The language of devotion was for them the language of emotions, human and personal, and at times so intense that it was painful. The goal they sought was salvation, but it was salvation in very personal terms: not union with the impersonal *Brahman* or even merging with the Supreme Person, but an eternal relationship of blissful devotion in which the distinction between the devotee and the deity would be preserved.

The spirit of their devotion was well expressed by the later Indian saint Śrī Rāmakrishna when he declared that he wanted 'to taste sugar, not become sugar'.[75] There seem to be relationships between personal devotion, intense feelings, a language of emotions, the validity of human feelings in establishing relationships with the Supreme Person and the experience of tasting, as all these convey an idea somewhat different than merging with impersonal *Brahman*. As such, perhaps these two modes of encounter with the divine ought to be slightly differentiated; on the one hand, 'the tasting of sugar', and on the other, 'becoming sugar'. The *Āḷvārs* were not mere emotionalists. They were clearly associated with the *Vedic* tradition, and its *Vedānta darśana*, so much so that in order to praise the Lord, they called him 'the divine light of the meaning of *Vedānta*'. From their hymns, we can see that some of the *Āḷvārs* are deeply conscious of Sanskrit literature; they speak of the *Veda* with great respect, and there is absolutely no evidence that they rejected or criticized the medium[76] or the message of Sanskrit literature. *Periyālvār* says he is well versed in the *Vedas* and worships the Lord with the chanting of the *Ṛg*, *Yajus* and *Sāma Vedas*.[77] He also praises sacred places by lauding the number of people who chant the *Vedas* in their precincts. Furthermore, he sees the Lord as the meaning of the *Vedas*[78] and also addresses him by the epithets *Cantokan*, *Taittiriyan*, *Cāmaveti*,[79] as well as the *Pauliyan.*[80] While the *Āḷvārs* were deeply influenced by the classical Tamil poems, we cannot ignore their respect for the *Vedas* and other Sanskrit literature. Indeed, their words are as much a product of the literature of two languages as are the later *Śrī Vaiṣṇava* works that proclaim the 'dual *Vedānta*' or *Ubhaya-Vedānta*.[81]

Not only did the *Āḷvārs* associate themselves with the *Vedic* Sanskrit literature, but they were later understood by their successors to have composed the new *Veda*. This was based upon the belief that a time will come in which the *Vedas* will no longer be accessible due to the influence of the Age of *Kali*, an idea which follows the tradition of the *Āgamas* and the *Purāṇas*. The *Āgamas* and *Purāṇas* of the fifth to seventh centuries CE emphasize the value of the new sectarian means of salvation in the *Kali Yuga*. This last of the four *Yuga* cycles, which is considered to be the present time, is described as a time of general deterioration of standards. In the past, it is said, men were purer and capable of greater learning and performance of religious duties. However, men in the *Kali Yuga* are not able to learn all the *Vedas* and engage in the extended practice of austerities. If the standards of the seers of the past were required, everyone in the *Kali Yuga* would fall short of salvation and be condemned to endless misery. For this reason an easier way has been given: devotion to the Lord and the use of mantras for purification.[82] Thus the *Āḷvārs'* mode of expression was religious poetry, and that was to replace the *Vedic* learning, which, as they believed, was a path of salvation in the past. A textual example of the *Āḷvārs'* poetry may be found in the *Tiruvāymoli*, addressed to Kṛṣṇa in a passionate manner:

You were gone the whole day,
Grazing cows, Kaṇṇā!
Your sweet words burn my soul.
Evening tramples like a rogue (elephant),
And the fragrance of the jasmine buds,
Unleashing my desires, blows upon me.
Embrace my beautiful breasts
With a fragrance of the wild jasmine
Upon your radiant chest.
Give me the nectar of your mouth,
And adorn my lowly head with your jewelled lotus hands.[83]

This poem evokes the sweet taste the devotee experiences in his relationship with his Lord. It is quite likely that songs such as this one, which reveal the divine reality through a rich emotional and poetic expression, represent the stratum upon which the *BhP*'s aesthetic and poetic parts were developed.

The northern Sanskritic culture was certainly not devoid of poetics and aesthetic expressions. One might note *Kāvya* in general, or a specific treatise of the *Kāvya* genre such as Vālmīki's *Rāmāyaṇa*, or a poet such as Kalidāsa – that should suffice to remind one of the richness of Sanskrit literature. Poetry was associated with *Vedic* literature quite directly, and the association of poetry with the vision of a transcendental reality has its roots stretching back as far as the *Vedic* era. The Indian spiritual guides have always been convinced of the necessity of having a direct experience of that transcendent reality which is the ground and essence of all empirical existence. Hence the continuous effort to transcend the empirical level – one of the most striking characteristics of Indian cultural history – and the belief that there are those, such as seers and *yogīs*, who, owing to a special gift or a wonderful exertion of will power, have access to the realm of the Unseen. The ancients were well aware of the resemblance between, and in many cases practical identity of, poets and visionary sages. A *Vedic* poet is a seer (*ṛṣi*), a gifted person who with his inner or spiritual eyes sees things divine and transcendental, and who through the power of his vision brings the past into the present.[84] Accordingly, in *Vedic* times, poets were seers, and vice versa, and as such, being a poet did not discredit one from transmitting the *Vedic* truth. It seems that the *Āḷvārs* ascribed to themselves a similar role of transmitting divine vision through poetry, a tendency which was to appear later in the *BhP.* A *Vedic* term referring to aesthetics which was to later gain importance was *rasa*, and it had *Upaniṣadic* roots. The *Taittirīya Upaniṣad* 2.7.1. reads,

> *raso vai saḥ*
> *rasaṁ hyevāyaṁ labdhvā 'nandī bhavati.*

> That which is known as the self-creator is verily the source of joy; for one becomes happy by coming in[to] contact with that source of joy.[85]

The *Upaniṣadic* usage of the term *rasa* might have been somewhat different than its later usage in the *BhP* and in classical *rasa* theory, but it still denoted 'joy' or 'taste'. Thus it is quite clear that traditionally poetry and even the term *rasa* are closely related to the *Vedic* and *Vedāntic* literature.

Considering all the above, we may evaluate our findings. It is evident that the *BhP* is an *opus universale* attempting to encompass both north and south, and thus has an 'all India' presence. It is also evident that the *BhP* possesses a deep *Vedāntic* character and a Brahminical ideology, combined with personal devotion and a great aesthetic and poetic sensitivity. However, it is not clear whether this aesthetic and poetic sensitivity is entirely of Tamil origin, or whether it shares a northern influence too. Considering the fact that Sanskrit literature had a well-developed aesthetic theory at the time of the *BhP*'s compilation, that this aesthetic sensitivity had clear *Vedic* roots, that the term *rasa* is explicitly mentioned at the *BhP*'s beginning and end, and considering the *BhP*'s author's passion for association with *Vedism*, it would be quite unlikely to presume that the *BhP*'s author had ignored the then available *rasa* theory and not integrated it with other literary and ideological ingredients in compiling this great treatise.

Having offered this deconstruction, we would like to offer alternative terms by which the attempt to deconstruct the *BhP* could proceed, for the purpose of shedding further light on its structure, meaning and notions of personhood. It seems that the terms 'northern' and 'southern' are touched with a certain obscurity, as the distinctions between them are not very clear – the north representing not only sober and formal Brahminical and *Vedāntic* ideology, but also poetic and aesthetic sensitivity, and the south representing not only aesthetic sensitivity and emotionalism, but also identification with *Vedānta*. We therefore wish to form two groups of generic terms, which can be associated with both north and south, and apply these for the purpose of studying the *BhP* and articulating its notion of an 'aesthetic self'. The first group is composed of *Vedānta* and *jñāna*, 'knowledge' and 'philosophy', and may be called 'The Knowledge Group', whereas the second group is composed of 'aesthetic expression', 'emotion', 'poetry' and *rasa*, and may be called 'The Aesthetic Group'. In order to reinforce the validity of this grouping, note Kane:

> Sanskrit writers also were aware of the fact that literature can be divided into two classes as De Quincey said viz. 'literature of knowledge' and 'literature of power'. The former teaches while the latter moves. The two kinds may be often mixed up in the same work but it is possible to keep them entirely separate. Literary criticism, whether in Sanskrit works or elsewhere, is mainly concerned with works of the second of the two classes mentioned above. No question of right or wrong arises as regards the second class of literature, which mainly comprises Poetry, Drama and Fiction. There is a distinction between intuitive consciousness and consciousness arrived at by reasoning.[86]

Apparently, the first type of literature appeals to reasoning while the second evokes an emotional response. Moreover, it may well be that each group represents a wider pattern of thought, or a paradigm, and as such a somewhat closer textual examination is warranted. The *Bhāgavata Purāṇa* opens with the aphorism *oṁ namo bhāgavate vāsudevāya*, translated as 'I offer my obeisance unto Śrī Kṛṣṇa, son of Vasudeva, who is the Supreme Person.'[87] This is followed by the aphorism *janmādyasya yataḥ*, translated as 'From whom emanates the creation and so forth (i.e. maintenance and destruction) of the universe.' This quotation from the *Brahma Sūtra*[88] points to the supreme or to *Brahman* as the source of the entire universe, thus indicating affiliation with the *Vedānta* school. The first three verses are quite condensed, carry a significant conceptual weight and end with the statement, 'Oh connoisseurs of *rasa*, always relish this treatise of the Supreme Person, which is full of *rasa* – on this earth and in the final state.'[89] It may well be that the application of these terms is not circumstantial, rather, it points at one of the *purāṇa*'s main themes, and that is the shift from philosophy to aesthetics. The understanding of these dynamics is essential to the understanding of the way in which the *BhP* intertwines philosophy and aesthetics. By understanding how these two are integrated, one may be able to recognize the *BhP*'s unifying structure, which is based on the development of the theme of divine personhood. The following discussion focuses on the two statements *janmādyasya yataḥ*[90] and *pibata bhāgavataṁ rasamālayaṁ muhuraho rasikā bhuvi bhāvukāḥ*.[91] We shall first elaborate on the meaning of the statement *janmādyasya yataḥ* as representing *Vedānta* tradition, and then elaborate on the notion of *rasa* as representing the *rasa* tradition.

As in their commentaries on *janmādyasya yataḥ* (*BS* 1.1.2), both Śaṅkara and Rāmānuja quote *Taittirīya Upaniṣad* 3.1. In order to explain this aphorism, it may be quoted here too:

> Bhṛgu, the well-known son of Varuṇa, approached his father Varuṇa with the (formal) request, 'O revered sir, teach me *Brahman*'. To him he (Varuṇa) said this: 'Food, vital force, eye, ear, mind, speech – these are the aids to the knowledge of *Brahman*.' To him he (Varuṇa) said: 'Crave to know well that from which all these beings take birth, that by which they live after being born, that towards which they move and into which they merge. That is *Brahman*.' He practiced concentration. He, having practiced concentration.[92]

This passage clearly points to *Brahman* as the source of birth, sustenance and reabsorption, which is, again, a mainstream *Vedāntin* teaching. It also clearly establishes that (the superiority of) knowledge, food, vital force and so forth, are all aids in achieving the goal: knowledge of *Brahman*. Thus for our purpose we would designate this passage as being spoken within a knowledge-oriented paradigm. We shall look deeper into five opening *Brahmasūtra* aphorisms, as it seems that the *BhP*'s first verse is closely related to these, and that there are many corresponding words and terms that relate the two. However, we shall first quote the *BhP* 1.1.1:

oṁ namo bhagavate vāsudevāya
janmādy asya yato 'nvayād itarataś cārtheṣv abhijñaḥ svarāṭ
tene brahma hṛdā ya ādi-kavaye muhyanti yat sūrayaḥ
tejo-vāri-mṛdām yathā vinimayo yatra tri-sargo 'mṛṣā
dhāmnā svena sadā nirasta-kuhakaṁ satyam paraṁ dhīmahi

> I Salute Śrī Kṛṣṇa, the Supreme Person who is the son of Vasudeva, from whom emanates the creation, preservation and destruction of this world. This can be inferred from his presence in all that exists and his absence from all that does not exist. He is fully knowledgeable, fully independent, and it is He who imparted the sacred *Veda*, about which even the learned are perplexed, into the heart of the original wise seer, the god Brahmā. By Him the three *guṇas* appear to be real like the illusory appearance of water in fire or land in water. On Him, who dispels illusion, I meditate.

We shall now quote the opening five *Brahmasūtra* aphorisms along with their English translations:

1. *athāto brahmajijñāsa*:[93] Then, therefore, an enquiry into *Brahman*.
2. *janmādyasya yataḥ*:[94] (*Brahma* is that) from whom arises the origin and rest of (the world).
3. *śāstrayonitvāt*:[95] Because scripture has *Brahman* for his source.
4. *tattu samanvayāt*:[96] But that follows from the concordance (that *Brahman* has scripture as his sole proof).
5. *īkṣaternāśabdam*:[97] Because (the creator) sees, (*Pradhana* is) not (the cause of the universe), it is not scriptural.

The word *paraṁ* appearing in the *BhP*'s first verse corresponds to the word *Brahma*,[98] as both denote the Supreme Being or ultimate reality. The word *dhīmahi* means to meditate, and Kṛṣṇa is the object of meditation. It corresponds to the word *jijñāsā*,[99] which means to desire to know the ultimate reality, or the knowledge of *Brahman*. The words *dhāmnā*, *kapaṭam* and *satyam* denote the idea that after the destruction of darkness, illusion and ignorance by the lustre, one makes an enquiry about *Brahman* and the nature of truthfulness, and as such *māyā* is destroyed by his own power. These correspond to the word *athātaḥ*,[100] which means that after the *pūrva mīmāṁsā* system, which is limited, impermanent and not free, one enquires into *uttaramīmāṁsā*, which represents the *jñānakāṇḍa* or *Vedānta*, which is considered unlimited, permanent and free. In other words, after epitomizing the *Vedic* rituals, it is *Brahman* which remains to be known. The phrase *janmādyasya yataḥ* means the effect and the material cause of the universe, and it points to Kṛṣṇa as the absolute who creates, sublimates and reabsorbs.

It corresponds to the same phrase,[101] which means the Supreme *Brahman*, the absolute from which proceed the creation, sublimation and reabsorption of the universe. The phrase *tene brahmā hṛdaye ādikavaye* means 'who revealed the knowledge of the *Vedas* to Brahmā'. This corresponds to *BS* 1.1.3, according to which *Brahman* is known only through scriptures. Joshi explains this phrase by saying that intellect is based on reasoning and argument, as one argument can be nullified by another stronger one. Subsequently, the Supreme *Brahman* is the revealer of the scriptures. The words *anvaya* and *vyatireka* have a sense similar to *BS* 1.1.4, according to which the authority of the scriptures is established by *samanvaya*, directly or indirectly, as they directly or indirectly establish the Supreme *Brahman* as the highest one. The word *abhijña* corresponds to the *BS* 1.1.5 word *īkṣa*, which means to think or to see. The thinking or seeing is only possible by a conscious being, and not by *pradhāna*, the intelligent substance.[102] All this points to deep relations between the first verse of the *BhP* and the five opening verses of the *Brahmasūtra*. Thus, the *BhP*'s opening verse comprises a clear statement by which the *BhP* associates itself with the *Vedānta* tradition.

The terms *Vedānta*, *Jñāna*, 'knowledge' and 'philosophy' seem to be closely related, but at the same time are distinct as well. In order to proceed with deconstructing the *BhP* into its literary and ideological elements, a closer definition of these terms may be warranted. *Vedānta* is one of the six orthodox systems of Indian philosophy, and primarily denotes the earlier *Upaniṣads* and their teachings. Metaphorically, *Vedānta* is also understood to represent the consummation or culmination[103] of the entire *Vedic* speculation, or indeed of all knowledge.[104] The Hindu philosophical tradition, however, generally recognizes three foundations (*prasthānas*, literally, 'points of departure') of *Vedānta*, namely the

Upaniṣads, the *Bhagavad Gītā* and the *Brahma Sūtra*.[105] The *Vedānta* tradition generally refers to a body of concepts and a number of schools of thought that claim as their primary referent and authority the Sanskrit-language *Upaniṣads*, a group of texts from the middle and late *Vedic* period.[106] In the *Upaniṣads*, speculation about the orthodox rituals of ancient India was increasingly accompanied by speculation on the nature of the world in which ritual is efficacious, on human nature and on the nature of the 'higher' or post-mortem reality that renders human experience ultimately significant. Inquiries into, and discourses about, the vital breath,[107] the self[108] and the corresponding spiritual and cosmic principles[109] are prominent in the *Upaniṣads*.[110] As such, *Vedānta* is engaged with topics such as the nature of the world, human nature, the nature of rituals, the nature of afterlife, the vital breath and ultimately *Brahman*. Simplifying issues, the nature of reality can be deconstructed into three: *Brahman*, *ātman* and *jagat*, or the supreme, the self and the world. These may correspond to the Western notions of God, the human being and the world, which are basic topics of philosophical enquiry.

The term *jñāna* is closely related to *Vedānta*. Within *śruti* a twofold division occurs: *karmakāṇḍa* and *jñānakāṇḍa*. The *Vedic Saṁhitās* and the *Brāhmaṇas*, which centre on the sacrifice, make up the 'part of action', systematized by *Pūrva Mīmāṁsā*, whereas the *Āraṇyakas* and the *Upaniṣads*, with their emphasis on speculation and intuitive knowledge, form the *jñānakāṇḍa*, the 'part of wisdom'.[111] As the *jñānakāṇḍa* is composed of the *Āraṇyakas* and the *Upaniṣads*, which comprise the foundation of *Vedānta*, these two terms, that is *jñānakāṇḍa* and *Vedānta*, are practically synonymous. The Sanskrit root *jñā* is cognate with the Old English *knawan*. Hence on etymological consideration one normally translates *jñāna* as 'knowledge'. Although this translation seems harmless in many contexts, in a philosophical text that deals with epistemology, or *pramāṇa-śāstra*, it will often be wrong and misleading. In fact, in non-technical Sanskrit *jñāna* often means knowledge.[112] As such, the term *jñāna* is used in two ways: whereas in non-technical Sanskrit *jñāna* often means 'knowledge', in specific epistemological texts, such as *nyāya* texts, the term would have a different meaning. For our purpose, taking *jñāna* to mean 'knowledge' may be acceptable, as we do not engage with *pramāṇa-śāstra* in this work. However, in Indian thought, knowledge is taken to have not only a cognitive significance, but a soteriological significance as well and, as such, the term *jñāna* also possesses a soteriological significance. It is almost unanimously claimed that some sort of *jñāna*, or *tattva-jñāna*,[113] is instrumental in bringing about the final release from bondage.[114] Underlying Indian thought is the idea of release from *saṁsāra*, and the acquisition of *jñāna* is no doubt a central path to release. Thus *jñāna* may affect one's cognitive state by removing ignorance or *avidyā*, thus enabling a process of self-knowledge or self-realization, leading to final liberation. Having briefly discussed the term *jñāna* and its relation to the term 'knowledge', and considering *Vedānta* to be one of the six *darśanas* or orthodox branches of Indian philosophy, the question ought to be asked: Can *jñāna* be considered similar or equivalent to the term 'philosophy'?

Here is a general definition of the term philosophy: 'The study of the fundamental nature of knowledge, reality, and existence, especially when considered as an academic discipline.'[115] This definition emphasizes the act of study and theoretical endeavour, the purpose of which is the understanding of reality. The term *darśana* is somewhat similar as it denotes having a view of the nature of reality and, as such, traditionally, Indian philosophy is referred to as *darśana*, which literally means 'view', in the sense of having a cognitive 'sight' of something. What is implicit in this is that what is 'viewed' or 'sighted' is the truth about the nature of reality, and this reflects the fact that understanding the nature of reality is the aim of philosophizing in India.[116] It seems that the concept of philosophizing as an 'intellectual activity meant for a rational understanding of the nature of reality' fairly well represents both Western philosophy as well as Indian philosophy. However, Indian philosophy has a trans-rational aspect too, and in that it may differ from Western philosophy. Implicit in the term *darśana* is the idea that human beings are able to gain an actual sighting, in the sense of experiential knowledge of a metaphysical truth. It seems that this trans-intellectual aspect of the term *darśana*, characterized by wisdom and insight, is related to the Indian idea of knowledge having a soteriological character. The Indian concept of 'knowledge' may be characterized as having two aspects: the rational and the trans-rational.[117] As for the Western concept of 'knowledge', we may treat it as sharing the rational aspect with its Indian counterpart, but not the intuitive aspect. This may be reinforced by the definition of the term 'knowledge' by *The New Oxford Dictionary*: 'Facts, information, and skills acquired by a person through experience or education; the theoretical or practical understanding of a subject. In philosophy: true, justified belief; certain understanding as opposed to opinion.'[118] This definition clearly refers to the theoretical aspects of knowledge, but not to any intuitive or trans-rational aspects of it. In summary, it may be said that all four terms – *Vedānta*, *jñāna*, philosophy and knowledge – share a rational aspect of attempting to grasp or deconstruct reality through a theoretical endeavour. However, the Indian terms share a second quality, which is a trans-rational, mystical and intuitive aspect of liberating wisdom, a concept not denoted by the Western usage of the terms 'knowledge' and 'philosophy'. In this book we shall avoid discussing the trans-rational, mystical and intuitive aspects of the Indian terms, and refer to their rational aspect only. This will enable us to simplify our terms and thereby concentrate on developing our argument.

Having discussed the *BhP*'s opening phrase, *janmādyasya yataḥ*, and having looked somewhat closer into the four terms associated with knowledge, we may now discuss the aesthetic aspect of the concluding phrase of the three introductory verses. The phrase is *pibata bhāgavataṁ rasamālayaṁ muhuraho rasikā bhuvi bhāvukāḥ*.[119] It is significant that the term *rasa* appears already in the opening stanza, as aesthetics would later occupy a major place in the *BhP*. Moreover, the idea of integrating *Vedānta* and *rasa* seems to be central and important enough, so much so that it not only opens the *BhP*, but concludes it as well.[120] Thus one of the concluding verses of the *BhP*'s final chapters reads as follows:

> *sarva-vedānta-sāram hi śrī-bhāgavatam iṣyate*
> *tad-rasāmṛta-tṛptasya nānyatra syād ratiḥ kvacit*

> The *Bhāgavata Purāṇa* is considered to be the essence of the entire *Vedānta* tradition; As such, for one who is satisfied by tasting its nectar-like *rasa*, there does not exist any other delight elsewhere.[121]

Apparently, the *BhP*'s author or group of authors were interested in emphasizing this integration of *Vedānta* and *rasa* at the formal opening and closing of the treatise, an integration out of which its unique structure evolves. It should be noted that in Indian thought, meaning could be conveyed not only through transmission of knowledge, but through the tasting of emotions as well. Consequently, complex theories on the nature of emotional flow and literary experience were developed in India. *Rasa* originally meant 'sap', 'essence' or 'taste'. Although *rasa* retains this original meaning, in the context of aesthetics it can perhaps best be translated as 'dramatic sentiment' or 'aesthetic enjoyment'.[122]

The term *rasa* is a central term in Indian aesthetics, so much so that a complex *rasa* theory was developed. It considered itself to have *Vedic* roots, comprised a cornerstone in Sanskrit dramaturgy and poetics and was associated with northern Sanskrit culture. The *rasa* theory originated with *Bharata* in the *Nāṭyaśāstra*, and claimed that the object or meaning that is sought to be conveyed in literary compositions is an emotional effect or a diverse human experience appearing in one's mind and heart. It is possible, *Bharata* demonstrated, to enumerate the whole range of emotions, or states of being born of experience, and to analyse the structure of those emotions in terms of cause and their physical effect. The theory thus became one of literary experience rooted in empirical human reality.[123] We shall leave the topic of *rasa* aside at this point and return to it later.

Knowledge and Aesthetics and their Relationship to Direct and Indirect Applications of Language

This section first looks into Sanskrit linguistic theory and poetics and offers examples of direct and indirect usage of language in the *BhP*. It then distinguishes between the philosopher's world – 'the Universe of Reason' – and that of the poet – 'the Universe of Feelings' – and concludes that poetics may better express the personal than philosophy.

Indian medieval theorists of language pointed to three ways in which verbal expressions are made – the denotative, the metaphoric and the suggestive. Regarding these three types of expression, or three types of *śakti* – powers inherent in language – language has a basic potential to say things as they are, to supply a denotative name to things, to nominate terms, to claim obliging assertions and so forth. This denotative ability is called *abhidhā*. The second capacity, that of *lakṣaṇā*, includes what we would call a metaphor. In this regard there exists a sophisticated and interesting literary theory related to Kuntaka, which speaks of a certain distortion in the usage of language as characterizing the poetic technique. Accordingly, the good poet always distorts his expression. His language is distorted from the normal and logical literary path, and it is only due to this distortion that penetrates language that this transformation in consciousness and emotion, which is the goal of the poem, occurs. The various types of distortions can naturally be analysed and categorized, and that is what Kuntaka does in his treatise *vakrokti jīvita* or 'The Life of Literary Distortion'. However, despite its sophistication, this theory has not become common in India. Instead, a different theory became acknowledged as the peak of medieval literary criticism, and this is the theory that emphasizes the third ability, the third potency inherent in language: suggestion – *vyañjanā* or *dhvani*. *Dhvani* means resonance. There is a continuous resonance in poetical language, which carries the real import of poetry. There is no good poetry without suggestion and, according to Indian poetics, suggestion is carried by the words' resonance and not by their explicit content.[124] Whether the denotative mode of expression attempts to grasp things as they are, whether it supplies a denotative name to things, whether it nominates terms or claims obliging assertions, it always applies language directly. In other words, it prefers terms that actually denote the specific intended meaning, in a concise, simple, straightforward and direct manner. However, the other two modes of expression are rather different. The metaphoric mode of expression uses some linguistic distortion in order to express itself, and the suggestive mode of expression relies on resonance, which hints at a meaning beyond the simple, normal and logical sense of the expression. As such, both of these literary techniques apply language indirectly, that is they intend to express something that is beyond the simple, normal, straightforward and logical meaning of the verbal expression. The poetical term *bhāva* may exemplify an indirect usage of language, and a definition is offered:

> *Bhāva*: A figure in which a literal truth is expressed for the purpose of conveying a hidden intention. For example; the girl is inviting the wayfarer to bed: 'I am alone and weak and innocent, and my husband has left this house for a far country; why do you ask refuge here? Don't you realize that my mother-in-law is about, deaf and blind? Stupid traveler!'[125]

This figurative mode of expression well exemplifies the indirect transmission of the girl's message to the traveller. Whereas attempting to read this statement as a direct verbal expression will result in mere confusion, the real message of inviting the traveller into the house is not explicitly stated but only hinted at indirectly.

The direct usage of language may be exemplified by the *catuḥ-ślokī bhāgavata*, the four verses spoken by Viṣṇu to Brahmā, perhaps epitomizing the *BhP*'s philosophy:[126]

> 32 I alone existed before the creation; there was nothing else but the supreme – neither real nor unreal. Since the creation of the universe that which exists is me, and that which will remain after the universal destruction will also be me alone. 33 That which appears to be of value, has no reality unless it is related to me. You should know it to be my illusion, *māyā*, just like a reflection in the darkness. 34 Just as the great elements, which have entered into all created things whether gigantic or minute, have also not entered into them,[127] similarly, I am within the creation, and at the same time not within it.[128] 35 This much should be known by him who desires to know the truth in regards to the soul, in all time and space, both directly and indirectly.[129]

This section clearly contains philosophical-theological statements regarding subjects such as the existence of the Supreme Person prior to the creation and after the annihilation, the existence and non-existence of the phenomenal world, and the reality of the soul. Moreover, it is specifically stated in verse 35 that these topics should be understood by one who seeks knowledge of the *ātman*'s reality. Thus it can be said that this is engaged with the Supreme *Brahman*, the *jīva* and the world. In essence, this section is characterized by a rational and consistent form of discourse: it conveys ideas in a condensed manner; it aims at a theoretical study of the subject; it has a soteriological aspect characterized by *jñāna*; it deconstructs the truth regarding the nature of reality into its essential components – the core issues dealt with being *Vedāntic* topics such as *īśvara*, *jīva* and *jagat* and their interrelations; and it aims to bestow a certain philosophical point of view, or *darśana*, upon the reader. In fact, it is a commonly accepted traditional view that these four verses are so condensed as to contain the entire *BhP* in essence. In regard to these four verses, Joshi writes,

> the traditional scholars of *Bhāgavata* recitation and exposition and a vast majority of Sanskrit commentators accept the four verses of *Bhāgavata mahāpurāṇa*[130] as *catuḥślokī Bhāgavata* [. . .] The common arguments put forward in support of the *catuḥślokī Bhāgavata* are 1. That the answer of Śrī Kṛṣṇa to the four questions of Brahmā is given in only four principal verses, 2. That all the twelve *skandhas* of the *Bhāgavata Purāṇa* are included in these four verses.[131]

The idea of these four verses including all 12 *BhP skandhas* further reinforces their character as a kind of philosophical *sūtra*, conveying *jñāna* in the most condensed and straightforward fashion. Therefore this section well exemplifies a direct and compressed exposition of knowledge, one that well represents a 'Knowledge Paradigm'.

A different application of language appears in the *BhP* where Kṛṣṇa expresses literal truth while conveying hidden intentions. In this manner he addresses the *gopīs*, who have left home and come to meet him in the forest, being enchanted by his playing of the flute in the full moon. The translation is as follows:

> 18 Kṛṣṇa said: Welcome, Oh blessed ladies! What can I do for you? Is everything well in *Vraja*? Please explain to me the reason for your coming here. 19 Oh slender-waisted ladies, this night is fearful and is infested with ferocious creatures. Please do return to *Vraja*, as this place is not fit for women to stay out at night. 20 Not seeing you, your mothers, fathers, sons, brothers and husbands must be searching for you. Do not create fear and anxiety in your family members. 21 You have now seen this forest, full of flowers, illuminated by the beams of the full moon, and beautified by the trees, whose leaves are quivering in the gentle breeze playfully blowing from the Yamunā. 22 Please return to *gokula* without delay; wait upon your husbands, suckle your children and feed the calves. 23 Or perhaps you have come as your heart is attached to me out of deep affection for me, as it is quite natural for all living beings to be affectionate towards me. 24 It is the supreme *dharma* for women to wait upon and render service to their husbands with sincerity of hearts, to look after the well-being of relatives and to take care of children. 25 The husband may be ill-natured or

> quarrelsome, unfortunate, old in age, dull-witted, sickly or poor, but women desirous of the heavenly world should not desert him if he is not fallen. 26 Resorting to an adulterous affair with a paramour by a woman of a noble family is a hindrance to the attainment of heaven: it ruins her reputation, it involves difficulties, is petty and creates fear. 27 Love for me arises by hearing about me, by receiving my *darśana*,[132] by meditating upon me and glorifying my noble deeds, and not by physical proximity. Therefore please return home.[133]

This passage applies language in a suggestive and indirect way. Kṛṣṇa advises the *gopīs* to return home, while indirectly suggesting that they stay in the forest with him. Kṛṣṇa preaches to them a sermon on the importance of following *dharma* by being chaste and loyal to their husbands, but at the same time compliments their thin waists, thereby implicitly suggesting they give up *dharma* for the sake of enjoying the *rasa*-dance with him. Kṛṣṇa asks the *gopīs* to return home, while mentioning the forest's floral beauty and the silvery beam of the full moon, and even propounds the theology of devotion to him, wherein physical proximity is secondary to meditation upon him. Saying that, he indirectly suggests that the *gopīs* give up even that doctrine for the sake of being in his physical proximity. This section indeed represents a very deep emotional reality shared by both Kṛṣṇa and the *gopīs*, and, in summary, is aesthetically very rich. Judging this same section from the theoretical or philosophical point of view, it seems quite dull. The information given is quite specific as opposed to universal, it is not at all condensed but rather is quite detailed and, ethically speaking, it is not very consistent, as it involves a sermon on morality accompanied with explicit bodily compliments. Moreover, it doesn't provide a coherent idea as to the nature of reality, neither does it deconstruct reality into its essential components. Similarly, its theological components depicting devotion to, meditation on and glorification of Kṛṣṇa are quite self-centred and self-glorifying, as opposed to a more balanced and distant discourse one might expect from a serious theological instruction. Thus this section well exemplifies an indirect and suggestive expression of an emotional reality, one spoken within an 'Aesthetic Paradigm'.

The nature of direct language (and philosophies) is to exist within the sphere of rationality and logic. It is characterized by its ability to extract the general and abstract principles from many specifics and particulars in a direct, exact and concise manner, thereby distinguishing the true from the false. The nature of literature and poetry is different as it is characterized by an ability to trigger and arouse emotions through an indirect and suggestive usage of language. Gerow sheds light on this:

> Theories of literary criticism develop in congenial literary contexts. Less abstract than philosophies, they can serve as grist for a *Wissenschaftssoziologie* that attempts to state the cultural preconditions of a formal intellectual theory. Literature is work of sensibility; that it takes as a principle some notion of 'taste' ties it to a certain time and place more radically and meaningfully than any of the forms of expression that have a more theoretical grounding.[134]

Gerow makes a few important points relevant to our discussion. He distinguishes between theories of literary criticism, of which the *rasa* theory is one, and philosophies, which he takes to be 'more abstract'. He says that these theories help one to understand the cultural preconditions within which an intellectual theory exists, and emphasizes literature's way of sensing reality, which is by tasting (as opposed to rationalizing). Finally he points out that literature ties a taste to a specific time and place more than other forms of expression, which are more theoretical. It may well be that philosophy focuses more on the substance, which is general, and less on the attributes, which are specific.[135] Thus, for example, when saying that 'a chair is a separate seat for one person, typically with a back and four legs',[136] philosophy would relate to an abstract chair, and not to any particular one with certain attributes related to a specific time and place. Similarly, logic is formal, as it perceives the form of an object and ignores its specific attributes.

Poetry, however, has the ability to intensify the specific and particular qualities of a specific object. Examining a flower, for example, the philosophical approach would concentrate on its 'flowerhood', that is, its essential and minimal components that are needed for it to be a flower. In order to do that, it will minimize a perception or, in other words, further a relaxation of its peculiar and personal characteristics in favour of emphasizing and intensifying its abstract and impersonal essence of 'flowerhood'. A poetic approach would, on the contrary, intensify its particular specific or 'personal' characteristics – its being red, its having thorns for protection, its being fragrant and its being mildly covered with morning dew – and at the same time further a relaxation, or minimize a perception, of its abstract and impersonal characteristics, that is, its 'flowerhood'. It follows that philosophical language favours abstraction, whereas poetic language favours specification, that is concentration on the detailed and peculiar.

It seems that the philosopher and the poet are each living in 'parallel worlds', so to speak, and are experiencing different realities. In regard to the possibility of reality being divided, the contention that reality, for human beings, is neither fixed nor singular seems to be commonly accepted. One has only to survey the diversity of cultures to be struck by the enormous variability in the ways of being human, and in people's sense of what is real and meaningful. Reality is culturally constructed and is not a given for human beings, who are not fixed psychologically, but instead manifest an immense plasticity in the arena of reality construction. Human nature enables an experience of a wide and seemingly endless range of possible realities.[137] As such, we shall attempt to further understand the two competing realities through looking closer into the way both the philosopher and the poet attempt to grasp the world and construct the reality in which they live. As Gerow indicates, literary criticism is congenial for stating the cultural preconditions of a formal intellectual theory, thus we may attempt to construct our theory or thesis based upon an analysis of its cultural preconditions, and we may arrive at that through literary criticism, or looking into the way the literature's founding texts are constructed.

In other words, by studying the issue of the direct and indirect modes of expression, we may better understand the two kinds of reality found in the *BhP.* Although both the philosopher and poet each attempt to grasp the truth, there is an irresolvable tension between them. Seen from the point of view of the rational philosopher, variety, specifics and diversity, including emotional diversity, are to be organized into a simple and concise unified truth, which extracts the abstract essence of the variegated phenomena. Thus, for example, the statement that 'All men are mortal' states simply and concisely that which is a reality for numerous people, past, present and future. There is no doubt a deep emotional and existential reality related to the phenomenon of death, but the philosopher has to distance themself from that emotional reality in order to make his statement. He would have to rise above his own feelings, which may obscure his judgment, and only then would it be possible for him to see and rationalize clearly. The more he widens his horizons and concentrates on the abstract, the deeper his experience of that reality becomes. Thus, his reality may be called 'A Universe of Reason'. The poet too tries to grasp the truth and express it, but his is a different truth and his mode of expression is also different. The reality he tries to grasp is an aesthetic and emotional reality, and he may be living in a different reality, which may be called 'A Universe of Feelings'. His mode of grasping is through tasting, and the more variegated reality is, the more opportunities for tasting exist for him. For the aesthete to taste a specific phenomenon, he has to come as close to it as possible, and in order to magnify his taste, he has to distance himself from any other tastes, as the more he narrows his horizons and concentrates on the specific, the deeper his experience of that reality becomes. The conclusion is that both the philosopher and the poet are trying to grasp the essence of reality, but they do it in entirely different ways and reach an entirely different experiential conclusion as to reality's nature. Stated differently, the philosopher lives within a 'Universe of Reason' whereas the poet lives within a 'Universe of Feelings'.

An example may be given of Romeo expressing his love to Juliet, described differently in two different languages, the rational and the aesthetic:

1. Romeo felt intense love for Juliet.
2. The brightness of her cheek would shame those stars,
As daylight doth a lamp; her eyes in heaven
Would through the airy region stream so bright
That birds would sing and think it were no night.
See, how she leans her cheek upon her hand!
O, that I were a glove upon that hand.
That I might touch that cheek![138]

The first statement is grounded in a knowledge-oriented paradigm, whereas the second is within an aesthetics-oriented paradigm. Although the two statements describe the same occurrence, each emphasizes a different aspect of it. The first statement articulates the occurrence concisely and briefly, whereas the second statement articulates the same phenomenon from a tasting perspective, through a suggestive or indirect use of language. In order to exemplify the different use of language, we may try to read Shakespeare's lines in a direct way and say that 'Romeo wanted to be the glove on Juliet's hand'. Obviously that was verbally expressed, but it does not reveal the reality fostered in that passage, and it leaves the reader in need of further interpretation and clarification. Gerow writes:

> The expressive goal, or sense, of verbal art is often not explicitly derived from the literal content of the words and sentences employed. The meticulous analyses of poetic utterance and poetic imagination that were the business of the *alaṁkāra* school, seemed to come to precisely this conclusion. Insofar as utterance can be deemed poetic, it must involve, as an essential element, some such detour in the usual or normal apprehension process – a *vakrokti* as Bhāmaha first called it; a sense grasped by the refined mind as a result of the word heard or read, but not directly by means of it. In the striking conceit of Shakespeare, 'O that I were a glove upon that hand – that I might touch that cheek...'. It is just the absurdity of the identification of the speaker (Romeo) with an inanimate glove that provokes the hearer to a leap beyond the language in an effort to make sense of that nonsense [...] If this is the case, then are we not invited to consider whether *qua* poetry, language is any more distinctive than gesture or character in the drama?[139]

In this way, the manner in which the aesthetic experience is transferred through verbal art is implicit rather than explicit. Moreover, looking into the relationships between language and drama in Indian thought, it is evident that language is not necessarily always taken to be the highest verbal expression. In summary of this issue, it may be stated that language applied indirectly is suitable for aesthetic expressions, and that aesthetic expressions lead to personal ones. The opposite seems to hold true too, as direct usage of language is suitable for rational expressions, which have a tendency to lead to impersonal findings. It may well be that language applied directly is suitable for a discussion of personhood and personalities up to a certain degree, and that from there onwards indirect language, represented by drama and poetry, can better depict the personal realm. Philosophy has the ability to define the general among the many particulars, and distinguish the true from the false. However, its strength constitutes its weakness as the general may be blind to the particular and personal, and therefore philosophical enquiry tends to result in general and impersonal findings. Therefore, a philosophical system, which is, by definition leaning on logic, will necessarily lead to the articulation of abstract principles, whereas an aesthetical system, which, by definition, leans on aesthetic principles, will necessarily lead to the particular and the peculiar.

Personal and Impersonal Theologies: Linguistic and Ontological Implications

This section first raises the topic of personal and impersonal theology. Following that it argues that traditionally the *rasa* school was considered to be engaged not merely in the sphere of poetics, but rather offered its own path of spiritual realization, just like the *Vedānta* school did. Finally, this sections looks into the ontological status of emotions and describes how in the Caitanya school of Bengali *Vaiṣṇavism*, emotions indeed constitute reality.

The dual application of language in the *BhP* has not only literary implications but theological ones as well. If philosophy favours abstraction and impersonalism, and poetics favours specification and personalism, it may well be that in a theological context, philosophy favours impersonal divinity, whereas poetics favours personal divinity. In other words, it may well be that the knowledge trend, which is associated with the direct usage of language, is also associated with the impersonal concept of *Brahman*. Similarly, it seems, the aesthetic trend, which is associated with the indirect usage of language, is also associated with the personal concept of *Brahman*. The two concepts of *Brahman* – the impersonal and the personal – coexist within the *BhP*, and the notions of divinity are constructed through various proportions of their mixtures. Although the two trends, impersonal and personal, are generally mixed, we propose to separate them methodically or theoretically and examine each of them on its own terms. That may be analogous to the study of grammar, in which theoretical forms such as roots and stems are examined for the purpose of understanding the structure of a given language. Although in spoken or written language stems and roots are not directly applied, they serve as the linguistic structure's foundation. Similarly, although it may be hard to point at textual sources entirely representing impersonal or personal worldviews, it may still be necessary to separate the two terms, even artificially, for the purpose of their study. As such one may be able examine how these two trends intertwine, thus supporting and constructing the notion of personhood in the *BhP*. We will begin by looking into the association of *jñāna* with the notion of Impersonal *Brahman*, and a similar association between *bhakti* and Personal *Brahman*, as indicated by Sharma:

> *Jñāna-yoga* is directed towards the realization of *nirguṇa Brahman* wherein the sole spiritual reality of *Brahman* leaves no room for any kind of distinction [...] *Bhakti-yoga* is directed towards the realization of *saguṇa Brahman*, and this *yoga* functions within the framework of a somewhat different set of presuppositions.[140]

What are the relationships between *jñāna*, knowledge, philosophy and Impersonal *Brahman*? Does the language of philosophy necessarily presuppose impersonal ideas? In what sense is the devotional language of *bhakti* directed towards personal *Brahman*? We shall first look closer into the personal–impersonal debate. Traditionally these concepts of the Supreme Being served as a major issue of sectarian debate. In general there are two principles at work in the Indian sublime: the first is the principle of non-differentiation and absolute non-representation, whereas the second is its very opposite, of excessive representation and differentiation. The latter principle makes its own way into the myriad of reincarnations that invade the Hindu religious universe, whereas the former into what is vaguely referred to as the mystical tradition in which the relationship between the one and the many is kept intact through an essentially mystic logic.[141] These two principles, the non-differentiated abstract and the differentiated particular, have deep roots in theology.

As such, more than in any other topic, it is concerning the personal character of the Supreme Being that the theists oppose the monist's concept of the supra-personal Absolute. They declare with relatively united voice that *Brahman*'s transcendent nature is most properly described by means of his being as the highest Person (*puruṣa-uttama*). Naturally, some of these attributes consist of peculiarly *Vaiṣṇava* theistic terms. Their distinct theological outlooks precluded any complete unanimity. Nevertheless, as serious theists they are at one in opposing the monistic view which, only by way of concession, ascribed a variety of personal qualities to *Brahman*, and considered this personalized *Brahman* a lower-order being. Thus the monist contends that the radical transcendence of *Brahman*'s real and essential nature demands a theological descriptive method that can reach beyond all such attributes. *Brahman*-with-qualities (*saguṇa*) must be replaced by *Brahman*-without-qualities (*nirguṇa*). Only in this way can the perfect identity of the inner self and the Supreme Self be maintained.[142] The monist arguing for *Brahman*'s transcendence cannot but consider *Brahman*'s personal form to be a lower manifestation, somewhat crude and imperfect, of the pure and unadulterated *Brahman* – impersonal form. However, the theist or the personalist sees things in an entirely different manner as for him this whole method appeared blasphemous, not only because it 'robbed' the Supreme Person of qualities essential to his being, but more specifically because it reduced his transcendent supremacy in relation to the individual self. It was just this divine supremacy that the theist experienced as the basis of worship, the highest human end, and it was the knowledge of the self's dependence on this supremacy that he declared as the only means to ultimate liberation. On this issue the divergence between monism and theism is at its most striking.[143] As such, for the theist the notion of impersonal *Brahman* represents only a limited aspect of the supreme. This aspect might represent *Brahman*'s eternal, conscious and blissful nature,[144] but fails to grasp the Supreme Person's various qualities, fails to incite in the worshipper feelings of dependence upon that Supreme Person and fails to supply a foundation upon which personal relationships can be developed between the minute and the Supreme Persons. As mentioned, the personal–impersonal discourse has not only religious, but philosophical and specifically ontological aspects as well. In other words, the impersonalist believes that underlying the whole of reality there exists an impersonal principle.

Conversely, the personalist believes that it is ultimately a person who underlies reality. We have already quoted Kohak on this point,[145] and indicated its existential implications. However, these two positions are not always perceived as conflicting or contradicting each other. There can and sometimes is a reconciliation between them, and this tension could also be viewed in a non-sectarian way, as two different ways of viewing reality. As such, it is commonplace in the discussion of Hindu philosophy to maintain that *Brahman* may be taken to mean either *saguṇa* or *nirguṇa*, although the two are not clearly mutually exclusive but represent two standpoints of viewing the same reality.[146] Although there have been numerous sectarian polemics on this very question, it still seems that one cannot exist without the other. Those maintaining an impersonal view practise some form of personal devotion, whereas those maintaining a personal view rely on impersonal philosophy in order to claim transcendence for their deity, and raise the object of their adoration from a mythical context to a theological one. In general, these two concepts are mixed with each other within Hinduism, as the one ultimate reality can be visualized either in personal or impersonal terms. However, the chronological order of priority of *Brahman* (neuter) and *Brahman* (masculine) cannot be determined with certainty. In fact, it is quite possible that the Hindu tradition did not consciously distinguish between the two, and that may be why we find monotheism and monism often mixed up with each other.[147] We may look now closer into the *BhP*'s position on this major question.

The *BhP* engages this subject matter in the first book, where the programme for the entire treatise is being laid out. The translation is as follows: 'According to *śruti*, those who possess knowledge of the Highest Truth say that this non-dual knowledge is *Brahman*, the Divine Person within the Heart and the Supreme Person.'[148] This fundamental statement establishes the *BhP*'s position on the truth as being non-dual. Moreover, this non-dual truth is designated in three different ways – *Brahman*, *Paramātman*[149] and *Bhagavān*.[150] *Brahman* may be considered as the impersonal feature of the truth, whereas *Bhagavān* may be taken as its personal feature. The term *Paramātman* may be situated inbetween the impersonal and the personal. However, this term is subtle and will be further looked into later.[151] Sheridan states:

> The non-duality of Truth or the reality (*tattva*) is such that no ultimate distinction between knower and knowledge can be made, though by giving the absolute reality different names, the *Bhāgavata* affirms that the richness of absolute reality cannot be exhausted by considering it from one angle only. With admitting any distinction within the absolute reality, the *Bhāgavata* draws on various traditions to aid the understanding. The terms '*Brahman*' and 'Highest Self' are drawn from the *Vedānta*, while '*Bhagavān*' is

> dear to the *Vaiṣṇavas*. The final position given to *Bhagavān* seems to raise it above the other two in importance, and this is borne out by the *purāṇa* as a whole. Thus non-dual knowledge which is the essence of the absolute reality, is, according to the *Bhāgavata*, ultimately personal.[152]

The important points made by Sheridan are: 1. the *BhP* conceives of the absolute to be a rich reality which cannot be considered from one angle only; 2. there are, according to the *BhP*'s theology, distinctions within the absolute; 3. the terms *Bhagavān* and *Paramātman* are associated with *Vedānta*, whereas the term *Bhagavān* is associated with *Vaiṣṇavism*; and 4. the position of the term *Bhagavān* seems to rise above the two other terms in importance. Another question that may be raised is: In what sense can the reality of *Bhagavān* be taken to be non-dual? We are prone to seek the answer in the various *Vaiṣṇava* theologies, and our preliminary idea would be to look deeper into the relations of the *BhP*'s *Vedānta* and some theistic form of *Vedānta*. However, as it is an important question, the final chapter will be devoted to looking further into four *Vedāntic* systems, with the purpose of shedding further light on the various systems' reconciliation of the reality of *Bhagavān* with non-duality, apparently influenced by the *BhP* in doing so.

Having pointed to the 'Universe of Feelings'[153] as representative of a reality parallel to the 'Universe of Reason', the question may be raised: What is the status emotional reality holds in Indian thought? For Indian thought, emotions and emotional reality do indeed seem to have an ontological status, and can therefore constitute reality no less than physical objects or rational thoughts. The idea of emotions being organized in universal patterns, and constrained by logical necessity, is quite natural for Indian thought and theology. As we suggest that the *BhP* gradually leads its reader from the rational reality into the emotional one, we aim at shedding further light on the Indian theological concept of emotional reality. Gerow raises the question whether *rasa* is applicable to other genres than Indian dramaturgy, in the context of which it was originally verbalized:

> In this light we want to put forth a related but apparently contrary problem: Is the *rasa*-aesthetic applicable to other genres and to the literature of other times and places? This is not to raise again the

> question of the *rasa*'s validity in the sense of psychological reality, or as a state of mind (or emotion) having epistemological or ontological implications; but rather to ask just how tightly circumscribed the *rasa* (as an aesthetic principle) is by the literature which conditioned its proposition. This kind of query should enhance our perception of the function of *rasa* by testing its critical limits.[154]

It seems that *rasa* was perceived as claiming to have a wide import right from the beginning of its usage in Sanskrit literature, as both in its field of application (poetry in the broadest sense) and in its theoretical justification (*śāstra*), the notion of *rasa* showed a marked imperialistic tendency. From its beginnings in the discussions of Sanskrit drama, its partisans have sought on the one hand to bring under its explanatory aegis many other genres of literary and artistic production and, on the other, have claimed for the *rasa* greater and greater psychological or ontological validity. Indeed, the notion of *rasa* that emerges today is a result of this agglomerating tendency, so much so that we must count universality as more an intrinsic than adventitious quality of *rasa.* Our task in seeking to determine the appropriate limits of the *rasa*'s applicability is thus not a static one. We must keep in view the apparent dynamics of *rasa* itself.[155] As such, *rasa* may well possess an apparent dynamic character that is not merely psychological but ontological as well. Moreover, *rasa* seems to possess an 'imperialistic' tendency and its universality seems to be an intrinsic quality. In other words, right from the beginning of its usage, the term *rasa* was taken to apply to a wide range of spheres, far beyond dramaturgy.

Rasa played a central role in medieval religious devotional schools, and was understood to be similar to the realization of *Brahman*. In regard to the views of Viśvanatha,[156] Jadunath Sinha writes:

> An aesthetic enjoyment is similar to the realization of *Brahman*. A person of taste experiences an aesthetic enjoyment even as a *yogī* experiences *Brahman*. Like the direct and immediate experience of *Brahman* the aesthetic experience is the direct and immediate experience of the *rasa* free from cognition of all other objects. In both kinds of experience there is immediacy. Just as in the intuitive realization of *Brahman* the subject is lost in *Brahman*, so

> in the aesthetic enjoyment of the *rasa* the subject is lost in the enjoyment.[157]

Apparently, in these medieval schools the experience of *rasa* was regarded as some kind of spiritual experience, similar to the experience of self-realization. As such, the experience of *rasa* would relate directly to the soul or *ātman* as well in certain medieval schools of thought. There, *rasa* transcended its aesthetic domain and became a general principle of awareness having profound implications on absolute consciousness (*ātman*).[158] What is the meaning of *rasa* being 'a general principle of awareness' and having 'profound implications on absolute consciousness'? Our understanding is that *rasa* may be taken by certain schools to be an essential characteristic of the *ātman* itself. As such it could express awareness and have profound implications for the *ātman* and its relationships with *Brahman*. Klostermaier argues that in one major school of thought, feelings possess an ontological status, as they structure reality and provide the criterion for its existence:

> There is [. . .] one major school of thought for which the universe consists of feelings – feeling elicited by and directed towards a transcendent person. I am speaking, of course, of Caitanya's *Gauḍīya Vaiṣṇavism* and its systematization in the works of his immediate followers, among whom Rūpa *Goswāmin* and Jīva *Goswāmin* stand out. Their is a universe of feelings – feelings providing not only the criterion of reality but also its structures.[159]

The ontological status awarded to emotions in the Caitanya school of *Gauḍīya Vaiṣṇavism* may provide an important clue to the understanding of the *BhP*, as it highlights the existence of an alternative pattern of thought, which does not perceive reality through rationality, but rather through aesthetics. Klostermaier describes this type of reality as 'very different': 'It is so different an approach to reality from what we have been brought up in that it takes considerable effort to see its point. Having seen the point, however, it begins to make sense.'[160] Klostermaier's describing this approach to reality as 'very different' is significant. As our work is theoretical and therefore confined to the realm of reason, it can but articulate the rational aspect of its subject, but not enter it or 'taste' it. We can, however, argue that the *BhP*'s aesthetic sections represent a mode of reality that is difficult for a Western mind to penetrate. *Rasa* awareness seems to be subject to the constraints of logical necessity and, more specifically, to the notions of cause and effect. The notion of cause–effect is really too powerful to explain the emergence of *rasa* awareness. It presumes a realistic determination, thus ignoring that the play is in an important sense a fiction, whereas its effect is real. More importantly, it is subject to constraints of logical necessity that do not hold in the case of fiction, where we often have causes without effect and effects without causes.[161] Fiction is differentiated from reality, in that fiction is not subjected to the constraints of logical necessity, whereas reality is. The emergence of *rasa* awareness is subjected to constraints of logical necessity, and is thus within the sphere of reality. For our purpose, it is important to note that the *rasa* theory is indeed subjected to constraints of logical necessity. This is similar to grammar, which represents rules organizing a language in logical patterns.

Not only is the aesthetic dimension organized and subject to logical patterns, but it represents a reality more real than its cause, the play that is, after all, a fiction. This is already enough to hint at a possible Indian religious interpretation: The world may be a type of illusion, just as a dramatic play is. However, it enables one to experience emotions that, when properly directed to the divine, become true and real. The experience of these emotions becomes the means of salvation or *mokṣa*, and the practitioner may continue to develop these emotions further after salvation, in a world more real than the present one. Gerow notes:

> In the period of vigorous Bengali *Vaiṣṇavism* (fifteenth to sixteenth centuries), we find a religion that takes its entire theological apparatus from the categories of the *rasa* aesthetics. In medieval Bengal, the critic ceases to be a sophisticate, and instead becomes the teacher of multitudes: a guide in the most important business of life – salvation. Of course, these atypical developments presume a religion of a certain type, one fully manifest in the Indian middle ages, wherein the immediacy of god was prized to the extent that only an emotional relationship with him was judged suitable, or even possible. For it is in the emotions only that the great majority of mankind can experience immediate being; it is their only way to god, a way called *bhakti* from the *Gītā* onward. Once the emotions

> are seen as the exclusive, or only suitable approach, to the divine, worship becomes the experience of the god in possession, and is most akin to human love. And where do we find the sentiment of love most clearly expounded and related to its psychic limits? In aesthetics, for love is the *rasa* par excellence. If such a system of religious devotionalism requires a theology, it will find it only in an aesthetic; and an aesthetic was most readily available.[162]

Gerow makes a few important points here. First, he acknowledges that Bengali *Vaiṣṇavism* takes its entire theological apparatus from the categories of *rasa* aesthetics. As Bengali *Vaiṣṇavism* considers the *BhP* to be its most important scripture, it is not unlikely that the roots of this concept are found in the *BhP* itself. Then he points to the idea of the immediacy of God to be gained only through emotional relationships with him. The roots of this idea may well be represented in the *BhP*, albeit in a more modest form. Thus the *BhP* may convey the idea that emotional relationships with God are the highest possible relationships between the human and the divine, but still not rule out other forms of human–divine exchange such as knowledge. His last important point here is that when a system of religious devotionalism requires a theology, it will find it in aesthetics, and that, moreover, aesthetics were indeed available – inter alia in the form of the *rasa* theory. Thus it was quite possible for the *Āḷvārs*' devotionalism to seek an aesthetic theory for the purpose of consolidating their theology, the result being the aesthetic element comprising the *BhP*. When the devotionalism further developed, it went beyond the *BhP*'s balanced approach to the devotional extreme, stating that only an emotional relationship with God was judged suitable. We should perhaps express a slight reservation, in that *bhakti* in the *Bg* was certainly not exclusively emotional. Rather, the *Bg* presents a careful and gradual path of progress from the conditioned state up to the state of surrender to the Supreme Person. That path is disciplined and philosophical, as can be understood by the term *jñāna yoga*, which is a key term in the *Bg*. Moreover, the *BhP* continues in the same pattern of gradual progress, relying much on knowledge and philosophy. Although it does aim at an intense emotional experience of the Supreme Person, the path is supported and guarded by knowledge all along. The interrelations of philosophy and aesthetics in the *BhP* may comprise its distinct feature.

We may leave aside the *BhP* for now and evoke a wider vision as to the possible contribution of aesthetics to philosophy and theology. Klaus Klostermaier questions the superiority of the knowledge paradigm over the aesthetic paradigm, and suggests openness to the idea of imagining God to be an artist or a lover:

> What determines our decision to reduce feelings to either mind or body rather than see mind and body as instruments of feelings? Why should one imagine God in terms of a mathematician or a judge, rather than in terms of an artist or a lover? Possibly the bias of our culture stems from a perception that feelings presuppose a material *sensorium* and an object felt, and that feelings, being by nature chaotic, require an ordering mind to make sense. Abstract order – mathematical and philosophical – is of the essence of our present civilisation. The physical sciences have dissolved matter into a network of mathematical formulae. Much of contemporary philosophy considers logic in its most formalised sense the essence of mind.[163]

Klostermaier points to the possible bias of Western culture, which considers feelings to presuppose a material *sensorium*, and to be by nature chaotic. However, following Klostermaier's line of argument, we have pointed out that Indian aesthetic theories take feelings and emotions to be organized in patterns and subjected to rules of logical necessity. Moreover, some Hindu theologies consider emotions to exist not only in the illusory or external realm, but in the essential realm, the realm of the *ātman*, too. Klostermaier continues to argue for the usefulness of the aesthetic pattern of thought:

> Doubts as regards the prevalent 'paradigm' are rising. The basic concepts of physics – space, time, matter and number – begin to be understood as metaphors for a reality which eludes the method of contemporary physics. The necessarily axiomatic character of all formal logic again has convinced some of us that it presupposes a reality which is not necessarily governed by the same logic. So, we may be more favourably disposed today to consider 'a universe of feelings', than many of our predecessors. It is, as we shall see, neither chaotic nor without its own logic, and it avoids a number

> of problems in theodicy which have proven insoluble in the context of the mind–body universe.[164]

According to Klostermaier, the application of logic is axiomatic or arbitrary, but not necessarily governed by the same logic. Therefore, applying patterns of thought such as the 'Universe of Feelings' may be more favourably regarded nowadays. Also, Klostermaier brings to light the possible contribution of this worldview to theology.

Keith Ward addresses the issue of understanding God through an aesthetic point of view, rather than through a scientific or philosophical one. He criticizes the attempt to treat religious language, whose function is to evoke eternity, as if it were treating scientific or philosophical language, and says:

> What needs to be done is to develop a sense that the world of finite things is able to express an infinite reality beyond and yet also infusing it [...] What can help us to evoke such a sense is not science or philosophy, but poetry or music. The language of religion is like the language of poetry; and it is a major heresy of post-Enlightenment rationalism to try to turn poetry into pseudo-science, to turn the images of religion, whose function is to evoke eternity, into mundane descriptions of improbable facts. In a sense, atheism is right – but only in its rejection of a God who never was, and of a belief which never touched the heart of religious faith.[165]

Ward compares religious language to the language of poetry, and considers its function 'to evoke eternity'. This is opposed to scientific or philosophical language which belongs to a different realm. Similar ideas may have been maintained by the *BhP*'s author or authors, who may have applied language poetically and indirectly, in order to reveal Personal Notions of Divinity through inviting their listeners to gradually enter into a 'Universe of Feelings'.

CHAPTER 2

THE AESTHETIC DOCTRINE OF THE *BHĀGAVATA PURĀṆA*

In proceeding to associate the *rasa* tradition with the *BhP*, one may justly ask whether this connection was previously made by scholars, implicitly or explicitly. Apparently, it seems that scholars have long been associating the *BhP* with *rasa*. As such, Sheth notes, 'When we turn to the *Bhāgavata Purāṇa*, we find that it is literally saturated with devotion; every page drips with the juice (*rasa*) of devotion. In its variety, elaborateness and intensity, it leaves the *Harivaṁśa* and *Viṣṇu Purāṇa* far behind.'[1] Sheth points to the *BhP*'s abundance of *bhakti rasa* (*rasa* of devotion), saying that it is distinguished by its variety, elaborateness and intensity. He goes on to analyse various types or modes of devotion, among them, *dāsya* – serving Kṛṣṇa as a servant,[2] *sakhya* – friendship with Kṛṣṇa,[3] *vātsalya* – parental affection toward Kṛṣṇa[4], and the lover–beloved relationship with Kṛṣṇa.[5] Although Sheth mentions these terms and analyses them, he doesn't link them directly to Sanskrit poetics. It is generally accepted that the *rāsa līlā* chapters[6] represent the *BhP*'s climax or peak, and that the *gopīs*' love for Kṛṣṇa represents the highest spiritual achievement, according to *Vaiṣṇava theology*. Flood addresses the relations of *Vaiṣṇava* mythology to Sanskrit poetics:

> Although much of the *Bhāgavata Purāṇa* contains reference to Kṛṣṇa's love-play with the *gopīs*, it does not mention by name Rādha who only appears with the *Gītāgovinda* and in later literature and visual art. In *Vaiṣṇava* mythology, she is an older

> married woman and the love between her and Kṛṣṇa is conventionally adulterous [. . .] This is theologically important and relates to a distinction in Sanskrit poetics between love-in-union (*svakīya*, one's own woman) associated with marriage, and love-in-separation (*parakīya*, another's woman) associated with adulterous love [. . .] In loving Kṛṣṇa, Rādhā disobeys wifely duty (*strīdharma*), for the love of God transcends social obligation. The love between Rādhā and Kṛṣṇa is love-in-separation characterized by longing – as the soul's longing for the Lord is the highest human spirituality.[7]

Accordingly, Rādhā's romantic love for Kṛṣṇa is considered the highest human spirituality in *Vaiṣṇava* theological terms. This assertion is based upon a relation between *Vaiṣṇava* theology and Sanskrit poetics, and seems to justify the mode of romantic love as being higher than other modes of devotion.

We may ask: What is this relation? Is *Vaiṣṇava* theology related to Sanskrit poetics? Could such a relation be articulated in a way that could possibly explain how the *gopīs*' love for Kṛṣṇa is 'the highest human spirituality'? By now it may be quite clear that the *BhP* has a deep aesthetic character and sensitivity, and it is also quite clear that the author or authors of the text were consciously aiming at associating the *BhP* with orthodoxy by conforming to orthodox philosophy – *Vedānta* – and to an archaic Sanskrit style. Given the fact that orthodox aesthetic theories were quite widespread at the time of the *BhP*'s compilation, a few questions may be raised: Was there a structured aesthetic theory available to the author of the *BhP*? Is it possible that the *BhP* had not only absorbed an orthodox philosophy and linguistic style, but an orthodox aesthetic theory as well? What types of aesthetic theories existed at the time of the *BhP*'s compilation? Would such an aesthetic theory or theories serve the *BhP*'s theme of expressing divine personhood, as indicated by its name – 'The *Purāṇa* of the Supreme Person'? As the *BhP* is such a sophisticated text, articulating itself through archaic Sanskrit composed in careful metre, and as it expresses a deep association with the *Vedānta* school, would it be possible for it to treat its aesthetic and dramatic portions in an amateur, casual or non-systematic fashion? Given the fact that the *BhP* is intrinsically dramatic, and that a Sanskritic Brahaminical aesthetic ideology associated with drama was readily available, would it be possible to presume that the *BhP*'s author would not make use of it? Could the *BhP*'s formal opening and closing with phrases combining *Vedānta* and *rasa* in fact be meaningless? To our mind it is quite clear that the *rasa* theory occupies a major place in the *BhP*'s structure, and the question remains: In what way is the *rasa* theory related to the *BhP*? Does it occupy an essential role in developing the *BhP*'s theme or is its role merely secondary? Does it underlie the *BhP*'s structure and thus comprise an intrinsic aspect of it, or is it applied for merely external reasons, such as adding an orthodox 'flavour' to the *BhP*? The following section will look into the deep relationship between *Vaiṣṇavism* and Indian dramaturgy, which combines theatre with poetry.

Indian Dramaturgy and Its Role in *Vaiṣṇavism*

The Indian concept of drama is characterized by soteriology, and hence we see early on that drama was held in South Asia to possess an edifying quality, because of its ability to produce a certain experience called *rasa*. Within the mythological account of the origins of drama as expressed in the *Nāṭya-śāstra*, we glimpse the intent to evoke within an audience a particular aesthetic–emotional experience, known as *rasa*, that would cope with or transcend the problems of egoism. From Bharata's time onwards, this was to be the central objective of any drama. One can readily understand from this, then, that dramatics developed in India in a very different direction than in the West, which for the most part followed Aristotle's assertion that plot was the soul and organizing principle of drama.[8] Plato and Aristotle agree with Indian theorists of drama in defining it as a kind of imitation.[9] Plato considered this to have damaging consequences and in the *Republic* he claimed that imitative arts lead us further from the truth. Plato argues that there are three types of people: the philosophers, who know the truth or the idea; the craftsmen, who copy the idea and produce appearances; and the imitative artists, who copy the appearances and are thus three steps removed from the truth. The product of the latter group, imitative art, tricks us into confusing appearances for the real thing and thereby leads us further from the truth. Plato declared that tragedy, or drama, is an imitative art to the 'highest possible degree' and therefore ranks among the worst of the arts. Plato therefore refuses to allow drama in his ideal republic.[10]

Aristotle, however, considered drama uplifting in that it created a valuable experience known as catharsis. He also assessed the value of drama in terms of what, or rather who, it imitates. All imitation imitates agents – human beings who can be better than we are, worse than we are or equal to us. For Aristotle, the worthiness of the agent determines the quality or affective meaning of the imitative art. Tragedy, he declares, is an imitation of the actions of worthy agents, and as such is a valuable source of learning and of catharsis.[11] *Rasa* theory is closer to Aristotle's ideas than to Plato's. Both Aristotle and Bharata considered the dramatic experience to be potentially edifying and uplifting. The drama's edifying qualities seem to be shared by both Greek and Indian theorists, and as the term *rasa* played a central role in the process of purification leading ultimately to liberation, it appears that drama in general, and *rasa* in particular, were rooted in theology already in Bharata's time.

Vaiṣṇavism is by nature dramatic. However, is there evidence of dramaturgy ever being associated with *Vaiṣṇavism?* It may well be that Vaiṣṇavism in general and Kṛṣṇaism in particular have been associated with drama since ancient times. A survey of the development of the Kṛṣṇa tradition in its various forms, especially those that centre upon his childhood and youth in *Vraja*, reveals a large number of dramatic elements that are highly significant for devotion. By reviewing certain prominent examples of such elements, it may be seen how pervasive drama – both as a concept and as a religious practice – has been in Kṛṣṇa worship generally.[12] Dramaturgy is not only an essential element of Kṛṣṇaism, but the association of the two may have preceded the compilation of the *BhP* by a millennium or so. Indeed, there seems to have been a flourishing tradition of vernacular Kṛṣṇa dramas in ancient Mathurā as early as the second century BCE.[13] Hein highlights the relations of *Vaiṣṇavism* and dramaturgy, and his discovery of several different theatrical styles that have grown up around the figures of Rāma and Kṛṣṇa leads him to go as far as claiming that 'our many evidences of drama among the *Vaiṣṇavas* indicate the existence of a strong sectarian theatre and a possibility that fondness for the stage was a special *Vaiṣṇava* characteristic'.[14] Hein mentions the word *citra* which appears in a passage in Patañjali's *Mahābhāṣya*. He mentions how in his commentary on Pāṇini III.1.26, Patañjali refers to the manner in which *śaubhikas*, *citras* and *granthikas* present *Vaiṣṇava* stories, and considers that these three terms involve possible substantiation of the existence of Kṛṣṇa dramas in the second century BCE.[15] Wulff joins Hein in claiming the centrality of dramaturgy in Kṛṣṇa worship, and the spread of this phenomenon far beyond the area of *Vraja* to much of the Indian subcontinent. Accordingly:

> Hein's investigations are by no means limited to Mathūra and the surrounding region of Braj, but range over much of the Indian subcontinent at the same time that they span a period of more than two thousand years; as such it may well be that drama has long been central in the worship of Kṛṣṇa.[16]

It seems that drama has been closely associated with *Vaiṣṇavism* right from its formative years, some 2,000 years ago or more.

In general, the *purāṇas* as a whole are dramatic by nature, so much so that neglecting to recognize the *purāṇas*' dramatic nature may pose a problem for their readers, who in the absence of such recognition may fail to understand them. This problem arises not from the *purāṇas*' self-describing statements, but from their present existence in printed and bound editions. In this form they give the impression of being books, intended for reading, commentary and annotation, but originally they would have been more accurately described as performances, intended to be seen, heard and enjoyed. Unless some appreciation of this is present, today's reader of the *purāṇas* may fail to understand them.[17] As such, certain passages depict Kṛṣṇa as an actor. In describing the worship of Mount Govardhana, for example, advocated by the child Kṛṣṇa in place of the former festival of Indra, Kṛṣṇa is portrayed as presenting himself on the summit with the words, 'I am the mountain', and partaking of the food offerings at the same time that he ascends the mountain in his familiar form, to offer worship (to himself) along with the other cowherds.[18] Kṛṣṇa's assumption of the form of the mountain is paralleled by the imitation of him by the *gopīs*, two of whom are represented in that text as saying, 'I am Kṛṣṇa'. And the *gopīs* in turn are taken as the exemplars of the tradition of enacting Kṛṣṇa's *līlās* by the directors of the modern troupes of *Braj*.[19] It is in the *BhP*, however, that the theme of Kṛṣṇa's paradoxical assumption of roles is developed most fully: the author of the *Bhāgavata* continually juxtaposes Kṛṣṇa's cosmic reality with his human form, and indicates at various points that Kṛṣṇa is wholly conscious of his true nature.[20] His human actions are thus necessarily represented as playacting.[21] All this suggests that a possible reason for the *BhP*'s central position among the *purāṇas* is that the theme of Kṛṣṇa's dramatic character is developed most fully in it.

Is there any fundamental principle in *Vaiṣṇava* theology that encourages the development of dramaturgy? The *avatāra* theme may be such a possible theological source, having its roots already as early as the *Bhagavad Gītā*, where a famous section[22] provides the earliest account of Kṛṣṇa's many births. The forms that the Supreme Person assumes seem to resemble forms of a dramatic performance. The parallel with actors who assume roles for a specific time is strengthened by the dramatic scene described in the eleventh chapter, in which Kṛṣṇa first reveals to Arjuna his awesome cosmic form, and then assumes once more his gentle appearance as Arjuna's charioteer. Before Kṛṣṇa resumes his human guise, however, Arjuna apologizes profusely for treating him as a friend, that is for mistaking Kṛṣṇa's temporary semblance for his true reality.[23] This, too, reinforces the scene's dramatic character. It may well be that there is hierarchy and order within the sequence of *avatāras* presented. In other words, it may well be that some *avatāras* are the objects of lower or simpler moods of worship, whereas others are the objects of more complex or higher moods of devotion. The term *līlā*, which represents a cosmic drama and is closely related to the term *avatāra*, may be considered too. It may be translated as 'play', both meanings of the English term being applicable. It designates the Lord's play, the spontaneous, unfettered activity manifest in each of his *avatāras* but expressed most fully in the playfulness of Kṛṣṇa. Because *līlā*, like the English word 'play', refers to a dramatic representations as well as to joyous activity free of any utilitarian purpose, its frequent use to designate Kṛṣṇa's actions suggests that they themselves constitute a divine drama in which Kṛṣṇa has the principal role. Kṛṣṇa's *līlā* is both a dramatic performance and an expression of his unpredictable playfulness and, as such, it is noteworthy that this term is applied in each of the three *purāṇic* passages in which *gopīs* are described as imitating Kṛṣṇa's actions.[24]

The question may be raised as to why the term *līlā* is expressed most fully in the playfulness of Kṛṣṇa. In order to answer that, the logic underlying the *BhP*'s aesthetic paradigm will have to be uncovered first. But it may well be that the role of Kṛṣṇa is the most complex and rich in aesthetic terms; that is, that it displays and attracts the finest, richest and most complex emotions, and arouses the same in his worshippers, followers and devotees. The dramatic elements have theological implications. Indeed, one such purpose of this playful drama, this divine revelation of the *avatāras*, is to provide humans with a model for perfection. Having achieved perfection, one participates eternally in those dramatic performances with the Supreme Person in the eternal world. Besides offering a model for perfection, the drama enables one to develop the desired emotional state. In a dramatic performance, the enacted play is illusory or fictitious, but the emotions invoked are real, and may remain in the mind or heart of the spectator as impressions long after the play has ended. The theological implication is that emotions are taken to be invoked in an illusory world, and to remain with the participant-observing *jīva* after the play has ended, that is after it has reached the stage of liberation. Besides the term *līlā*, the term *māyā* needs to be looked into, as it also holds an important role in the *BhP*'s theology. Its significance lies in a somewhat distant or critical perception of reality, resembling a dramatic performance taking place on the world stage. The spectator is beholding the divine play revealed to him or her through the *BhP*. The play describes the Lord descending to deliver the souls captured in the material world, the observer being one among them. At the same time, by hearing and envisioning the story and play the spectator makes progress towards liberation. As such, the *Vaiṣṇava* mode of 'textual dramaturgy', in which the texts themselves are not explicitly considered dramaturgical, but still carry dramaturgical features, is somewhat complex. Not only is the reader or hearer of the story a spectator in a dramatic performance, but a participant-observer, too. In other words, when the story speaks of the Supreme Person descending to the world in various *avatāra* forms, for the purpose of delivering those *jīvas* deluded by *māyā* and suffering in *saṁsāra*, it is the spectators who apparently are those *jīvas*. Similarly, when the text tells the stories of the divine person, which are meant for the deliverance of the world, the audience is to be delivered, too. So in that sense, the enactment of the *BhP* does not really take itself to be fictitious, but rather grounded in reality.

Rasa: History and Theory

The concept of *rasa* has its roots already in the *Upaniṣads*, specifically the *Chāndogya*[25] and *Taittirīya Upaniṣads*. A famous quote from the latter reads, 'He is indeed *rasa*. Having obtained *rasa* this one becomes blissful.'[26] The term *rasa* may denote sap, juice or liquid and, by extension, flavour, pleasure and essence, and is also closely associated with the term 'delight' or *ānanda*.[27] Also, it could possibly be translated as 'taste', 'aesthetic enjoyment', 'dramatic sentiment' or 'aesthetic rapture'.

The earliest discussion of *rasa* as an aesthetic term takes place in the canonical text *Nāṭyaśāstra* attributed to Bharata Muni. Opinions regarding the *Nāṭyaśāstra*'s date vary, but we shall accept the period between the second century BCE to second century CE as a reasonable possibility. In general, this period marks a Hindu reaction to Buddhist rule characterized, inter alia, by a rise of the arts. The last ruler of the Maurya dynasty, Bṛhadratha, was assassinated by his general, Puṣyamitra Śuṅga, during a parade of his troops during the year 185 BCE. The usurper then founded the Śuṅga dynasty, which continued for 112 years but about which very little is known. Puṣyamitra is reported to have been a Brahmin and it is said that his rise to power marked a Brahmin reaction to Buddhism that had been favoured for such a long time by previous rulers. Puṣyamitra once again celebrated the *Vedic* horse sacrifice. It was certainly a clear break with Aśoka's tradition, which had prohibited animal sacrifices altogether. There is some other evidence, too, for the inclination of Indian kings to violate the rules established by the Mauryas and to revive old customs that had been forbidden by them. King Kharavela stated in an inscription of the first century BCE near Bhubaneshwar that he had reintroduced the musical festivals and dances that were prohibited under the Mauryas.[28] Apparently the Mauryas had discouraged arts such as music and dance, and encouraged the fostering of quiet, religious and more meditative forms of expression, which were more in line with Buddhist ideas. The Brahminical reaction to their rule involved a return to *Vedic* ideas such as the horse sacrifice, and the rise of *Vedic* arts as theorized by Bharata in his *Nāṭyaśāstra*, and as such, the *Nāṭyaśāstra* may be considered a post-Buddhist or even a contra-Buddhist *Vedic* revitalization. *Rasa* first emerged as an aesthetic term in regard to drama, being related to its poetical aspects. However, beside the realm of drama, the term *rasa* entered the poetical tradition too. The *Nāṭyaśāstra* apparently had a number of early commentaries that were lost, with the exception that some parts of these were mentioned in the tenth-century commentary of Abhinavagupta. The first writer to treat *rasa* in poetics was Bhāmaha,[29] who in his

Kāvyālaṅkāra treated *rasa* as a variety of figures of speech, or *alaṅkāras*. The next major writer to follow him was Daṇḍin[30] in his *Kāvyādarśa*. Rudraṭa[31] in his *Kāvyālaṅkāra* laid more emphasis on *rasa*, insisting that it be a part of the experience of all poetic works. The term *rasa* gained a new and central place in poetic theory with Ānandavardhana[32] and his treatise *Dhvanyāloka*, in which he related *rasa* to the concept of *dhvani*, or the suggestive power of language distinct from its direct usage.[33] Thus *dhvani* became recognized as the essence of poetry, and *rasa* became the highest criterion of fine poetry, and *rasa* became the aesthetic determinant of both drama and poetry. The new *rasa-dhvani* school found its most powerful formulation a century later, in the commentaries of Abhinavagupta[34] on the *Nāṭyaśāstra*[35] and on Ānandavardhana's *Dhvanyāloka*.[36]

Following Abhinavagupta, a rich tradition of *rasa* aesthetics emerged in the succeeding centuries, largely inspired by his works. Bhoja of Dhāra was approximately a contemporary of Abhinavagupta, and his two great works are *Sarasvatī-kaṇṭhābharaṇa* and *Śṛṅgāra-prakāśa*. The latter is the largest known work in Sanskrit poetics, and deals with poetics and dramaturgy. Bhoja's works[37] exerted a great influence on the section of the *Agni Purāṇa* that deals with poetics[38] and on Śāradātanaya's *Bhāva-prakāśana*.[39] A major figure of the tradition was Mammaṭa Bhaṭṭa[40] and his work *Kāvya-prakāśa*. This aesthetic tradition became known as the central or classical tradition of Sanskrit aesthetics throughout India and formed a creative intellectual force, even after its last great reformulation by Jagannātha Paṇḍitarāja.[41] Despite the changes and developments the tradition went through, there emerged a recognizably unified manner of understanding the aesthetic experience with *rasa* being its core.

As mentioned, the oldest work to mention *rasa* as a definable aesthetic principle is the *Nāṭyaśāstra* of the legendary Bharata. Consequently, an examination of the *rasa* theory of Bharata is the starting point for any foray into an Indian understanding of dramatic experience.[42] The *Nāṭyaśāstra* annunciates a theory of aesthetics and the techniques of dramaturgy in 36 chapters, and discusses dramatic evolution, theatrical and stage construction and the presentation of drama. Drama is viewed as a re-enactment of the cosmos, which is composed of celestial and mundane worlds. It is compared to a ritual performance[43] and aims at emancipation or release[44] gained through the purification of emotion (*rasa*).[45] Apparently, the *Nāṭyaśāstra* possesses clear *Vedic* orthodox characteristics: as such, drama reenacts the cosmos, its underlying metaphor is that of a *yajña* and it aims at *mokṣa*. The marked difference between the *Nāṭyaśāstra* and the *Vedāntic* tradition is that *Nāṭyaśāstra* aspires to achieve *mokṣa* through the purification of emotion, as opposed to the *Vedāntic* idea of achieving *mokṣa* through an epistemological purification, that is the attainment of true knowledge. It appears that drama in general and *rasa* in particular were related indirectly to theology already in Bharata's time through claiming to be of a divine origin. The *Nāṭyaśāstra*'s theological nature is expressed by its consideration of itself as the fifth *Veda*, meant for the uplifting of humankind from a lower state, characterized by absorption in pleasure and pain, greed, avarice, jealousy and anger. The *Nāṭyaśāstra* opens by conveying this idea:

> Long, long, very long ago, said Bharata, people of this world of pain and pleasure, goaded by greed and avarice, and jealousy and anger, took to uncivilized ways of life [. . .]. Various lords were ruling. It was the gods among them who, led by Mahendra, approached God Brahma and requested him thus: please give us something which will not only teach us but be pleasing both to eyes and ears. True, the *Vedas* are there but some like the *śūdras* are prohibited from listening to them. Why not create for us a fifth *Veda* which would be accessible to all the *varṇas*?[46]

The idea of the *Nāṭyaśāstra* being the fifth *Veda* given by Brahma may help to explain its *Vedic* authoritative position, how deeply it has affected Hindu traditions, and why religious dramas came to occupy such a central place within Hinduism, a practice that continues to this very day. Similar to *Vedānta*, which aspired to transcend the problem of egoism, the *rasa* school also had the very same aspiration – of transcending egoism through a transformative process. So, from Bharata's time onwards, the central objective of any drama was to 'evoke within an audience a particular aesthetic-emotional experience, known as *rasa*, that would cope with or transcend the problems of egoism'.[47]

The topic of *rasa* appears in the sixth chapter of the *Nāṭyaśāstra*, and is followed by a discussion of *bhāva* or enacted emotion, which appears in the seventh chapter. In analysing human nature, Bharata defined 41 different emotional states or *bhāvas*. These are divided into eight primary emotions and 33 secondary emotions.[48] The eight primary emotions were considered by him to be especially prominent, so much so that while experiencing them a person forgets everything else. These eight *bhāvas* are called *sthāyin* or *sthāyi-bhāvas* and are: amorous love – *rati*; laughter – *hāsa*; sadness – *śoka*; anger – *krodha*; courage – *utsāha*; fear – *bhaya*; disgust – *jugupsā* and wonder – *vismaya*. The eight primary emotions or *stāyi-bhāvas* correspond to eight *rasas*: erotic rapture – *śṛṅgāra*;[49] comedy – *hāsya*; compassion – *karuṇa*; fury – *raudra*; heroism – *vīra*; horror – *bhayānaka*; revulsion – *bībhatsa* and astonishment – *adbhuta*. Some versions of the text as well as Abhinavagupta in his commentary add a ninth *rasa* named tranquility – *śānti*, based on the *sthāyibhāva* of equanimity – *śama.*[50] We can arrange the primary emotions and their corresponding *rasas* in a table (Table 2.1).

The gap between the *sthāyibhāva* and its corresponding *rasa* may shed light on the transformative potential of this theory. Whereas the primary emotion is touched or tinged by a certain amount of egotism, the experience of its corresponding *rasa* is pure. Thus the process of transcending the ego involves the relinquishment of the ordinary emotional experience in favour of a pure emotional experience. Hence the soteriological nature of the *rasa* theory, which considers the pure emotional experience a liberating experience, just as the experience of true knowledge in the *Vedānta* tradition is a liberating experience, too.

A question may be raised: If all 41 *bhāvas* are instrumental in producing *rasa* when coming into contact with the human heart, how can it be said that only primary emotions directly produce *rasa*? The

Table 2.1 The nine primary emotions and their corresponding *rasas*

Primary emotion (*sthāyibhāva*)	**Corresponding** *rasa*
amorous love	erotic rapture
laughter	comedy
sadness	compassion
anger	fury
courage	heroism
fear	horror
disgust	revulsion
wonder	astonishment
equanimity	tranquillity

answer given in the *Nāṭya-śāstra* draws on the example of a king and his followers: although all are born similar, some become leaders due to family, character, education, action, artistic skills and so forth, while others become their followers. Similarly, the other *bhāvas* are dependent and follow the primary emotions or *sthāyibhāvas*. Thus these eight or nine primary emotions occupy a superior position in regard to the other 33 emotions in Bharata's doctrine. Another question raised is: Where do these emotions exist or abide? Bharata maintains that these eight (or nine) prominent emotions exist in the heart or mind in the form of unconscious latent impressions or *vāsanās*. These may be there from previous lives and are ready to manifest under certain conditions.

Bharata queried what means or conditions are needed for evoking these various *sthāyibhāvas* and to raise them to a conscious and relishable state. Bharata divided these conditions into three components: the environmental conditions or causes – *kāraṇa*; the external responses or effects – *kārya*; and the accompanying supportive emotions – *sahakārin*. When these three are manifested as components of artistic expression distanced from the realm of everyday life they are sublimated as they wrest free from egoistic notions. Thus they are renamed as *vibhāvas*, *anubhāvas* and *vyabhicāribhāvas*, respectively. These terms may be better understood by the standard example of a young couple depicted in a romantic setting such as a moonlit garden. The couple cast furtive glances at each other, they tremble upon touching each other, and experience fleeting emotions such as shyness, euphoria or jealousy. When that scene is acted in a drama the members of the audience may taste or share these emotions, and that tasting is defined by the *Nāṭyaśāstra* as *rasa*. In the example cited above, the primary emotion tasted (*sthāyibhāva*) is amorous love (*rati*). The *vibhāvas* are the characters, objects or settings that make the observers taste a particular emotion. In our example the young couple as well as the moonlit garden comprise the *vibhāvas*. In this way the *vibhāvas* supply the settings of a particular drama such as the time, place and characters involved. The later tradition recognizes two types of *vibhāvas*: the first is the substantial or *ālambana*, which consists of the actual characters of the play, whereas the second is the enchanter or *uddīpana* which comprises the setting of the play, such as the moon or the garden in our example.

Physical, mental or verbal actions, either pre-planned or spontaneous, are called *anubhāvas*, and these form the primary emotions actually sensed. As such, they are the actions of the play. In the example cited above, the *anubhāvas* would be the furtive glances and the trembling. The *anubhāvas* add a deeper dimension to the play. Whereas the *vibhāvas* convey the primary emotion displayed, the *anubhāvas* add the dimension of direct experience of the primary emotion, and that through the actors' dialogue or physical actions. The *anubhāvas* include words, gestures as well as involuntary physical expressions such as trembling, which are named *sāttvika-bhāvas*, and can be considered a subcategory of the *anubhāvas.* The eight *sāttvika-bhāvas* are involuntary states that are physical reactions that accompany some feelings, such as tears or perspiration. These are paralysis, perspiration, horripilation, faltering voice, trembling, change of colour, tears and fainting.[51] Besides the actions, words or expressions performed by the actors, there are various transitory emotions being expressed by the actors, such as shyness, euphoria or jealousy, and these are called *vyabhicārins*. These serve to enhance or adorn the primary emotions by expanding the emotional variety, by verifying the authenticity of the primary emotions aroused by the *vibhāvas* and *anubhāvas* and by beautifying these primary emotions. The *Nāṭyaśāstra*[52] explains the etymology of the term as based upon the verbal root *car*, meaning movement or motion, prefixed by the prefixes *vi-* and *abhi-*, *abhi-* expressing motion towards something or approaching it. The reason is that the *vyabhicārins* lead a subtle movement towards the *rasa*, in the same subtle way the sun leads the day. The *Nāṭyaśāstra* lists 33 *vyabhicārins* and these are: weariness,[53] physical weakness, anxiety, envy, intoxication, fatigue, laziness, depression, worry, confusion, remembrance, peace of mind, shame, rashness, joy, panic, lifelessness, pride, dejection, longing, sleeping, apoplexy, dreaming, awakening, resentment, dissimulation, violence, attentiveness, sickness, insanity, death, fright and perplexity.[54]

The *Nāṭyaśāstra* provides a list of different *vibhāvas* and *anubhāvas* which are compatible with various *sthāyins*, as the proper combinations are important to the emerging of these primary emotions. Table 2.2 lists some examples of compatible mixtures of secondary emotions (*vyabhicāribhāvas*), external settings (*vibhāvas*) and their expressions (*anubhāvas*).[55]

The *Nāṭyaśāstra* says, 'From the union of the *vibhāvas*, *anubhāvas* and *vyabhicārins*, *rasa* is produced.'[56] The balanced combination of the *vibhāvas*, *anubhāvas* and *vyabhicārins* in a drama or a poem allows the appearance of the primary emotion, that is, the *sthāyin* or *sthāyibhāva*, and the enjoyment

Table 2.2 Compatible mixtures of secondary emotions (*vyabhicāribhāvas*), external settings (*vibhāvas*) and their expressions (*anubhāvas*)

Vyabhicāribhāva	*Vibhāva*	*Anubhāva*
depression, weariness	poverty, disease, insult	crying, hesitation
joy	achieving one's desires, meeting one's dear ones	cheerful face, embracing
sorrow	calamity, incompletion of work undertaken	sighing, seeking help
fortitude	bravery, pure conduct, prosperity	not grieving over what is not achieved
memory	loss of peace of mind	shaking the head, looking down
shame	confession, repentance	hiding one's face, writing with the toe on the ground

of this primary emotion is called *rasa*. The *rasa*, however, is a deep and meaningful aesthetic experience: 'a meaning which touches the heart creates *rasa*; the entire body feels the *rasa* like fire consuming a dry stick'.[57] The careful and expert mixing of settings, expressions and secondary emotions is compared by the *Nāṭyaśāstra* to the process of cooking, and that, in turn, is relished by the expert and sensitive taster:

> Let me begin with the explanation of *rasa* first, because there is no *Nāṭya* without *rasa*. *Rasa* is the cumulative result of *Vibhāva*, *Anubhāva* and *Vyabhcāribhāva*. For example, just as when various condiments and sauces and herbs and other materials are mixed, a taste (different from the individual tastes of the components) is felt, or when the mixing of materials like molasses with other materials produces six kinds of tastes, so also along with the different *Bhāvas* the *Sthāyibhāva* becomes a taste (*rasa*).[58]

Just as the different gastronomical ingredients combined together in a certain way during the cooking process produce *rasa*, similarly does the combination of the dramatic components produce *rasa*.[59] What is the difference between an emotion and its corresponding *rasa*? The emotion is by nature worldly, and is therefore touched by some egoistic impurity.

Thus, following our example, a lover may feel some possessiveness for or jealousy towards his beloved. However, in the dramatic context, the enacted emotions are *alaukika*, meaning not belonging to this world, and are therefore experienced in a pure form. The primary emotion, or the *sthāyin*, which is an internal mental state, is not experienced directly by the audience of the drama, rather it is experienced indirectly, through the experience of *rasa*. The reason is that the relishing of a drama requires a certain detachment or distance from the play itself, as opposed to day-to-day life when one is absorbed in experiencing various emotions directly. For this reason the drama is always enjoyable when properly conducted and when enacted to a balanced and sympathetic spectator,[60] even when depicting grief or tragedy. This is opposed to real tragedies which may occur in quotidian life, which are not enjoyable to the participants or to the sympathetic spectators. Using the previous example, it may be said that in the play enacting amorous love between a young couple, the audience as well as the actors do not experience the *sthāyin* of love, and if they were to experience that, it would have made the enacting and relishing of the drama difficult if not impossible. In other words, if the actors were really in love with each other, they probably would have found it difficult to concentrate on performing their roles. Similarly, if a spectator had fallen in love with the actress, he probably would have not been able to relish the drama, being absorbed himself in various emotions such as jealousy directed at the male actor acting as the actress's beloved.

The notion of *rasa* carries a universal flavour. The discussion of *rasa* in the *Nāṭyaśāstra* begins with a statement regarding the central role *rasa* plays within a drama, and states that 'apart from *rasa*, nothing indeed exists'.[61] In other words, the arising of *rasa* is taken to be the essence of dramaturgy. This statement can be taken in a more general way, meaning that nothing in the world can exist or proceed without *rasa*. The generality of this statement implies, however, relevance beyond just the topic of drama. It suggests a broader view according to which nothing in the world can exist or proceed without *rasa*, in the wider sense of delight as in its *Upaniṣadic* application.[62] In a sense, it can be said that *rasa* sustains the world, as without deep aesthetic tastes life could barely go on. Examining the world from the point of view of quotidian life, it could be said that the teacher would not teach and the student would not study, unless they tasted some taste in those activities, and similarly a mother couldn't be carrying the heavy burden of motherhood unless there would have been a deep taste of motherhood in this role. In that sense, as a deep aesthetic experience underlying various emotions, the principle of *rasa* may be taken as pervading all spheres of life, and sustains the functioning of each and every individual. In summary of the brief survey of the notion of *rasa*, the *Nāṭyaśāstra* characterizes *rasa* as the spectator's 'tasting'[63] of the primary emotion[64] related to a set of *vibhāvas*, *anubhāvas* and *vyabhicāribhāvas*, which are parts of a dramatic or poetic presentation. Furthermore, as a 'tasting', the experience is pleasurable. Second, it arises because the emotions represented in drama or poetry are both familiar and fictitious. Drama or poetry is, therefore, essential to the arousal of *rasa*, and that is to say that *rasa* is not a quotidian experience. Third, *rasa* is an experience, related to, but different from, the experience of quotidian emotion,[65] and, finally, it occurs in a spectator who is well disposed (*sumanas*).[66] Stated briefly, *rasa* is the pleasurable tasting of familiar but fictitious emotions through drama or poetry by a sensitive and well-disposed spectator, and is different from the quotidian experience of emotions. The discussion of the *vibhāvas*, *anubhāvas* and *vyabhicāribhāvas* as well as the other dramatic components hints at the complex, elegant, authoritative and systematic nature of *rasa* theory. It therefore occupies a unique position among aesthetic theories both East and West, similar to the position Pāṇinī's grammar occupies among systems of grammars due to its complex, elegant, authoritative and systematic nature.

Rasa Theory's Division in the Middle Ages between Impersonal and Personal Trends: The Poetical Theories of Abhinavagupta and Bhoja

The polarization among the *Vedāntin* sects, represented by the divergence into Śaṅkara's and Rāmānuja's theological positions, is one of the major characteristics of medieval Indian philosophy. On the one hand, it represents the development of the doctrine of illusion, while on the other hand, it represents the development of its opposing view, that is the philosophy of personal theism. This very same divergence had occurred in the aesthetic tradition, too. Just as the philosophical position of Śaṅkara differed much from the *Vaiṣṇava* position, the aesthetic position of Abhinavagupta differed much from Bhoja of *Dhārā*'s position. The split had the same theme at its core: the impersonal versus personal conception of *Brahman*, the highest reality. Abhinavagupta held *śānta rasa* to be supreme, as its corresponding emotional state of mind is similar to the state of relaxed individual consciousness of one who aspires to attain oneness with *Brahman*. Bhoja, however, held *śṛṅgāra rasa* to be supreme, as its corresponding state of mind is similar to the state of the intense individual consciousness of one who aspires to experience deep love for a personal God.

Abhinavagupta was born approximately 950 CE, and his main period of literal activity was between 990 and 1015. His two surviving works on aesthetics consist primarily of his commentaries on Ānandavardhana's *Dhvanyāloka*, which was the earlier, and on Bharata's *Nāṭya-śāstra*, which was the later. Abhinavagupta was influenced by his predecessor Bhaṭṭa Nāyaka, who was a Kashmiri writer of the tenth century, and who maintained that drama has a special power to overcome the illusion covering individual consciousness. As *rasa* theorists maintain that the experience of *rasa* is always an enjoyable experience, the question may be raised: How can an experience of a tragedy be enjoyable? Bhaṭṭa Nāyaka considered it to be a generalized experience, and therefore different from the personal experience of ordinary life. Generalization is a state of identification with the world of dramatic representation, which transcends any practical interest or egoistic concerns of the limited self.[67] It represents a process of idealization by which the sensitive viewer transcends his own personal emotions to a state of serene dramatic contemplation. Thus the dramatic experience transcends the pleasures and pains of the personal ego and reaches a state of impersonal joy. The artistic distance ensures a pure dramatic pleasure, as the spectator's life is not personally affected by the scene on the stage. It is due to the process of transcending one's personal emotional world of happiness and distress, and entering into a serene world of pure emotional pleasures. That dramatic experience was considered by the Kashmiri school to have the power of overcoming illusion, or at least of distancing oneself from it. The reservation expressed is due to the fact that the dramatic aesthetic experience still depends on unconscious emotional impressions (*vāsanās*), which consist of acquired personal experience, which are taken to be illusory. It may well be that Bhaṭṭa Nāyaka was the first person to make the famous comparison of *yogic* ecstasy and aesthetic experience,[68] and as such directly relate aesthetics and theology. Abhinavagupta's aesthetic theory was indirectly associated with *Advaita Vedānta*.

Before examining the aesthetic theory of Abhinavagupta, it may be useful to understand something of the religious context within which he was writing, for his conception of aesthetic and religious experience assumes a particular notion of religious experience. Abhinava was deeply involved in the religious world of the twelfth-century *Kashmir Śaivism*, which was informed by the philosophical system of *Advaita Vedānta*.[69] He showed interest in Bharata's *rasa* theory and in Ānandavardhana's *dhvani*[70] theory, and wrote commentaries on both. His interpretation of Bharata's *rasa sūtra*[71] is that *rasa* comes from the force of one's response to that which already exists, as opposed to the idea that it is produced. Thus *rasa* is experienced when the unconscious latent impressions rise to consciousness by the *vibhāvas* and other dramatic inciters. Abhinava's entire treatment of *rasa* theory displays a deep concern with the parallels between aesthetic experience and the experience of the *Vedāntin* mystic.[72] He writes:

> Watching a play or reading a poem for the sensitive reader[73] entails a loss of the sense of present time and space [. . .]. We are not directly and personally involved, so the usual medley of desires and anxieties dissolve [. . .] Our hearts respond sympathetically but not selfishly [. . .] The ego is transcended, and for the duration of the aesthetic experience, the normal waking 'I' is suspended [. . .] Now that the hard knot of 'selfness' has been untied, we find ourselves in an unprecedented state of mental and emotional calm [. . .] We experience sheer undifferentiated bliss.[74]

It is apparent that the experience described gradually leads to the peak of undifferentiated impersonal bliss.

Regarding *rasa* Abhinavagupta writes,

> *Rasa* is the enjoyed form of the operation of relishing the joy of one's own delicate consciousness colored by the impressions of love etc., which were previously instilled, that are appropriate to (or aroused by) the beautiful *vibhāvas* and *anubhāvas* conveyed in sound,[75] that appeal to the heart. And it, falling only within the

> ken of the operation of poetry, is *rasa*-suggestion (*rasa-dhvani*). It, indeed, is suggestion itself, and being primary, it is the essence of poetry.[76]

This passage represents Abhinavagupta's early concept of *rasa*, the essence of which is the experience of one's own consciousness when it is coloured by different emotions or *sthāyins*. These emotions have been latent in one's consciousness either from a previous life or the present one, but have been aroused by the beautiful *vibhāvas* and *anubhāvas* that touch the heart. The meeting of the external emotions with the internal emotions in the realm of one's consciousness creates the *rasa*. Moreover, that occurs within the realm of poetry and the suggested sense is the *rasa* itself. These descriptions may seem somewhat obscure, but later writings shed further light on the notion of *rasa* in Abhinava's theory. The experience of one's consciousness in Abhinava's thought takes the form of *hṛdaya-saṁvāda*, meaning 'response of the heart', or literally 'a conversation with the heart'. It is taken as a prior condition for the *rasa* experience.[77] If something has appeal to the heart, then its presentation in drama through its *vibhāvas* and *anubhāvas* was thought capable of producing *rasa*. Referring to this, Abhinava expands the notion of *rasa*:

> Nor is *rasa* a thing like the joy aroused when one hears, 'your son is born'. Nor (is it aroused) by indirect meaning (*lakṣaṇā*). But rather, being tasted, when the *vibhāvas* and *anubhāvas* are perceived, by means of identification with that from the strength of its appeal to the heart.[78]

This description clearly distinguishes the *rasa* from the primary emotion. The experience of *rasa* occurs in a favourable atmosphere created by the *vibhāvas* and *anubhāvas* in which the heart is open. At that time, the emotions latent in one's heart and the emotions expressed in the poetry or drama become one, and that opens one to experience the bliss of one's own consciousness, which is, according to Abhinavagupta, the essence of *rasa*. In other words, it seems that there are different emotions stored in the heart that obscure it, and these various emotions cloud one's consciousness. However, in a certain favourable atmosphere created by drama or poetry the heart opens, and when the emotions stored within it meet with the same emotions arriving from external sources, such as the *vibhāvas*, *anubhāvas* and *vyabhicarins*, at that time the emotional cloud is cleared as one's heart becomes ordered and transparent. At that time one can experience the bliss of one's own consciousness, which is the essence of *rasa*. In summary of the major components of Abhinava's early work, and his idea of *rasa*, it may be said that the major elements of his early theory are, therefore, the latent impressions[79] that appeal to the heart,[80] from which arises identification.[81] The consciousness in this identification is coloured by the impressions, and the experience of its joy in that state is *rasa*.[82]

In Abhinava's later work, *Abhinava-bhāratī*, the idea of generalization is added to the notion of *rasa*. The main components are still maintained, as the experience involves freedom from identifications such as 'one's own' or 'another's', but the *rasa* experience becomes more of a shared communal experience rather than an individual one. Due to a loss of any notion of ego or individuality, the emotions tasted do not have one's own limited self as their basis, rather they are based on unobstructed or undifferentiated consciousness, and thus they do not produce other dependent mental states. That is different from ordinary emotions, which are based on one's limited self and therefore produce other dependent mental states, such as a sense of loss or sorrow. In summary, Abhinava's view is that in dramatic experience one may overcome one's personal emotions, undergo a repose of his personal limitations and join in a shared emotional experience brought about by the drama. As the heart opens to these emotions, one experiences *rasa*. These ideas are best depicted by Abhinava himself:

> That singular mental state [. . .] is freed from identification such as 'one's own or another's' [. . .] Because of appearing without having one's own or another's limited self as its basis, it is incapable of producing other mental states like a sense of loss, etc. as arises with one's ordinary sexual love or sorrow caused by women etc. Thus, because it is grasped by a process also known as 'tasting' which is characterized by a repose whose nature is unobstructed consciousness, it is conveyed by the word *rasa*.[83]

Thus is the state of experiencing *rasa* characterized by a repose or relaxation of personal awareness, followed by a state of unobstructed consciousness.

The number of *rasas* is an especially important issue, for while many continued to maintain the concept of multi-*rasas*, most writers interested in the religious quality of the dramatic experience tended to single out one *rasa* among the many as the supreme culmination of all *rasas*. A given religious assessment of aesthetic experience is then somehow dependent upon the nature of the one *rasa* chosen as supreme. Bharata had produced a list of eight *rasas* in the *Nāṭyaśāstra*. Two major figures deeply involved in the endeavour to single out one particular *rasa* as special are Abhinavagupta and Bhoja.[84] Abhinavagupta, following others before him, added a ninth *rasa* to this list: *śānta rasa*, the tranquil sentiment. Abhinava's words on *śānta rasa* are at times difficult to comprehend, but it is the opinion of most scholars that for Abhinava, this *rasa* is qualitatively different from the eight standard *rasas*. In fact, this is the argument Abhinava provides to explain why Bharata did not mention the *śānta rasa* along with the standard eight. The special place of the tranquil *rasa* in the thought of Abhinavagupta perhaps can best be seen in his discussion of its *sthāyi-bhāva*. In the Abhinavabhāratī, his commentary on the *Nāṭya-śāstra*, he states that the knowledge of the truth,[85] the knowledge of the *ātman*,[86] or simply the *ātman* itself, is the *sthāyi-bhāva* of the *śānta rasa*.[87] It appears that for Abhinava the *śānta rasa* holds the position of the supreme *rasa*. The idea that the knowledge of the truth[88] or the knowledge of the *ātman*[89] is the *sthāyi-bhāva* of the *śānta rasa* is most interesting, as it equates knowledge with emotions.

Accordingly, both knowledge of the truth and knowledge of the self, that is *tattva-jñāna* and *ātma-jñāna*, and even the *ātman*, are considered to correspond to *śānta rasa*. This is a clear meeting place between the *jñāna* or knowledge paradigm and *rasa* theory, and as such the state of true knowledge is the primary emotion or *sthāyi-bhāva* from which *śānta rasa* emanates. The understanding of this passage from knowledge to aesthetics is important for understanding the *BhP*'s structure, as there, too, the state of true knowledge becomes equated with *śānta rasa.*

As Abhinavagupta was a monistic philosopher, an ascetic and an aesthete, all three aspects of his personality were expressed in his *rasa* theory. As a philosopher he belonged to the school of Kashmiri *Śaivism* who propounded the *Śaiva Siddhanta*, which was close to *Advaita Vedānta*. As an ascetic he may have been practising some form of *tantra* or *yoga*, in which the mental fluctuations are quieted and one gains direct perception of the self,[90] and as an aesthete, he was engaged in articulating *rasa* theory. It seems that his aesthetics combine the experience of transcending the limits of one's personality while aiming to merge with *Brahman*, with the *yogic* experience of bringing the mental fluctuations to cessation. As *jñāna* may serve as a vehicle for attaining oneness with *Brahman*, so may aesthetics serve that very same goal, too. Thus, his system may be considered to be 'the path of aesthetics', as the experience of *rasa* is not the goal in itself, rather it serves as a gate to the ultimate experience of *sat-cit-ānanda*, or the self becoming one with the Supreme Self or *Śiva*. In some ways, the aesthetic experience is for Abhinavagupta similar to the mystic's experience of *Brahman*. Both are uncommon – *alaukika* – in both the self is forgotten, and both are brought by a removal of obstacles, are beyond present time and place, are marked with bliss and are underlain by wonder or astonishment due to experiencing a different dimension of reality. However, there are also differences between the two: the aesthetic experience is temporal, it is not expected to change one's life radically and after the end of the performance the spectators once again return to their separate selves; *mokṣa*, however, is permanent and does change one's life radically. The implication of Abhinava's position is that the dramatic bliss places one in a mental repose, by which egoistic illusions can be shattered. However, whereas *mokṣa* is beyond illusion, the aesthetic experience, although higher than ordinary life, still partakes to some degree in illusion.

The tradition also included several writers who held different views than those held by Abhinavagupta and the *Rasa-dhvani* school. One of the most important and innovative thinkers among them was king Bhoja of *Dhārā*, who lived and ruled in present day Rajasthan, and who was approximately a contemporary of Abhinavagupta. Three possible dates of his birth are 982, 986 and 989 CE.[91] His coronation took place probably about 1000 CE and he ruled for the next 55 years, that is until the year 1055 CE or so. Bhoja of *Dhārā* was not only a great patron of poets, but a theorist of poetry as well. His two great works are *Sarasvatī-kaṇṭhābharaṇa* and *Śṛṅgāra-prakāśa*. The latter is the largest known work in Sanskrit poetics, and it deals with poetics and dramaturgy. Regarding its authenticity and unity of authorship, it seems that all the writers who have known the *Śṛ-pra* have quoted it as a work of king Bhoja. The peculiar views propounded in the work have been cited as Bhoja's, and the work *Śṛ-pra*, despite its size, undoubtedly exhibits a unity of authorship.[92] It is apparent that, in writing this masterpiece, Bhoja perceived himself as continuing an ancient tradition of Sanskrit poetics originating in Bharata, and made explicit efforts to associate himself with Bharata's *Nāṭyaśāstra*. It also seems that Bhoja attempted to imitate Bharata whose *Nāṭya Śāstra* speaks of poetics, though its main subject is dramaturgy. Bharata wrote his work in 36 chapters and so did Bhoja. Bharata dealt with Sanskrit language and its grammar to some extent and Bhoja dealt with both more elaborately.[93] However, although Bhoja was highly aware of the previous tradition upon which he developed his theories, and although his authorities were the ancients, it is interesting to note that Bhoja didn't have knowledge of Abhinavagupta. There is not the slightest indication of Bhoja's knowledge of Abhinavagupta, the end of whose literary career coincided with the beginning of Bhoja's.

The authorities for Bhoja are the ancients and as such he refers to Bharata and Daṇḍin, and the only other writer whom he quotes and considers in the formulation of his own *rasa* theory is Rudraṭa, who just preceded Ānandavardhana.[94] Though he claimed originality for his *rasa* theory, he nevertheless cited the earlier writers and specifically the *Kāvyādarśa* of Daṇḍin as the source of his *rasa* aesthetic theory. Moreover, it may well be that Bhoja's *rasa* theory was a culmination of a then existing tradition, in regard to which writes Pollock, 'His work would more rightly be viewed as the culmination of a tradition rather then a departure from it.'[95] As such, it may be possible to consider that although the *BhP* had preceded Bhoja, it may have still absorbed an earlier version of similar ideas. Bhoja's works[96] exerted a great influence on the section of the *Agni Purāṇa* on poetics[97] and on Śāradātanaya's *Bhāva-prakāśana* (thirteenth century). Both of these works, and especially the *Agni Purāṇa*, played a major role in spreading Bhoja's influence to other parts of India;[98] as such, the *Agni Purāṇa* may have finally crystalized in Bengal during the twelfth century, and its section on poetics had its greatest influence in Bengal, eastern Bihar and Orissa. As opposed to the classical tradition, the tradition following Bhoja emphasized the aesthetic experience as a feeling, which transcends the contemplative non-affective awareness of emotion.

The *Śṛṅgāra-prakāśa* purports to explain or treat the *śṛṅgāra rasa*. Thus the main part of Bhoja's huge work, which Bhoja himself considers important enough to serve as the basis of the name of the work itself, is the exposition of his new-found theory of the one *rasa* of *Ahaṅkāra*,

Abhimāna or *Śṛṅgāra.* Besides this *Śṛṅgāra* or *Ahaṅkāra*, the lower *śṛṅgāra rasa* of *Rati* between men and women is also elaborately treated. Thus the chief subjects of the whole work are the two, major and minor, *Śṛṅgāras*. Hence the work is called *Śṛ.Pra.*[99] It appears that the theorizing of the *śṛṅgāra rasa* occupies the heart of the treatise, and indeed Bhoja in his *Śṛṅgāra-prakāśa* writes, 'That is *rasa* which, rising beyond the path of contemplation, is only tasted in the identifying heart.'[100] This statement seems to award *rasa* an essential, realistic or ontological value, as opposed to the illusory or idealistic status it occupies in Abhinavagupta's thought. Moreover, it seems that some sort of hierarchy exists within Bhoja's philosophy of aesthetics, as there are two kinds of *Śṛṅgāras*, major and minor. Examining the *Śṛṅgāra-prakāśa*, it becomes evident that it amplifies ideas articulated earlier in the *Sarasvatī-kaṇṭhābharaṇa.* The *S-ka* is the earlier work of Bhoja in *Alaṅkāra*. The *Śṛ-pra* followed, as an amplification and also a more systematic exposition of the original ideas of Bhoja on various subjects, notably *rasa*. The new theory of *rasa* had already risen in Bhoja's mind in the *S-ka* and the very opening verses of chapter 5 of the *S-ka* state this theory: poetry is beautiful because of the presence of *rasa*, and *rasa* is called *śṛṅgāra*, *abhimāna* and *ahaṅkāra.* It is by reason of the experiences of many births that one gets it in one's soul. It is considered the germ from which other qualities grow, and it is the inner *tattva* of ego, or the idea of the 'I', the *ahaṅkāra.* It is one's love for one's own self. It is that which makes one receive even pain as pleasure.[101] These ideas constitute the heart of Bhoja's theory. We shall first discuss Bhoja's remarkable universality, and then the unique position the *śṛṅgāra rasa* occupies in his thought.

A notable feature of Bhoja's thought is its remarkable universality. Thus the dramaturgical realm expands into the realm of *kāvya* or poetics. The *Śṛṅgāra-prakāśa* is therefore at once a treatise on both poetics and dramaturgy. Bhoja states that *rasa* is the greatest element by virtue of which men are called *rasikas*, that this *rasa* is conveyed to responsive hearts through drama and poetry – *kāvya* – that poetry or *kāvya* is *śabda* and *artha*, word and sense united.[102] Bhoja's doctrine continues to cross boundaries and, as such, it freely applies terms derived from the orthodox *darśanas*, such as *dharma*, *Sāṅkhya* and *Vedānta.* However, despite applying these classical terms he nevertheless treats the sense of ego in a unique manner: in his thought the ego becomes a positive force, to be developed through aesthetics and turned into a vehicle for aesthetic liberation. In regard to Bhoja's *dharmic* or social aesthetics, Sheldon Pollock writes:

> There are [. . .] themes in Bhoja's treatise centrally concerned with the social aesthetic that I want to concentrate on here [. . .] In brief, Bhoja's conception seems to me as follows: literary texts make moral arguments. A moral argument is a general discursive phenomenon, however, not specific to literature. What is specific is *rasa*, and Bhoja shows that the moral order is inseparably connected with it: passion, *śṛṅgāra* – the one *rasa* – is moral force. This is no Platonic-Christian conceptual scheme were the virtues and passions are at war with each other; passions are virtues.[103]

Pollock attributes to Bhoja a holistic approach, where his aesthetics have social and moral implications. In other words, the aesthetic experience of *rasa* is also a moral experience, presumably strengthening social stability and morality, or uplifting *dharma*. A different way of expressing it would be to say that action performed according to *dharma* carries with it an aesthetic aspect, too. We shall not expand the discussion on the philosophy of action, but suffice it to say that action performed according to *dharma* and with proper motives is considered in *Sāṅkhya* terms to be *sāttvika*, and similarly, the experience of *rasa* is considered by Bhoja to be *sāttvika*. We shall hence look into Bhoja's relation to *Sāṅkhya* philosophy and highlight this relation as another source for the universality of his ideas. Bhoja's position is contrasted with the Platonic-Christian approach, which according to Pollock sees passions and morality at war with each other. The philosophical implications of Bhoja's social aesthetics are that this associates Bhoja with Rāmānuja's *pariṇāma* doctrine, which awards an essential status to acts of devotion and indeed to any action performed according to *dharma*. It seems that, according to Bhoja, the quality of being a *rasika* is a result of good deeds over many births. He clearly says that not all men are *rasikas*, rather one must have done numerous good deeds in past lives to possess it.[104] This is the application of dramaturgical ideas to *Vedāntic* ideas, of accumulating good deeds and striving for liberation birth after birth. It seems that the state of being a *rasika*, being able to taste *rasa*, becomes in Bhoja's thought synonymous to the liberated state. In this regard, the *Bhagavad Gītā* may be quoted: 'At the end of many births, the wise man surrenders unto me, thinking that "Vasudeva is all in all"; it is indeed very difficult to find such a great soul.'[105]

It appears that Bhoja maintains a similar idea, according to which the soul undergoes many births before it can taste *rasa* and achieve liberation. As such, the soul may have potential to experience *rasa*, but that is covered by some kind of a power such as ignorance or the lower *guṇas*. Accordingly, souls who have attained the state of being *rasikas* are rare indeed. All men are not called *rasikas* and some explanation must be found for calling only a choice few *rasikas*, as this refers to one who has *rasa* in him. Bhoja says that this cannot be due to any known cause. It is due to past adherence to *dharma*, and he adds that if the *rasika* tastes *rasa*, it must be present in him as a *guṇa* of his *ātman*.[106] Bhoja clearly treats the quality of being able to taste *rasa* in orthodox philosophical terms.[107] This ability seems to potentially be there in the *ātman* and the term *satkāryavāda* indicates that the cause precedes the effect, that is that this potential has been there previously, presumably since time immemorial or even eternally. Bhoja's indebtedness to *Sāṅkhya* thought is seen in another aspect of his *rasa* theory. It is the *Sāṅkhya* which speaks of *buddhi* as being made up of the three *guṇas* of *sattva*, *rajas* and *tamas*.

The first, *sattva*, is *sukhātmaka*. This *sattva-guṇa* must be made to predominate in one's character by incessant good deeds that purify one during the many migrations of the soul through numerous bodies. This *sattva-guṇa* can be called *rasa* and *āsvāda*, and Bhoja says expressly that his new *ahaṅkāra-śṛṅgāra-rasa* is an excellence in ourselves pertaining to our *sattva-guṇa.*[108] This refers to a somewhat more external layer, or the subtle coverings of the *ātman* bound in *saṁsāra* such as *buddhi.* Here, the state of *sattva* is characterized not only by happiness as it usually is, but by the ability to taste *rasa* as well.[109] The idea of *rasa* as relating to the *sattva guṇa* may be further clarified by considering Bhoja's idea of *ahaṅkāra* or ego. Bhoja's *ahaṅkāra* is called also *abhimāna*, because of its quality of giving pleasure to all experiences, including pain. It is also called *śṛṅgāra*, because it is itself the peak (*śṛṅga*) and takes one to the peak of perfection.[110] This interesting idea of the ego as a positive force sheds further light on Bhoja's ideas. This is not a concept of an ego that is a cause of pleasure and pain, such as in Buddhist or *Advaitin* thought, rather this ego seems to be essential or eternal. At the same time, this kind of ego experiences pleasure in everything, including pain. This is a most interesting mingling of dramaturgical and soteriological ideas, as this seems to be the foundation of the 'Aesthetic Self of the *Bhāgavata Purāṇa*'. This is an aesthetic *ātman*, who is characterized not by knowledge, rather by the ability of tasting *rasa* or the quality of being a *rasika*. This *ahaṁkāra* is not one of the vices such as haughtiness or egotism, rather it means ego in the *sāttvika* sense. Bhoja says that it is the peculiar virtue one gains by good deeds done during countless births which makes him more and more *sāttvika*. When this sense of 'I', personality and individuality are not developed, this person may be called a rustic or a *grāmya*, whereas by *rāsikya* Bhoja refers to the full bloom of one's emotional nature as emanating from *ahaṅkāra*.[111]

This concept of ego is clearly distinct from the Buddhist and the *Advaitin* concept, as it is not considered to be a vice, but rather a blessing. The development of this kind of ego is a worthy goal, to be pursued and strived for birth after birth. As this type of aesthetic ego seems to be essential and therefore eternal, it may well continue to exist in the post-*saṁsāra* state, that is the state of *mokṣa*. When the self is taken to be essentially aesthetic, it follows that artistic expressions are desirable, as they enable one to expand one's aesthetic qualities, and thereby make progress towards perfection. Thus, Bhoja treats the 64 classical arts favourably and considers them to be enchanters or *uddīpanas*. Bhoja treats the 64 arts as *uddīpana vibhāvas*. These arts, crafts and miscellaneous skills and dexterities of the mind and hand constitute the accomplishments of persons, helping them to become more attractive and irresistible personalities. These are qualities like beauty and pertain to the character or *ālambana vibhāva*. They kindle another's love and thus are classed among *uddīpana vibhāvas*.[112] The worldview unfolding here is that of spiritual pluralism. As opposed to the tendency to overcome pluralism in favour of an undifferentiated monistic view, the direction unfolding here is rather the opposite – as variety increases, emotional pleasure increases. As it expands, the *ātman* is able to taste deeper emotional tastes, and the more he is able to do so, his personhood unfolds and he comes closer to the state of *mokṣa*, were he continues to experience a variety of emotional tastes through a pure ego. Although this interpretation may sound like imposing *Vedāntic* ideas on Bhoja's thought, Raghavan clearly explains Bhoja's doctrine in those terms, when he writes:

> It will be plain when we go into the new *ahaṅkāra*-theory of *rasa* of Bhoja that the cultured individual as such is the seat of *rasa*. The

> *ātman* of the *rasika* is the *āśraya* of *rasa*. The *rasika* may be the spectator and the connoisseur, the poet, or the characters like Rama in the story. Thus primarily sentient and cultured beings are the seat of *rasa*.[113]

It is quite evident that *rasa* is the quality of the *ātman* and is therefore essential as opposed to contingent. The *Vedāntic* terms *vyavahāra* and *paramārtha* may be applied. Regarding the ordinary sentiment of love, in the ordinary plane of *vyavahāra*, love is called *abhimāna* because of its being enjoyed by one's heart, which considers or thinks the object to be pleasurable, though in fact it may be painful. When there is nothing in the object itself to warrant bliss, the *rasa* enjoyed must then be located in oneself.[114] The term *Vyavahāra* denotes the empirical reality as opposed to the highest reality, and it presumes the concept of hierarchical reality. It is interesting to note that in this case, it is applied to aesthetics, as opposed to the more common *Vedāntic* application of *saṁsāra* and illusion. It seems that Bhoja has articulated a worldview where aesthetics constitutes both empirical reality as well as the highest reality. As the *Vedāntic* tradition considers the worldly experience to be illusory or based on false knowledge, and the liberated experience to be based on true knowledge, similarly Bhoja considers the worldly emotional experience to be lower, and the liberated emotional experience to be higher, characterized by the experience of pure *rasas*.

Raghavan differentiates the worldly love from the higher love, which presumably exists in the liberated plane:

> [. . .] the one and only *rasa* which Bhoja accepts and which he calls *śṛṅgāra* is not the *sāmprayogikaśṛṅgāra*, the love in the ordinary sense, sex love [. . .] Bhoja's *śṛṅgāra* is not the *śṛṅgāra* of man and women in love. To distinguish the two, we can say that the *ahaṁkāra-śṛṅgāra*, the real *rasa*, is the *paramārtha-śṛṅgāra* or the higher *śṛṅgāra*.[115]

This 'real *rasa*' called *paramārtha-śṛṅgāra* seems to characterize the liberated post-*mokṣa* state, and is a natural outcome of Bhoja's system. As opposed to the well-known concept of undifferentiated *sat-cit-ānanda* state characterizing *mokṣa*, Bhoja's doctrine implies an aesthetically differentiated *sat-cit-ānanda* liberated state.

We may now look further into Bhoja's concept of a single and supreme *rasa*, and consider its implications in regard to the nature of the *ātman* or *jīva*. A final reduction of all *rasas* into one supreme *rasa* is found in Bhoja's *Śṛṅgāra-prakāśa*, wherein he writes that at an initial level, any of the emotions listed by Bharata[116] can become a *rasa*. He continues to say, however, that finally all *rasas* are based on the truly central and permanent ego,[117] and it is only by means of their association with the ego that the other emotions are enjoyed as *rasa*. Hence all *rasas* ultimately resolve into this *ahaṅkāra-rasa*, which Bhoja calls Love (*śṛṅgāra* or *prema*),[118] and as such for Bhoja the supreme *rasa* is *śṛṅgāra* or *prema*. It is to be noted that in Bhoja's thought all *rasas*, including the supreme *rasa* of love, are based on a permanent ego or personality. The implication is that his system is essentially personalistic, in that personality is never lost at any stage, nor even in the supreme state of liberation. Moreover, this ego or notion of personality is the foundation or a precondition upon which the *rasa* experience is tasted. Thus is the *jīva* taken to be ultimately and essentially personal and, similarly, it seems that the supreme is perceived by this system to be personal too, as the emotional exchange in the liberated state takes place between the *jīva* and the Supreme Person. Raghavan reinforces the idea, that for Bhoja the *jīva* is personal: Bhoja 'explains the term *rasika* as pointing to the fact that *rasa* which manifests later in the *rasika* was already existent in his soul'.[119]

The idea of *rasa* as existent in the soul may be parallel to the *advaitin* and the *viśiṣṭādvaitin* idea of knowledge comprising the essence of the soul. The soul's aesthetic sensitivity and its ability to experience *rasa* imply its personhood, given, of course, that personhood is defined in aesthetic terms. This idea is reflected in the *BhP*, where both the *jīva*, the minute person and *Brahman*, the Supreme Person, are essentially personal in this world, as well as in the liberated world, where they exchange various pleasurable emotions even in the post-*mokṣa* state. In this school of thought, the supreme *rasa* is *śṛṅgāra*, and it is not awakened by knowledge, but rather by beauty. Bhoja maintains that the amorous sentiment,[120] originating from the dominant love-instinct perpetually associated with the soul and awakened by manifestations of beauty, is the ultimate source of all *rasas*. Thus it is the only *rasa*.[121] Bhoja differentiates this kind of pure emotion, experienced by the *ātman*, from an ordinary or worldly emotion. He expands the realm of the *rasa*.

Bhoja goes further than both Rudraṭa and Lollaṭa, who perhaps restricted themselves to the 49 *bhāvas* described by Bharata, and claimed all of them *rasas*, as he calls almost anything *rasa*.[122] It seems that not only did Bhoja expand the *rasa* experience beyond the realm of dramaturgy into the realm of poetics, but from his point of view *rasa*, or the aesthetic experience, is universal and underlies almost every experience. This reflects on the dramaturgical question of who experiences *rasa*, too. He does not restrict the state of being *rasika* to the reader of poetry or the spectator of drama but applies it to all cultured votaries of art, the poet, the characters in a composition, the actors and the spectators.[123] There are differing opinions on the question of who experiences *rasa*, and Bhoja, whose concept of *rasa* is characterized by universality, naturally awards it not only to the spectators, but to all involved, including the drama's actors. Despite Bhoja's explicit plurality, his doctrine possess a unifying element, which is the concept of the one and supreme *rasa*. From the extreme idea of considering all aesthetic experiences to be *rasas*, Bhoja goes to the other extreme and says, none of these really deserves the name *rasa*. They are called *rasa* only by courtesy. The real *rasa* is only one.[124]

The concept resembles *sāṅkhya* through the idea of devolution, as all *rasas* devolve into one supreme *rasa* which is *śṛṅgāra*. The third stage of *rasa* is called by Bhoja the *uttara-koṭi* or 'the other end'; it is a synthesis of all these scattered *bhāvas* again in a phase of the fundamental *ahaṁkāra*, the phase called *preman*. That is, the *bhāvas* return to the one *rasa* from which they sprang up. They pass the *bhāvanā*-stage after attaining *prakarṣa* and dissolve in the *rasa* of *ahaṁkāra* through the stage of *preman*. In the stage of *preman*, every *bhāva* is a kind of love, *preman*, and finally every kind of love is a kind of love of *ātman*, *ahaṁkāra*, *abhimāna* or *śṛṅgāra*. Bhoja holds that his new theory of this three-dimensional *rasa* – *ahaṁkāra*, *bhāva-prakarṣas* and *preman* – is based on Daṇḍin's verse on the three emotion-figures called *ūrjasvi*, *rasavat* and *preyas*.[125]

What is the meaning of the statement 'In the stage of *preman*, every *bhāva* is a kind of love'? Our understanding is that it refers to the liberated stage, where numerous and multifarious *rasas* are exchanged between the minute and the Supreme Persons. However, underlying all of them is the state of *preman* or love. As such, whether in servitude, friendship or parental affection, love underlies the various exchanges. This certainly is an interesting rationale establishing the supremacy of love, and the close relations between dramaturgy, aesthetics, theology and philosophy are also rather remarkable. Besides the idea of loving the other, Bhoja's idea of love extends to love of oneself. This is illustrated by Bhoja: a man is glanced at by a beautiful damsel and at once goes into ecstasies over himself, and bows again and again to himself. The love for the woman is because he loves himself as being loved by her and, as such, he congratulates himself.[126] We find the same idea if we analyse the ordinary expression of men when they attain some prized object: 'I should congratulate myself, I am proud of it', and so on. Bhoja analyses human experiences and arrives at this fact of *ahaṅkāra* which enables enjoyment, and from its being the root cause of enjoyment, he calls it *rasa*. It is called *śṛṅgāra* not only as that which takes one to the state of perfection but also because it is love, it is the very life of *ātmayoni* or *kāma*. *Kāma* is not meant here as sexual love, even as *śṛṅgāra* is not used by Bhoja here in the sense of love between man and woman, and even as Bhoja's *āhaṅkāra* here is not egotism.[127] The view expressed is unique in that it values the ego as a positive force, both in worldly life as well as a vehicle on the path towards perfection. This stands in stark opposition to the Buddhist and *Advaitin* conception of the ego, as a notion to be deconstructed or overcome. In summary, Delmonico's description of Bhoja's aesthetic theory may be cited:

> His [Bhoja's] aesthetic is laid out and the answers to the four questions are elicited.[128] Bhoja claims that all forms of rapture are really forms of erotic rapture (*śṛṅgāra*) since they originate out of the quality of self that makes possible the experience of love (*preman*). *Rasa* is the experience of love and the *rasas* are experiences of love for different objects or activities, presenting a potentially unlimited realm of possibilities. In the experience of *rasa* the identity, instead of becoming relaxed, as with Abhinavagupta, becomes intensified and one's self-valuation is increased. Moreover, *rasa* is the 'peak experience' of lovers (*śṛṅgārins*) in the world and is experienced only indirectly by the same through drama and poetry.[129]

Here the experience of love is there in the self. It is not external or illusory but an essential quality of the self. The experience of *rasa* requires objects external to the self. It is not a monistic experience, but rather is dualistic, as *śṛṅgāra-rasa* is based on the existence of at least two distinct persons, without which that *rasa* cannot take place. There are unlimited possibilities of *rasas*, presumably by different combinations of *rasa*'s various components, and by different levels of intensity or depth. As opposed to the repose or relaxation of personal characteristics in *śānta rasa*, the experience described by Bhoja entails an intensification of personal characteristics, and a rising of self-valuation or self-identity. *Śṛṅgāra*'s supreme position represents its being the most intense and tasteful aesthetic experience. Here drama and poetry cannot supply the direct experience, but rather an indirect representation only. The full manifestation of this *rasa* can be experienced, thus, may one presume, in the liberated state only, where the self is free from any clouding or obscuring coverings.

A Comparison of Abhinavagupta's and Bhoja's Position on Three Major Questions

In order to focus on the differences between the two approaches of Abhinavagupta and Bhoja, a comparison of three key issues will be made and implications highlighted. The issues are: 1. the location of *rasa*; 2. the ontological status of emotions; and 3. the supreme *rasa*. It seems that whereas Abhinava's position clearly supports the impersonal position, Bhoja's position clearly supports the personal one.

Who can experience rasa?

Rasa theorists have been divided on the question of who can experiences *rasa*. Although there is an agreement that during a dramatic performance the audience may experience *rasa* under suitable conditions, there are differing opinions on the question of whether the actor can experience *rasa* too. Abhinavagupta refuses to grant the aesthetic experience of *rasa* to the actor, as the actor is too involved. Thus in his system it is only the spectator who experiences *rasa*. According to Bhoja, though, every cultured individual (*rasika*) can experience *rasa*. The condition of one's inner nature and his mature emotional condition is the determining factor, regardless of whether the person is the spectator, the poet or the actor. This discussion has a deep effect on the reading of the *BhP*. If the *BhP* is to be read as a cosmic drama, as we propose, both the Supreme Person in his *avatāra* forms acting his *līlā*, and the readers playing the role of participant-observers partake in the experience of *rasa*. Therefore, according to Bhoja's theory, readers can relish *rasa* regardless of their position as participant-observers, and their only requirement for experiencing *rasa* is their being *rasika*; that is, sensitive cultured individuals. I believe that this is the way in which the *BhP* was traditionally understood – as a liberating drama meant to release from *saṁsāra* the audience who are in the position of participant-observers.

Indeed, the *BhP* opens by addressing its audience as *rasikas* and calls them to enjoy the *BhP*, just as an actor calls the audience to enjoy the drama he is about to observe.[130] However, were Abhinava's theory to underlie the *BhP*, the spectators or readers, being participant-observers themselves, would have been too involved, and therefore excluded from tasting the *bhakti rasa*. Therefore, it seems that Bhoja's position of acknowledging the experience of *rasa* in the spectator well fits the logic underlying the *BhP*.

The ontological status of emotions

Abhinava's position is that the *sthāyi-bhava*[131] is worldly, whereas *rasa* is not of this world and therefore exists only in art. Whereas the *sthāyi-bhava* is the experience of the unconscious latent emotional impressions rising to consciousness in the world of everyday life, *rasa* is the experience of the unconscious latent emotional impressions rising to consciousness in the controlled and impersonal environment of the theatre,[132] and can therefore be tasted only there. For Bhoja the relations between the *sthāyi-bhava* and *rasa* are developmental. The examples he gives are the production of juice from sugarcane, oil from sesame, butter from curds and fire from wood. Therefore for him both *sthāyi-bhava* and *rasa* are of fundamentally the same nature, but represent different stages of evolution. This controversy among Indian aesthetes is deeply rooted in theology, concerning the nature of the ultimately real and its relation to the world. Haberman writes:

> One group, the *pariṇāma-vādins*, represented here by Bhoja and Viśvanātha, maintain that the world is a transformation or development (*pariṇāma*) of ultimate reality (*Brahman*); whereas the second group, the *vivarta-vādins*, represented here by Abhinavagupta, hold that the world is a false appearance

> (*vivarta*) of ultimate reality. The *pariṇāma-vādins* use the simile of the production of curds from milk to explain the existence of the world, whereas the *vivarta-vadins* favour the analogy of a rope being mistaken for a snake, to explain the world's (false) existence. The perspectives of these two schools on the evaluation of aesthetic experience are clear. *Pariṇāma-vādins* see a developmental relationship existing between art (*rasa*) and the world (*sthāyi-bhāva*); ordinary emotions are simply an underdeveloped form of *rasa*. The *vivarta-vādins*, on the other hand, insist that there is no direct correspondence between art (*rasa*) and the world (*sthāyi-bhāva*); art totally transcends the emotional experience of everyday life.[133]

Although aesthetics seemed at first to differ from *Vedānta*, we have returned to the core issues debated among *Vedāntins*, such as the realism or idealism of the world, this time expressed through aesthetics. The *vivarta-vādins* insist that the emotions experienced here in this world are false and unessential, and must therefore be given up. Contrary to that, the *pariṇāma-vādins* hold the view that ordinary emotions experienced in this world are but an underdeveloped form of pure emotions or *rasas* and, as such, should be sublimated and purified in order to become *rasas*. The implication is that when the Supreme Person appears in his *avatāra* forms, those who feel for him, and even those who don't encounter him directly but hear of him through the *BhP* with an open heart, all experience various emotions towards him. These emotions may represent various degrees of clarity, but they are nevertheless essential and real. When purified and sublimated by hearing the *BhP*, they turn into *rasas* and carry the devoted to the spiritual realm of *Vaikuṇṭha*, where they can be experienced in a pure and intense form. Therefore, the reading of the *BhP* according to Bhoja's *pariṇāma-vadin*'s position seems to fit the logic underlying the *BhP*.

The supreme rasa

We shall now look closer into the question: What is the supreme *rasa* according to the two positions? In articulating the impersonal aesthetic position, Haberman quotes Abhinavagupta's commentary on the *Nāṭyaśāstra*, the *Abhinavabhāratī*:

> Therefore, the *ātman* alone possessed of such pure qualities as knowledge, bliss, etc., and devoid of enjoyment of imagined sense objects, is the *sthāyibhāva* of *śānta* [...] For *rati*, etc., which arise and disappear due to the emergence and disappearance of their respective causes, are called *sthāyibhāvas* in so far as they attach themselves for some time to the canvas [wall] in the form of the *ātman* which is of an unchanging nature relative to them. But knowledge of the truth is the canvas behind all emotions, and so it is the most stable of all the *sthāyibhāvas*.[134]

Abhinava considers the essential self, namely the *ātman*, to consist of *sat*, *cit*, *ānanda* and to be devoid of enjoyment of objects external to it. Therefore, the state of experiencing the eight *rasas* is a state in which the *ātman*, the essential self which is unchanging by nature, is still clouded by some illusory variety and distinctness. However, being in its original and pure position of true knowledge, it experiences the bliss of *Brahman* through *śānta rasa*. In other words, according to Abhinavagupta, *śānta rasa* represents the *ātman*'s essential position. In articulating the personal position, Haberman writes:

> Another final reduction of all *rasas* into one supreme *rasa* is found in Bhoja's *Śṛṅgāra Prakāśa*. Therein he writes that, at an initial level, any of the emotions listed by Bharata can become a *rasa*. He continues to say, however, that finally all *rasas* are based on the truly central and permanent ego, and it is only by means of their association with the ego that the other emotions are enjoyed as *rasa*. Hence, all *rasas* ultimately resolve into this *ahaṅkāra-rasa*, which Bhoja calls love (*śṛṅgāra* or *prema*).[135]

In considering Bhoja's position it is to be noted that the various 41 emotions all produce *rasas*. These seem to pertain to the essential self and to be experienced in the *ātman*'s pure and original state. As opposed to the position of Abhinavagupta, Bhoja's position is that the *ātman* maintains a sense of ego or personal identity in its original and pure state, too. This is corroborated by the *Vaiṣṇava* position of the self maintaining a sense of personal identity even in the liberated state or in *Vaikuṇṭha*, and experiencing in that state a variety of emotions. Once this emotional reality is established as essential, Bhoja proceeds to analyse it, and resolves that *śṛṅgāra* or *prema* represents the ultimate *rasa*, or the *ātman*'s purest state. If the *ātman*, in its liberated state, lives in the variegated world of *Vaikuṇṭha*, and exchanges various worshipful relationships with the Supreme Person, it may well be that, according to Bhoja, love is the highest form of exchange with the Supreme Person. Haberman concludes:

> Bhoja maintains that the amorous sentiment, originating from the dominant love instinct perpetually associated with the soul and awakened by manifestations of beauty, is the ultimate source of all *rasas*; thus it is the only one *rasa*. We see then that both Abhinavagupta and Bhoja finally reduce all *rasas* into one single and supreme *rasa*, which they claim, compares to the religious experience of *brahmāsvāda*.[136]

Bhoja's position supports two of the *BhP*'s central themes. First, it explains why the *rāsa līlā* episode reigns supreme. According to Bhoja, *śṛṅgāra* or *prema* reigns supreme, and the *rāsa līlā* episode expressing amorous relations with the supreme is considered to be the *BhP*'s peak. Second, it supports the idea of maintaining a personal identity after achieving the liberated state. According to Bhoja, all *rasas* are based on a permanent ego, and as this ego is permanent and not lost at the liberated state, it is possible for the *ātman* or the minute person to continue and exchange *rasas* with the Supreme Person after achieving the liberated state. This is a central idea found in the *BhP*. Accordingly, the world of *Vaikuṇṭha* is depicted as variegated and full of personal expressions. Yet on the contrary, Abhinava's idea of the *ātman* being devoid of enjoyment and being representative of *śānta rasa* in its pure form doesn't seem to underlie the *BhP*. It deprives the *rasa līlā* episode of its supreme position, and excludes the *ātman* from having a sense of permanent ego after liberation. Therefore it seems that it is again Bhoja's position underlying the *BhP*.

In contrasting the two main *rasas* of *śānta* and *śṛṅgāra*, two extreme aesthetic positions may be found. The *śānta rasa* represents a quietening and settling of emotional expressions, a quietening of the mind and a cessation of all relationships with other persons. Thus it follows the *advaitin* ideal of the reposing of personal expressions as a stage higher than ordinary life, leading to the complete rejection of all personal characteristics and mental fluctuations, and merging with the undifferentiated *Brahman*. However, the *śṛṅgāra rasa* represents the other superlative – an extreme emotional excitement, a state of ecstatic ferment and intense relationships with another person. So it follows the *Vaiṣṇava* idea of intense emotional expressions that are pure and free from egotism, directed towards the Supreme Person. This stage is certainly considered higher than ordinary life, as expressed and exemplified by the *Ālvārs* and by the central protagonists of the *BhP* – the *gopīs*. It appears that the meeting of the *Vedānta* and *rasa* schools may have produced two basic kinds of hybrids: the first emphasizes the *ātman* being peaceful and serene, whereas the second emphasizes the *ātman*'s intense emotional expression towards the Supreme Person. The first position refers to the *ātman* as pure consciousness, and seems to imply that the *ātman* does not possess personal characteristics. The second position seems to view the *ātman* in a more personal manner. If the *ātman* is exchanging relationships with the Supreme Person in the liberated state, while separated from *pradhāna* and free from the *guṇas* and from *saṁsāra*, it may well be that in the theology of the *BhP*, the *ātman* is taken to be a person too. As opposed to the Supreme Person, the *ātman* could be taken as a minute person, defined by his/her/its exchange of pure emotions, that is, *rasas*, with the Supreme Person.

The *Bhāgavata Purāṇa* Interpreted According to *Rasa* Theory in the Sixteenth Century

Is there any clear evidence of the application of *rasa* theory in the interpretation of the *BhP*? Can a clear association between *rasa* theory and the *BhP* be recognized? Is there any traditional source that claims that *rasa* theory actually underlies the *BhP*? Is there a traditional *Vaiṣṇava* source which grades different stages from *śānta* to *śṛṅgāra*, thus supplying a rationale for analysing the *BhP* in this way? The *Caitanya Caritāmṛta* of Kṛṣṇadāsa Kavirāja is a later text, completed during the early seventeenth century in Bengali.[137] It analyses the relations between *bhakti* and the various *rasas*, and often refers to the *BhP* as a major source representing exactly that. The work provides a gradation of *rasas* from *śānta* to *śṛṅgāra*, along with a rationale justifying the gradation. Thus, although it is a later text, it may be considered a useful source in shedding light on our topic and providing some clues, not only as to how the *BhP* has been traditionally understood, but as to its structure and doctrine as well.

As the *Caitanya Caritāmṛta* of Kṛṣṇadāsa Kavirāja is a text central to *Gauḍīya Vaiṣṇavism*, we may look into the relations between *Gauḍīya Vaiṣṇavism* and classical Sanskrit poetics. Flood observes that:

> Devotional traditions focused on Kṛṣṇa the Cowherd developed in northern India, and found articulation in Sanskrit devotional and poetic literature as well as in more popular devotional movements, particularly around *Vṛndāvana* and in Bengal [. . .] The *Gauḍīya Vaiṣṇava* tradition developed a theology in which the categories of aesthetic experience, described in classical poetry (*kāvya*), came to be applied to devotional religious experience.[138]

Flood points to the clear link between Sanskrit poetics and the theology of popular medieval devotional movements, *Gauḍīya Vaiṣṇavism* included. Some of the main *Gauḍīya Vaiṣṇava* theological treatises were written by the highly orthodox *Gosvāmins* of *Vṛndāvana*. Flood continues: 'The works of the *Gosvāmins* are, indeed, highly orthodox in the sense that they accept the authority of the *Veda*, but they include within the category of revelation the *purāṇas*, especially the *Bhāgavata Purāṇa*.'[139] Flood points to the *Gosvāmin*'s acceptance of the *BhP* as authoritative, along with the *Vedas*. It may well be that their interpretation of the *BhP* was orthodox too, that is according to the norms prevailing during their times. Therefore the association of the *BhP* and Sanskrit poetics might have been seen as the generally accepted way to understand the *BhP*.

We may now look more closely into the *Caitanya Caritāmṛta* of Kṛṣṇadāsa Kavirāja. The work depicts the life story of the medieval Bengali saint Śrī Caitanya,[140] and is divided into three sections: the *Ādi Līlā*, *Madhya Līla* and *Antya Līla*. The chapter under discussion is the nineteenth chapter of the *Madhya Līlā* in which Śrī Caitanya instructs his disciple Rūpa through a metaphor of *jīva*-gardeners.[141] Certain *jīvas* gain the seed of the *bhakti* creeper. They plant the seed and nourish it through *śravaṇa* and *kīrtana*,[142] up to the point at which the tree grows and bears the fruits of *prema*.[143] The metaphor ends this way: 'And there he serves that wishing-tree, and in happiness tastes the *rasa* of the *prema*-fruit. For this is the best of fruits, and the highest end of man, before which the four ends of man are like straw.'[144] In other words, according to this text, the process of *bhakti* achieves its fructification in tasting *prema-rasa*, or the *rasa* of love for Kṛṣṇa. This is considered to be the highest end. Kṛṣnadāsa continues and describes how *bhakti* should be pure in order to produce this fruit:

> 147 From pure *bhakti* is produced *prema*; thus these are the signs of pure *bhakti*: 148 Abandonment of desire for other things, of *pūjā* of others, and of *jñāna* and *karma*, and with the aid of all the senses, constant dedication to Kṛṣṇa. 149 This is pure *bhakti*, and from it *prema* comes. These signs are given in the *Pañcarātra* and *Bhāgavata*.[145]

Two points may be highlighted: the exclusiveness of *bhakti* and the reference to the *BhP*. As far as the exclusiveness of *bhakti*, it is interesting to note that in the final stage, the stage of *prema*, knowledge or *jñāna* is rejected. It seems that knowledge, or *jñāna*, is judged according to its contribution to the experience of *rasa*. It is justified as long as it aids the *jīva* to develop *prema*, and at a certain point it becomes an obstacle and is consequently rejected. The *BhP* is mentioned as a reference, along with the *Pañcarātra*. Following this, Kṛṣṇadāsa quotes the *Nārada Pañcarātra* and the *BhP*.[146] The second *BhP* verse quoted reads as follows: 'The mark of *nirguṇa bhakti-yoga* is cited as *bhakti* not separate from me and spontaneous; it is not the fruit of examination, nor of knowledge of works.'[147] This verse further highlights the fact that *bhakti* is not caused by examination or empirical knowledge, nor by knowledge of works. It re-emphasizes the nature of knowledge as being subservient to *bhakti*, being neither its cause nor its goal. Kṛṣṇadāsa goes on to mention various stages of *prema*, and concludes,

> 154 All these are *sthāyi-bhāvas* of *Kṛṣṇa-bhakti-rasa*. When the *sthāyi-bhāvas* are mixed together with *vibhāva* and *anubhāva*, 155 and when mixed with *sāttvika* and *vyabhicārin bhāvas*, *Kṛṣṇa-bhakti rasa* comes about, as sweet as nectar to the taste.[148]

Here we see a clear application of the *rasa* theory components of Kṛṣṇaite theology.

Now Kṛṣṇadāsa goes on to analyse *bhakti rasa* as comprised of two groups: primary or chief *rasas* and secondary or subordinate *rasas*. He writes,

> 159 *Śānta*, *dāsya*, *sakhya*, *vātsalya*, and *madhura-rasa* are their names, and among the *rasas* of *Kṛṣṇa-bhakti* these five are chief. 160 *Hāsya*, *adbhūta*, *vīra*, *karuṇa*, *raudra*, *bībhatsa*, and *bhaya* – these are the seven *rasas* subordinate to the five kinds of *bhakti*. 161 The five *rasas* are *sthāyi*, and remain spread in the heart of the *bhakta*; the seven are secondary, and gain their cause as guests. 162 *Śānta bhaktas* were the nine Yogendras, and Sanaka and the others. *Bhaktas* of the *dāsya-bhāva* are his numberless servants everywhere. 163 *Sakhya bhaktas* are Śrīdāma and the rest, and in the city Bhīma and Arjuna. *Vātsalya bhaktas* were mother, father, and many elders. 164 The *bhaktas* of *madhura-rasa* are primary, and are the *gopīs* in *Vraja*, the *mahiṣīs*, the *Lakṣmīs*, too numerous to count.[149]

This passage conveys two ideas important for our discussion. First, it divides the *rasas* into two groups: primary and secondary. Second, it categorizes the devotees into groups characterized by the primary *rasas*. All the devotees mentioned are also in the *BhP*. Thus Sanaka and the others are mentioned in the third book of the *BhP*,[150] the nine Yogendras are included in the eleventh book,[151] Bhīma and Arjuna are in the first book,[152] the fathers[153] are in the tenth book,[154] and so are the gopīs.[155] It is evident that Kṛṣṇadāsa considers *prema rasa*, or love, to be the highest, as opposed to *śānta rasa*, and this is further reinforced by his considering *bhakti* to be exclusive, so much so that in its highest stage of *prema*, knowledge or *jñāna* is rejected. Our understanding is that knowledge is rejected at that stage, because of its association with *śānta rasa* and impersonal realization. The detailed description of the various *rasa*-theory components does not leave much doubt as to his sources. Kṛṣṇadāsa clearly builds upon classical *rasa* theory, applying the terms *sthāyi bhāva*, *vibhāva*, *anubhāva* and so forth within a theological context. He divides the *rasas* into two categories – primary and secondary, a division that may be a *Gauḍīya* innovation, as generally the nine *rasas* are undivided. He goes on to group the different devotees according to their predominant *rasa*, and that is another clear link to the *BhP*, as all the stories of the various devotees mentioned appear in it.

The following section will look closer into the developmental relations between the *rasas*. It looks into Kṛṣṇadāsa's analysis of each *rasa*'s components, and highlights the structure upon which the *rasas* are organized. The question of development naturally arises: Is there a sense of progress among the five primary *rasas*? Are they listed circumstantially or is there some rationale underlying their order, beginning with *śānta* and ending in *mādhurya*? Kṛṣṇadāsa goes on to articulate the rationale behind the order presented and writes:

> 173 In the *śānta-rasa*, by knowledge of his true form, Kṛṣṇa is established as the one. 'With knowledge of me, tranquillity is established.' This is a verse from the holy mouth: The fixing of knowledge on me is tranquillity, so says *Bhagavān*. Thus, without *śānta rati*, the fixing of knowledge on him is difficult. 174 The abandonment of desires except those for Kṛṣṇa, this action is to be honoured. Thus I know the *śānta* [person] as one [type of] *Kṛṣṇa bhakta*. 175 The *Kṛṣṇa-bhakta* considers heaven and *mokṣa* as hell. The fixing of Kṛṣṇa [in the mind] and the abandonment of desires – these are the two qualities of the *śānta* man.[156]

The position of the *śānta* devotee is characterized by knowledge and detachment. On the one hand, the devotee gains knowledge of Kṛṣṇa and, on the other hand, he relinquishes desires and develops detachment from the world. This is exemplified by his considering heaven as hell. His consideration of *mokṣa* as hell also, is interesting, and seems to be a feature of personalistic theology. The rationale seems to be that compared to the pleasures of exchanging *rasas* with Kṛṣṇa, the *Upaniṣadic mokṣa* representing merging with *Brahman* and a loss of personality is like hell. However, *śānta rasa* is devoid of affection since it is remote and somewhat impersonal: 'The nature of *śānta* is without a hint of affection for Kṛṣṇa, but is learned in the knowledge [of Kṛṣṇa as] *parambrahma* and *paramātmā*.'[157] This analyses *śānta rasa* still deeper. It is devoid of affection for Kṛṣṇa and is characteristically compatible with knowledge of *Brahman* as well as *Paramātman*.[158]

Now the text goes on to analyse the next *rasa*, *dāsya*:

> 178 In the *śānta-rasa* there is only knowledge of his true form; in *dāsya* there is additional knowledge of Prabhu with full divinity.

> 179 [In] knowledge of Īśvara, reverence for his glory is great, and serving him gives infinite pleasure to Kṛṣṇa. 180 In addition to the qualities of *śānta*, there is more of service in *dāsya*, and thus the qualities of *dāsya* are double.[159]

Dāsya-rasa is taken to contain additional knowledge, and that may mean that Kṛṣṇa is seen from a closer perspective. *Dāsya* is characterized not only by reverence for his glory but by service that gives him infinite pleasure. Naturally, that pleasure radiates to the devoted servant too and in this way the master and servant relish the exchange of relationships. As the experience of *śānta* is included in the experience of *dāsya*, the qualities of *dāsya* are said to be double. Thus, the experience of *dāsya* is more complex than the experience of *śānta*, including not only knowledge and renunciation, but also the pleasure of pleasing the master and exchanging relationships with him. Beside complexity, the experience of *dāsya* is more intense than that of *śānta*, as the qualities of *dāsya* are double. The picture emerging is of development characterized by two parameters – complexity and intensity. Next *sakhya rasa* is analysed:

> 181 The qualities of *śānta* and the service of *dāsya* are doubled in *sakhya*. In *dāsya* is reverence for his majesty, and service; *sakhya* is full of faith. 182 Riding on their shoulders, and having them ride on his shoulders, and playing at fighting: they serve Kṛṣṇa, and cause Kṛṣṇa to serve them. 183 Faith is primary in *sakhya*, and reverence for majesty less; thus are the signs of the three qualities of *sakhya-rasa*. 184 There is more affection for Kṛṣṇa, and knowledge of him as equal to the self; thus in *sakhya rasa Bhagavān* is controlled.[160]

It seems that the qualities of both *śānta* and *dāsya* are present within *sakhya rasa* but the notion of awe and reverence is diminished, whereas feelings of confidence, friendly intimacy and a sense of fraternity arise. The distinction of master and servant characterizing *dāsya* is replaced with egalitarian feelings, so much so that Kṛṣṇa's friends not only serve him but have him serve them. The phrase 'knowledge of him as equal to the self' can also be taken as 'think themselves equal to him'.[161] Still, as the first two *rasas* are present, here too some sense of knowledge, detachment and service is still present.

From this the text goes on to develop the notion of parental affection:

> 185 In *vātsalya* are the qualities of *śānta* and the service of *dāsya*, and those various services called by the name '*pālana*'. 186 The qualities of *sakhya* are the essence of non-difference and non-reverence for majesty, and in deep affection chastisement and reproach are common. 187 Knowledge of the self as protector, and of Kṛṣṇa as protected; with the qualities of the four *rasas*, *vātsalya* is like nectar. 188 He himself drowns with his *bhaktas* in the bliss of that nectar, and those who perceive his divinity say that Kṛṣṇa is controlled by his *bhaktas*.[162]

The *vātsalya rasa* includes the qualities of the other three *rasas*, but a new sense is added and that is the sense of maintenance.[163] Not only is there knowledge, servitude and fraternity but a sense of protection and maintenance is added. The devotee in *vātsalya rasa* is therefore lovingly controlling Kṛṣṇa out of parental affection and may even reproach him.

Following the discussion of parental affection is the discussion of *mādhurya* or conjugal love, taken by Kṛṣṇadāsa to be the peak of emotional experience:

> 189 In *madhura-rasa* is the establishment of Kṛṣṇa and very intense service, and the non-difference and most loving care of the *sakhya*. 190 In the manner of a lover, one serves him with the whole body. Thus in *madhura-rasa* are the qualities of all five. 191 The qualities of sky, etc., are in each of the other elements; the first, second, third, and up to earth, the fifth. 192 In the same way the *madhura* is the aggregate of all the others, and thus the taste of it is most wonderful.[164]

This section summarizes the topic and establishes the supremacy of *mādhurya rasa* based upon the two parameters of complexity and intensity. This traditional application of the *rasa* theory to Vaiṣṇava theology is an important source for the understanding of the *BhP*'s structure. Although its date of composition is doubtlessly later, the *Caitanya Caritāmṛta* provides us with a traditional rationale of how to understand the *BhP*. Perhaps these views were developed later than the *BhP*'s time of composition, or perhaps the *BhP* was composed by those who held views not that different from these later views, and these were echoed and amplified by the commentary tradition. Therefore the analysis of *rasa* theory, culminating in *madhura*, may well be an aid to understanding the *BhP*'s theology. At any rate, the commentary tradition considers *śānta rasa* to be characterized by knowledge and detachment, and to be devoid of affection. *Dāsya* includes the characteristics of *śānta*, but service is added. Therefore it is more complex and more intense. In *sakhya* confidence and fraternity are added, and in *vātsalya* the sentiment of maintenance is appended. *Mādhurya* is the richest of all, and represents the culmination of all *rasas*.

In summation, the classical Indian aesthetic theory underwent a polarization during the middle ages, similar to that which occurred in the *Vedānta* school. Whereas the *Vedāntins*, represented by Śaṅkara and Rāmānuja, opposed each other on the question of whether the absolute is impersonal or personal, the aesthetic theorists, represented by Abhinavagupta and Bhoja, held opposite views on the very same questions. In the aesthetic tradition it was Abhinavagupta who supported the impersonal school, and Bhoja supported the personal. As Bhoja's aesthetic theory held *śṛṅgāra rasa* to reign supreme, the *BhP* held the same view; that is, that the episodes revealing *śṛṅgāra rasa* represent the treatise's climax. The unique structure of the *BhP* emerges from the convergence of the *Vedānta* and *rasa* schools. Their union results in the emergence of an aesthetic type of *Vedānta*, the centre of which is the expression of divine personhood. Thus the Supreme *Brahmin* becomes not only known but tasted as well, through various personal relationships. As a *rasa* theory similar to Bhoja's underlies these tasting experiences, the notions of personal divinity are systematically arranged from those evoking *śānta rasa* to those evoking *śṛṅgāra rasa*. Therefore the famous *rāsa līlā* chapters[165] are considered the *BhP*'s peak. Had it been otherwise, that is, had Abhinavagupta's *rasa* theory underlain the *BhP*, these *rāsa līlā* chapters would have been considered a preliminary exposition of the divine, while the highest exposition of the divine would have been through the tasting of *śānta rasa* or the complete merging of *ātman* with *Brahman*.

CHAPTER 3

NOTIONS OF PERSONAL DIVINITY IN THE *BHĀGAVATA PURĀṆA*

Having argued for the integration of *rasa* theory with the *Vedāntic* school in the formation of the *BhP*, this chapter aims to shed light on the outcome of this; the *BhP*'s underlying structure, which is comprised of a systematic sequence of notions of divine personhood, gradually leading the devote reader deeper and deeper into the realm of the 'aesthetic personhood of the *BhP*'. The *Vedāntic* influence is expressed in that the notions of divinity represent the Supreme *Brahman*, the highest reality and the non-dual absolute. The *rasa* school influence is expressed in that the notions of divinity evoke an emotional reality, leading or inviting the *BhP*'s listener into higher and higher, or deeper and deeper states of aesthetic awareness of the divine. The development of the notions is represented by an increase in their aesthetic qualities, manifesting through the parameters of intensity and complexity. The *BhP* serves as a meeting place between the impersonal and the personal conceptions of *Brahman* and reconciles the two seemingly opposing concepts. On the one hand, it contains the realization of Impersonal *Brahman*, which is the highest possible concept to be articulated by the knowledge–*jñāna* paradigm. On the other hand, realization of Impersonal *Brahman*, when seen from an aesthetic point of view, represents an emotional or aesthetic experience of the absolute through *śānta rasa*. The historical example of associating the two is found in Abhinavagupta, who, as mentioned, was both a philosopher and an aesthete. In that sense, the

BhP reconciles the two conflicting ideologies and presents them as two aspects of the same truth: *Brahman*, when realized philosophically is abstract and impersonal, and the same *Brahman*, when realized aesthetically, carries the taste of eternity through *śānta rasa*. When the same *Brahman* becomes further realized through a growing aesthetic awareness, it becomes manifested as a person, personhood expressed in aesthetic terms. That personal manifestation which is first vague and remote, becomes gradually closer, more complex and more intense, and evokes higher and higher *rasas*.

Kṛṣṇa's personality as appearing in the four chapters engaged with the *rāsa līlā*,[1] represents the aesthetic climax of the *BhP*. In this way the *BhP* maintains a balanced position, which allows both conceptions of the absolute – the personal and the impersonal – to intertwine and to develop on their own ground, and so satisfies various types of readers. In other words, those who are inclined towards the impersonal conception relate more to the *Advaitin* trend within the *BhP*, whereas those who seek a more personal and emotional experience with the supreme find that in abundance within the text. Seen from the aesthetic point of view, the *Vedāntic* philosophical assertions stimulate further emotions, and therefore support the *rasa* personalistic trend. In other words, the idea that it is the Supreme *Brahman* who is crawling in Yaśodā's yard serves to intensify devotional emotions towards baby Kṛṣṇa. Seen from the philosophical point of view, the *rasa* trend expands the philosophical horizons of the text, as the Supreme *Brahman* is not confined just to the impersonal realm, but pervades the personal and aesthetic realm as well.

In developing the theme of personal divinity, the *BhP* first equates the experience of knowing Impersonal *Brahman* with *śānta rasa*. Therefore, further progress is made from that state towards higher states of realization – realizing or tasting the supreme through servitude, realizing the supreme through friendship, realizing the supreme through parental affection and, ultimately, realizing the supreme through romantic love. The progress is not a philosophical one, rather it is a progress of an increased aesthetic and personal awareness. That same divinity which appears at first to be utterly impersonal gradually starts manifesting personal characteristics, and the devoted reader becomes aware of the divine presence in a more personalized way. Thus in his progress towards personal awareness, he may first become conscious of the divine as an enormous cosmic person, present everywhere and in everything gross or subtle. At the next stage, the devoted reader internalizes this conception, and finds the divine in a personal form in his own heart. Both of these states represent mainly the emotional state of *śānta*, as they are serene and tranquil, and don't involve much relationship with the divine other than quiet contemplation. The text then progresses further to present notions more personalized and more specific, which comprise the main topic of the *BhP* – the *avatāras*. These are personalized divine forms which display a variety of qualities. They have specific forms (some human, some non-human), have purposes to fulfil, evoke various kinds of feelings, play role models and divinize history. The reader who hears of these *avatāras* develops an increasing awareness of divine personhood, expressed mainly through *dāsya*. In other words, observing or hearing about the *līlā* or cosmic play of these *avatāras* fosters a service attitude towards that deity. For the hearer to fully experience a particular emotion, he must actually be in a state of mind corresponding to a particular deity's nature. For example, when hearing about an *avatāra*, the listener would have to identify as a servant of that deity in order to fully experience the corresponding emotions which would naturally be in the category of *dāsya rasa*.

The text takes a dramatic turn in the tenth book, often considered the 'heart of the *BhP*',[2] where notions evoking *sakhya*, *vātsalya* and then *mādhurya* are presented, thereby leading the *BhP* to its theological climax in the *rāsa līlā* section of the tenth book. It is in this way that the text presents notions of divine personhood, the understanding or appreciation of which requires the listener to be in the mood of *sakhya*, or to feel friendship towards the divine. Being in that mood furthers the emotional awakening of the spectator, where he experiences more refined and intense emotions towards the divine. These intensify and become finer while ascending to the *vātsalya rasa*, and peak at the revelation of the divine through *śṛṅgāra rasa*. As the stories of the *avatāras* comprise the *BhP's* main topic, their central position may be reinforced through a textual reference from the *BhP*'s very first chapter:

> 16 What person desirous of purity of heart will not be eager to hear the glorious deeds of the Supreme Person, which are praised by elegant verses, the hearing of which is the means for cleansing the

> impurities of the age of *Kali*. 17 Please speak to us who are eager to hear, of the noble and magnanimous acts he playfully performs as he descends in his various incarnations, acts which are eulogized by the godly souls. 18 Oh wise Sūta, please narrate to us the auspicious narratives of the *avatāras* of the Supreme Lord Hari, who by his own mystic power indulges in his cosmic play.[3]

It seems that the text considers the hearing of the *avatāras*' narratives (or the acts of the different forms assumed by the venerable Lord and the incarnations of Hari) to be the process by which the evil influence of the *Kali* age is negated. As the age of *Kali* is characterized by a contamination of the heart, the hearing of the *BhP* is supposed to negate just that; that is, to purify one's heart. It seems that an aspect of this internal purification is the development of gradual awareness of divine personhood, in which the devoted reader progresses in internal moods, from *śānta* up to *śṛṅgāra*. The question may be raised: Is this idea of purification related to dramaturgy? The idea of drama as edifying and being morally uplifting exists already in the *Nāṭyaśāstra*'s introduction, and was already mentioned in this work.[4] This edifying aspect of drama underlies the structure presented here: the more one hears, identifies with and progresses in absorbing the *BhP*, the more one undergoes an internal edifying experience. Therefore, it seems that this idea of purification is deeply rooted in ancient dramaturgical theory.

A question arises: According to which order should the emotional effects be categorized? One option is to arrange them according to Abhinavagupta's system as follows: 1. erotic rapture – *śṛṅgāra*; 2. comedy – *hāsya*; 3. compassion – *karuṇa*; 4. fury – *raudra*; 5. heroism – *vīra*; 6. horror – *bhayānaka*; 7. revulsion – *bībhatsa*; 8. astonishment – *adbhuta*; 9. tranquillity – *śānta*. Although no doubt ample examples could be found to demonstrate each emotional effect, it seems that this system of categorization does not highlight the *BhP*'s structure. However, a more fruitful direction may be to analyse the *BhP* according to Rūpa Goswami's system, as it offers a sequential and dynamic line of textual development. Accordingly, the sequence will be as follows: 1. tranquillity – *śānta*; 2. servitude- *dāsya*; 3. fraternity or friendship – *sakhya*; 4. parenthood – *vātsalya*; 5. conjugal love – *mādhurya* or *śṛṅgāra*. This system has been accepted by traditional commentators as a way to interpret Kṛṣṇaite theology[5] and, moreover, I believe that Rūpa's aesthetic theory is well in line with Bhoja's. Delmonico writes:

> My suggestion is that Rūpa's familial, ancestral and social connections with the South [...] were responsible for the surprising direction that Rūpa's sacred aesthetic took and for the similarity between Bhoja's aesthetic and Rūpa's. The most striking implication of this similarity is a shared philosophical orientation that valued individual identity and refused to accept any outlook that ultimately required its dissolution.[6]

Delmonico clearly relates Rūpa to Bhoja not only on aesthetic grounds, but on philosophical grounds as well. The philosophical grounds referred to seem to indicate the value these two thinkers award 'individual identity', or the personal view of reality as opposed to the impersonal one. Delmonico highlights the philosophical similarity by pointing to the doctrine of *pariṇāma* as unifying both theorists: 'There seems to be a strong *Sāṅkhya* influence, with its resolution of spirit into monads and its principle of transformation (*pariṇāma*), in both writers, though Rūpa's *Sāṅkhya* is the theistic *Sāṅkhya* of the *Bhāgavata Purāṇa*.'[7]

It seems that not only do Bhoja and Rūpa share similar philosophical assumptions, but that these assumptions underlie the *BhP*, too. One may still question whether we are not imposing a *Gauḍīya* point of view on the *BhP*. However, it may well be that the *Gauḍīya* view which followed the *BhP* chronologically by a few hundred years is not an imposition on the *BhP* but rather its derivative. In other words, it may have well been that the *BhP* had first consolidated, and had its theology articulated by, the commentary tradition only hundreds of years later. We will therefore classify the textual references not by sequential order, but rather by their emotional effect, or the *rasa* they carry, beginning with *śānta* and ending with *śṛṅgāra*. It is to be noted that as the nature of emotional expression is variegated, there is generally a pleasurable mixture of emotional effects. Accordingly, a section that is dominated by a certain *rasa* is likely to carry other flavours as well, and for the simplification of the issue we have therefore aimed at merely highlighting the primary *rasa*. This chapter will, therefore, attempt to tie all these components together, showing that applying a personalistic philosophy in the line of Bhoja and Rūpa highlights the *BhP*'s structure and presents it as a unified personalistic theological treatise. Before progressing to discuss these notions in detail, a brief sketch will be offered of the *BhP*'s structure.

A Sketch of the *Bhāgavata Purāṇa*'s Structure

We now gradually progress from theory to a textual encounter. As such, before presenting a detailed articulation of the *BhP*'s structure, a short and abbreviated sketch is offered to help conceptualize this idea. This sketch follows the development of *BhP*'s notions of divinity, from the notion tasted through *śānta*, that is, Impersonal *Brahman*, to the notion tasted through *śṛṅgāra*, which is the notion of Kṛṣṇa, the sweet lover. This is backed by a concise and at times paraphrased scriptural reference.

1. Impersonal *Brahman*: Impersonal or *nirguṇa Brahman* is the state of realization which is generally aspired to by the followers of the path of knowledge, or the *jñāna mārga*: 'The Supreme is pure, abstract, all pervading, complete, is the embodiment of knowledge, without beginning or end, free from the association of the *guṇas*, eternal and non-dual. Oh seer, only when their minds and senses rest in peace,[8] can the sages realize that.'[9] Abhinavagupta considered the emotional state of *śānta* to correspond to the realization of Impersonal *Brahman*. As such, seen from an aesthetic point of view, the cognitive state of realizing Impersonal *Brahman* is accompanied by the emotional state of *śānta*, or feelings of serenity, both representing two aspects of the same internal state: the cognitive and the aesthetic.

2. *Vairāja Puruṣa* – The Universal Person is a mental construction, according to which one imagines the entire universe as comprising the divine body of a cosmic giant:

> The cosmic person has the lower planets as his soles, the middle planets as his waist, and the upper planets as his head [. . .] *dharma* is his chest and *adharma* is his back [. . .] Prajapāti is his penis, while Mitra and Varuṇa are his testicles [. . .] The rivers are his veins, the trees are his hair, the wind is his breath, time is his movement [. . .] The birds are his artistic expression [. . .] The

> *brāhmaṇas* are his mouth, The *kṣatriyas* are his hands, the *vaiśyas* are his hips and the *śūdras* are his legs.[10]

This form evokes a variety of qualities such as reverence, awe, astonishment, amazement and wonder. It spiritualizes one's vision of the world and makes one develop a kind of divine consciousness through nature, as well as through examination of the social structure. Although this notion is in the serenity or *śānta* category, it is nevertheless more complex and personalized than Impersonal *Brahman*.

3. *Antaryāmin* – The Person in the Heart: This form is also in the *śānta* category, or serenity. However, it is more internalized and attracts one's attention inwards:

> The Divine Person resides in the heart and is spanful in size [. . .] He has four hands holding a lotus, disc, conch and mace [. . .] He has lotus eyes, yellow garments and beautiful ornaments [. . .] He wears a garment of forest flowers [. . .] He is the Lord of the universe and is above the gods.[11]

This form is usually associated with *yogic* or mystic contemplation, and naturally evokes very serene and peaceful moods, which are representative of quietist and mystic states of mind.

4. Varāha – The Boar *avatāra*:[12] Similar to most *avatāras*, the Boar *avatāra* evokes emotions in the *dāsya* category, which are a response to his heroic deeds:

> As the earth sank into the universal ocean, a thumbsize boar dropped down from the god's nose, and in a moment, expanded to the size of an elephant [. . .] He dove into the water and rescued the earth [. . .] He then turned to fight with the demon Hiraṇyākṣa, and killed him after a severe fight.[13]

This *avatāra* is powerful and awesome, but also protective and kind-hearted. He is more personalized than the previous form, that of the person in the heart. The Boar *avatāra*'s personality is more distinct and is described through a more complex and detailed narrative.

5. *Nṛsiṁha* – The Lion Man *avatāra*: The *Nṛsiṁha avatāra* is in the same category as the *Varāha avatāra*, as he invokes *dāsya.* However, his

personal expressions are different, the devotion of his devotee Prahlāda is unique and his extreme wrath is extraordinary:

> Following a terrible roar, there appeared Viṣṇu as a terrible Lion Man from the pillar [. . .] His eyes fierce and his mane majestic [. . .] His terrible tusks and face struck terror [. . .] He touched the sky with stature, his mouth and nostrils were like a mountain cave [. . .] He had terrible tusks, his tongue sharp like a blade of a razor [. . .] His eyes fierce, his face majestic and his mane hair dazzling.[14]

It can be seen that the *avatāras* in this category express more personal characteristics than in the first two. They have desires, they exchange relationships and their personal characteristics are more specific.

6. *Vāmana* – The Gigantic Dwarf: The gigantic dwarf belongs to the major group of *avatārs* – those evoking servitude. Although each evokes it in a different way, evokes different emotional states and highlights different personal qualities, the principle still remains the same:

> The dwarf miraculously expanded to such an extent as to include the earth, the sky and the entire universe [. . .] The dawn and dusk on the garment of that gigantic person, the gods of creation on his genital organ, the demons in the anus, the seven seas in his sides, and the string of constellations on his chest [. . .] The *Vedas* his speech [. . .] *māyā* in his laughter.[15]

7. Viṣṇu – The Celestial Ruler: The Celestial Ruler Viṣṇu represents a majestic form of the divine, and evokes feelings of subordination and servitude, just like a king to his servants:

> You are the inner ruler of all [. . .] You have created the entire universe [. . .] You reactivate my power of speech, You control the illusory power of nature [. . .] Bless me with the companionship of those who are devoted to you with a pure heart [. . .] By hearing about you I shall easily cross the terrible ocean of *saṁsāra*.[16]

This form represents *aiśvarya* or royal sovereignty and Lordship. A similar form is that of Nārāyāṇa.

8. Kṛṣṇa – The Beloved Friend: Kṛṣṇa, the beloved friend represents a further progress to the higher category of *sakhya*, evoking feelings of friendship and fraternity:

> Early in the morning, Kṛṣṇa called his cowherd boyfriends by blowing his horn, and they all joyfully tended their cows to the forest [. . .] The boys were decorated by various ornaments, and were playing on their flutes and laughing [. . .] When Kṛṣṇa had gone to a distance to observe the beauty of the forest, they would compete among themselves who would run and touch him first.[17]

9. Baby Kṛṣṇa: A category still higher is the parental category, evoked by Kṛṣṇa the baby:

> While Kṛṣṇa's mother, Yaśodā, was churning curd, baby Kṛṣṇa climbed on her lap desiring to suck her breast [. . .] Yaśodā was overcome by maternal affection, and milk began flowing from her breasts as she gazed upon her smiling baby.[18]

The emotions expressed here are still finer than the previous ones, namely the fraternity category, and articulate the state of parental affection.

10. Kṛṣṇa – The Sweet Lover: The text reaches its aesthetic climax at the *rāsa līlā* or the love dance. Here, Kṛṣṇa is presented as a sweet lover, who attracts the village girls to a romantic dance in the forest. This is the most complex and most intense emotional expression found in the *BhP*:

> Hearing that music which increased their love for him, the damsels of *Vraja* whose hearts were captivated by Kṛṣṇa arrived hastily [. . .] Though prevented by their husbands, brothers and relatives, they all hastened to Kṛṣṇa's presence [. . .] Kṛṣṇa excited amorous sentiments in the *gopīs* by embracing them, indulging in jokes, pricking them gently with his nails [. . .] Then commenced formally the festive dance called *rāsa*, where Kṛṣṇa and the *gopīs* danced in a circle, Kṛṣṇa expanding himself and entering between every two girls.[19]

As one of the main goals of the *Bhp* is evoking personal awareness of the divine, it gradually evokes in the devoted reader emotions, from the relatively simple and serene to the most complex and intense, directed to the personal form of divinity. We may now survey the various components of the *BhP*'s structure with more scrutiny.

The Concept of Impersonal *Brahman*

This section is engaged with the first notion of divinity delineated in the *BhP*, which is the notion of Impersonal *Brahman*. This notion corresponds to *śānta rasa*, which is the *rasa* characterized by the most relaxed personal characteristics. With regard to the question of the status of *śānta* among other *rasas* we find two positions: the position of Abhinavagupta who takes *śānta rasa* to be the bedrock of all *rasas* and the peak aesthetic experience, and the position of Bhoja, who accepts *śānta* as a lower stage on the aesthetic path leading to *śṛṅgāra*. As previously argued in this work, the position of Bhoja seems to be compatible with the theology of the *BhP*, as it allows personal devotion, whereas the position of Abhinavagupta seems to be incompatible with the theology of the *BhP*, due to its predominant *advaitin* nature. In general, this section and those that follow consider the *BhP*'s structure according to Rūpa Gosvāmī's typology, in regard to which Haberman writes, 'The particular typology of religion Rūpa presents in the *Bhaktirasāmṛtasindhu* utilizes all the aesthetic components of the classical tradition. The chief elements of this, however, are the varying objects (*viṣaya*), shifting vessels (*āśraya*),and the resulting different religious experiences (*bhāvas*).'[20] Accordingly, Rūpa articulates his theory that intertwines theology and aesthetics. This theory enables the understanding of the sections depicting non-duality in a non-*advaitin* way, that is, as simultaneously representing both the state of *Brahman* realization and the state of *śānta rasa*. In regard to *śānta rasa* Haberman writes:

> Rūpa represents the resulting emotional experience (*bhāva*) as being somewhat similar to the joy of the *yogīs* (3.15). Jīva glosses the joy of the *yogīs* as an experience of the unqualified Absolute reality (*nirviśeṣa-brahman*). However, the object of the *yogīs*' quest is said to be the self (*ātman*), whereas the object (*viṣaya*) of this *rasa* is the Lord (*īśa*).[21]

The *Upaniṣadic* tradition views the essence of *Brahman* which is the *yogī*'s object of meditation, to be *sat-cit-ānanda.* Rūpa and Jīva focus on the *yogī*'s quest for *nirviśeṣa-brahman*, and consider it in terms of a peaceful *rasa*, having the self as its object, and as such, hold a similar position to Abhinavagupta.[22] However, they differ from *Abhinavagupta* by considering the object of this *rasa* to be *īśa* or *īśvara*, and by doing that, they open the door for developing further relationships with him, by entering into deeper or higher moods. In regard to this *rasa* Rūpa Gosvāmin writes:

> [Hari] is the Substantial Excitant and has the following qualities: he is a concentrated form of being, consciousness, and bliss (*saccidānanda*), the crest jewel of the pleasure of the self (*ātmārāmaśiromaṇi*), the Highest Self (*paramātmā*), the Highest Reality (*parabrahman*), tranquil, patient, pure, self-restrained.[23]

This exemplifies Rūpa's view of *nirviśeṣa-brahman* as the substantial excitant of *śānta rasa.* Two examples of the *BhP*'s referring to the supreme as *nirviśeṣa-brahman* may be quoted:

> 30 This form of the Supreme Person who is indeed formless, and whose true constitution is the pure consciousness of the self, has been created by the various elements of nature. 31 Just as a mass of clouds is attributed to the sky or the dust is attributed to the wind, similarly the quality of being seen is attributed to the seer by the unintelligent.[24]

> Your honourable self is that *Brahman* which is the Reality and pure consciousness – *Brahman* wherefrom proceeds the beginning, the end, the middle of this universe, but who due to being unchangeable is not affected by these.[25]

In both of these examples, *Brahman* is referred to as *nirviśeṣa* and its essence being pure consciousness. Following Bhoja's path, we may interpret these monistic passages as conveying a certain experience of divinity, which may be taken to be in the category of *śānta*. The monistic experience of divinity is a non-worldly position above the world of *saṁsāra*, and therefore can be defined as transcendental. In that state the *jīva* is considered to be separated from the *guṇas* and therefore situated beyond *saṁsāra*.

However, it is a preliminary stage in the *BhP*, as exemplified by the story of Śuka, who was situated at the realization of *Brahman* but was later attracted to the Lord's personal *līlā* and to higher modes of devotion. As the narrative develops, it is Śuka, or Śukadeva, who recites the *BhP* to Parīkṣit, the king who is about to die. As Śuka had previously undergone a transformation, Sūta is conversing with Śaunaka about it. Śuka was established in the state of *Brahman* realization, being devoid of any worldly attachments. Still, he was compelled to hear the *BhP* from his father, Vyāsa. Śaunaka expresses his surprise in that having achieved such an exalted state of realization, Śuka is still interested to hear the narrations of the *BhP*, and Sūta responds by saying that even those who have achieved that state are still compelled to hear about the excellent attributes of Hari. This sheds light on the progress from *śānta rasa* upwards, into the realization of more personalized forms of the divine, which are more attractive and emotionally satisfying. The *BhP* states:

> 9 Śaunaka enquired: As the sage Śuka was no doubt situated in the state of extinction, indifferent in every respect and fully satisfied within himself, for what reason did he undertake the study of this great treatise? 10 Sūta said: Hari is of such wonderful qualities that even sages who are fully satisfied within themselves, and whose knots of worldly bonds are severed, perform motiveless devotion to Viṣṇu.[26]

It seems that Śuka has achieved the state of *Brahman* realization and was completely satisfied with that, or delighted within himself. However, he was still attracted to the personal qualities of Hari, not for the purpose of achieving liberation, which was achieved by him already, but for the experience of *rasa*. Later in the text, Śuka himself confirms the same point: 'Oh seer among kings, although I was firmly established in meditation on the quality-less *Brahman*, I still studied this treatise, as my mind was attracted by the cosmic play of the supreme, which is described through the best of verses.'[27] The conclusion is that in the *BhP* the state of Impersonal *Brahman* realization serves as the basis from which higher or deeper states develop. This height or depth is defined not philosophically but aesthetically.

It seems that the realization of impersonal *Brahman* is the meeting place of the *Vedāntic* and *rasa* traditions. It represents the ultimate state of *Vedāntic* realization, and at the same time represents the emotional state of contemplating the divine in *śānta* or serenity. Thereby, one is encouraged to deepen his emotional state in relation to the divine, and enter emotional states which are more complex and more intense. The *BhP* reconciles the two positions, and presents them as two aspects of the divine. Philosophically, realization of Impersonal *Brahman* is the highest, while emotionally, the state of experiencing *śṛṅgāra rasa* is the highest.[28] Seen in this light, there is no real contradiction between the two positions, as both represent the truth from a different point of view, the one pointing at Impersonal *Brahman* as the highest cognitive state of realization, while the other pointing at the experience of *śṛṅgāra rasa* towards a personal form of the divine, that is *Bhagavān*, as the highest emotional and aesthetic achievement. The *BhP* attempts to reconcile the impersonal reality of *Brahman* with the personal reality of *Bhagavān*: 'According to *śruti*, those who possess knowledge of the Highest Truth say that this non-dual knowledge is *Brahman*, the Divine Person in the Heart and the Supreme Person.'[29] We believe that the *BhP* presents a balanced view of the two, allowing each to develop according to its own premises.[30] Thus it attracted some commentators in the *Advaitin* line, such as Śrīdhara Svāmin, and at the same time attracted commentators such as Jīva Gosvāmin, arguing for the supremacy of Kṛṣṇa.

The Universal Person: A Preliminary Notion Exemplifying *Śānta Rasa* with a Tinge of *Dāsya*

Śānta rasa may also be expressed somewhat more personally, that is with some consciousness of a remote person as an object of veneration and reverence. Quoting Schweig, it may be said that

> the soul loves the Supreme Person from a distance, as a great and powerful emperor is loved by subjects who are not personally serving him. Here the soul is removed from the direct presence of the Beloved, due to the soul's awareness of his or her finite existence in relation to the overwhelming majesty and omnipresence of the

> Lord. This love is characterized as quiet veneration and admiration; reverential love is passive and contemplative, unlike the dynamic and more intimate forms that follow.[31]

As opposed to the previous notion presented, which was utterly impersonal, the present notion depicting the *Virāṭ Puruṣa* represents progress towards a preliminary personalistic concept of the divine. This section[32] resembles the famous *Puruṣa-Sūkta*[33] as well as a similar section within the *BhP.*[34] It examines a universal notion of God, who not only fills the entire universe but also comprises it and is therefore physically perceived. This kind of 'personal pantheism' is, in one sense, fictitious, as that huge figure does not display the full characteristics of a person, such as consciousness, desires, exchange of relationships and so forth. However, it has the quality of being, as it certainly exists physically, and, moreover, once meditated upon, it exists in the mind of the meditator in a personal form. As scholarship has generally treated this notion either as mythology or as representing a *Vedic* orthodox worldview, we here aim to shed light on this notion from a new angle, that is, by emphasizing its theological significance in developing a personalistic awareness.

As the narrative unfolds, Parīkṣit has just retired to the bank of the river Ganges, having been cursed to die within seven days. He asks Śuka what one who is about to die should hear, chant, do, remember and worship.[35] The topic under discussion is, therefore, how one should end one's life. The *purāṇa* says that at the last stage of life, one should cast off all fear and sever with the weapon of detachment all attachments to one's body and its expansions, such as family, property, fame and so forth. One should leave home and travel to a place of pilgrimage, bathe there and sit in solitude. One should practice *yoga*, control his breath and concentrate on the sacred syllable Oṁ. One should gradually detach one's self from sense objects, and fix one's mind in meditation on Viṣṇu, a form of meditation that will soon yield *bhakti*. The object of meditation is the huge, gross, qualified form or body of the Lord, in which past, present and future existence is experienced:

> 24 This particular body of the Supreme is all encompassing, and within it is seen the past, present and future of the entire phenomenal universe. 25 The Supreme Person in the form of a Universal Person whose body is comprised of this egg-like

> universe, covered by seven layers, is the object of meditation.
> 26 Accordingly, the *pātāla* planets situated at the bottom of the
> universe comprise the soles of his feet, the planets named *rasātala*
> comprise his heels and toes, the *mahātala* planets form the
> ankles of the Universal Creator, while the *talātala* planets form the
> shanks of this Cosmic Person. 27 *Sutala* comprises the knees, while
> *Vitala* and *Atala* are the two thighs of this Universal Person.
> Oh King, they consider *Mahītala*, the earth to form his hips, and
> the vault of the sky to be his lake-like navel. 28 The host of stars
> form the chest of this Primeval Person, the *maharloka* planets are
> his neck, the *jana-loka* form his mouth, the *tapo-loka* planets are
> his forehead, and the *satya-loka* are the heads of Him who has a
> thousand heads.[36]

The description of the cosmic person starts with equating the entire universe to a gigantic person, starting from the lower planets, and going all the way up to the higher planets, representing his thousand heads. The text goes on to describe his senses:

> 29 The bright gods headed by Indra are his arms, the ten directions
> are his ears, the sound is his sense of hearing, the two *aśvinī*
> *kumāras*, Nāsatya and Dasra, are the nostrils of the Supreme,
> fragrance is his sense of smell and the burning fire is his mouth.
> 30 The sky comprises his eyes, the Sun is his eyeball and his sense of
> seeing, the day and night are Viṣṇu's eyelids, Brahmā is the
> movement of his eyelashes, Varuṇa is his palate while *rasa* is his
> tongue. 31 They say that the *Vedic* hymns are the head of the
> infinite Lord, Yama, the god of death is his fangs, feelings of
> affection are his teeth, the cosmic illusion, *Māyā*, which maddens
> the people is his laughter, and the unending creation of the world
> is the casting of his glance. 32 Bashfulness is his upper lip while
> greed is his lower lip, *dharma* is his chest and *adharma* is his back,
> Prajāpati is his penis while Mitra and Varuṇa are his testicles, the
> oceans are his belly, and the mountains are his heap of bones.[37]

Having heard about his senses and some of his organs, the text describes further bodily features along with subtle qualities – his movement,[38] his action,[39] his intelligence[40] and his heart:[41]

> 33 Oh best of kings! The rivers are his veins, the trees are the hair of his cosmic body, the wind of infinite force is his breath, time is his movement, and the incessant flow of the three *guṇas* through the ages is his action. 34 Oh best of the Kurus, the wise know that the clouds are the Lord's hair, the twilight is the garment of the all-pervading Supreme Lord, the unmanifest *pradhāna* is his heart, and the moon which is the reservoir of all transformations is his mind. 35 It is known that the *mahat*[42] is his intellectual power, and that Śiva is the internal organ[43] of the Lord who dwells in the hearts of all, the horses, mules, camels and elephants are his nails; all beasts and deer are at his hips.[44]

Finally, his artistic qualities are described, along with the famous *Vedic* metaphor – his social body comprising the four *varṇas*. The description ends by encouraging the reader to contemplate this form:

> 36 The various kinds of birds are his artistic expression, Manu is his depth of wisdom, the human race is his dwelling place, *Gandharvas*, *Vidyādharas*, *Cāraṇas* and *Apsaras* are his musical notes and the armies of *asuras* are his valour. 37 The Universal Soul has the *brāhmaṇas* as his mouth, the *kṣatriyas* as his arms, the *vaiśyas* as his thighs and the dark complexioned *śūdras* as his feet. The various hosts of gods are made up by him, and it is unto him that goods and works should be offered. 38 Such is the extent of the Supreme Lord's form described to you by me. One should concentrate one's mind and intelligence upon this huge body of the Cosmic Person, as there is nothing greater than this.[45]

This description no doubt resembles *Ṛg Veda* 10.90, the famous *Puruṣa-Sūkta*.[46] In regard to the *Puruṣa-Sūkta* Wendy Doniger O'Flaherty writes:

> In this famous hymn, the gods create the world by dismembering the cosmic giant, *Puruṣa*, the primeval male who is the victim in a *Vedic* sacrifice. Though the theme of the cosmic sacrifice is a widespread mythological motif, this hymn is part of a particularly Indo-European corpus of myths of dismemberment. The

> underlying concept is, therefore, quite ancient; yet the fact that this is one of the latest hymns in the *Rig Veda* is evident from its reference to the three *Vedas* and to the four social classes or *varṇas*, as well as from its generally monistic worldview.[47]

O'Flaherty emphasizes the cosmic giant's mythological significance and the monistic worldview expressed by it. However, can O'Flaherty's way of reading the text, a way that would presumably be accepted by most scholars, be taken as the only way? Does this hymn convey only information regarding the Universal Person? The association of *Vedic* literature with poetry has already been pointed out earlier in this work,[48] emphasizing the *Vedic* poet's visionary qualities. However, *Vedic* poetry was not only visionary, but as poetry had poetical characteristics as such. Michael Witzel writes:

> The oldest *Vedic* text, the *Ṛgveda*, is composed in archaic, highly stylized poetical Sanskrit. It contains verses of praise addressed to the *Vedic* gods and to some early contemporary chieftains; it also includes some speculative hymns and some (probably) non-ritual poetry.[49]

Was there a poetical structure or theory underlying this 'highly stylized poetical Sanskrit', and the '(probably) non-ritual poetry'? It appears that there have been some poetic aspects in the *Ṛg Vedic* hymns, and these may well have been amplified when quoted more than 20 centuries later or so, in a rather poetic literary environment. In analysing the language of the *Vedic* hymns, it is common to refer to the *Vedic* language's instrumental aspects, conveying concrete information or furthering some performance such as ritualistic or meditational.

However, *Vedic* poetry has apparent non-instrumental features, which have to be taken into consideration in attempting to uncover its meaning, about which David Shulman writes:

> Undoubtedly, while reading Sanskrit poetry we shall meet conventions which will seem peculiar to our taste. It may be said that in general, this literature stems from a culture which perceives the world in a manner different from that to which we are used

> [...] We have to enter into the spiritual world of the ancient Indian people. To use a classical Sanskrit term, we have to be *sahṛdaya*, that is, to become connoisseurs who know how to taste poetry.[50]

Shulman points to the difficulty of deciphering the Sanskrit poetic language, and emphasizes the quality of tasting poetry as necessary for uncovering its meaning. He goes on to explain that the *Vedic* language should not be taken to be instrumental:

> We shall first ask: what are the relations between the poetical language and the truth expressed through the hymn, the poet's truth. What can the language express and what can't it express? [...] If we shall ask what the *Veda* says on the poetic language and on its distinctiveness, we shall realize that for the *Vedic* poet language is not an instrument. It is hardly possible to say that instrumental usage of language is known in the *Veda* [...] Language is not taken as transmitting information or explicit contents. It doesn't make clear assertions and is not related to conventions connecting a word to its meaning, and as such, doesn't denote names to phenomena.[51]

In concluding Shulman's view, he doesn't consider the *Vedic* language to be instrumental, rather his view is that poetical sensitivity would better qualify a reader of the *Vedic* hymns to taste its meaning. This discussion refers to the *Vedic* hymns. However, our discussion refers to a *Vedic* hymn cited in a devotional *purāṇa* some 2,000 years or so later. Given the devotional context, it is quite likely that any poetical characteristics implicit in the original *Ṛg Vedic* hymn were amplified considerably in its being quoted in the *BhP*. Therefore, it may be justified to ask: What kind of emotional impact does this notion of a Universal Person generate?

Indira Viswanathan Peterson, in a footnote on a hymn to Śiva by Appar, associates the *Vedic Puruṣasūkta* and the *Bhagavad Gītā*'s eleventh chapter: 'This verse evokes the vision of the Lord as the Cosmic Person (*Puruṣa*) as described in the *Vedic Puruṣa Sūkta* (*Rig Veda* X. 90) and in the *Bhagavad Gītā* (XI.9–12).'[52] With regards to the emotional impact of the *Bg*'s eleventh chapter's Universal Person, Julius Lipner writes:

> The *bhakti* of the *Gītā* for example is hardly unemotional [. . .] or (during the revelation of the Universal Form in Ch. 11) 'Bowing humbly, prostrating my body, I beg of you, the Lord to be adored, to bear with me as a father his son, a friend his friend, a lover his beloved, O God' (11.44). There are different kinds of emotions involved here, especially awe and wonder.[53]

According to Lipner, the emotional impact generated by the *Bg*'s Universal Person is that of awe and wonder. We may presume that the form of divinity under discussion evokes similar feelings in the devoted mind, that is, awe and wonder. In his introduction to the *BRS*, Haberman writes:

> Rūpa begins his presentation and analysis of the primary *rasas* with an examination of the peaceful *rasa* (*śānta-bhakti-rasa*). The particular form (*viṣaya-ālambana-vibhāva*) in which Kṛṣṇa is encountered in the peaceful *rasa* is one appropriate to *yogic* meditation, the four armed Viṣṇu (3.1.7–8) which is described as being appropriate for *yogic* meditation in texts such as the *Bhāgavata Purāṇa*. The vessels of this *rasa* are peaceful (*śānta*) devotees, defined as those who have achieved tranquility and then go on to experience a love for Kṛṣṇa. Examples given are the four mind-born ascetic sons of Brahmā: Sanaka, Sananda, Sanātana, and Sanatkumāra (3.1.12). Enhancing excitants include listening to the principal *Upaniṣads* and residing in isolated places (3.1.18–19).[54]

Rūpa clearly associates *śānta rasa* with *yogīc* meditation, and considers the peaceful *rasa* to be a preliminary stage on a path leading to higher *rasas*. The mention of listening to the *Upaniṣads* and residing in isolated places clearly associates Rūpa's conception of *śānta rasa* with the *Vedāntic* tradition and with *jñāna*. Haberman mentions the *BhP* as describing the form of the four armed Viṣṇu, which is appropriate for this kind of *yogīc* meditation, and specifically *BhP* 2.2.8–14, which is the subject matter of our next section entitled 'The *Antaryāmin*: The Divine Person in the Heart'. However, we believe that the present section involves the same mood of peaceful devotion as the next section, and evokes similar feelings with a slight difference of emphases, the former being more external and the latter being more internal.

The present section is, however, more detailed than the *Puruṣasūkta*. It maintains a similar monistic worldview and puts less emphasis on the sacrificial motif. It seems to be presented more for quiet contemplation and meditation, as the text explicitly states.[55] However, the second *BhP* section describing the Universal Person[56] lays more emphasis on the idea of sacrificing that person in order to worship him.[57] This notion of a gigantic universal and divine person, who represents the first notion of personal divinity after the notion of Impersonal *Brahman*, can be perceived in a most tangible way. The feelings evoked by holding such a conception are those of deep awe and reverence, of the greatness of the divine as opposed to the human being who is minute and almost insignificant. An illustrative example may be that of an ant on an elephant's back. The hair on the elephant's body will seem to the ant to be as big as trees. Moreover, the elephant is so gigantic that the ant can't see it, let alone conceive that it is situated on the elephant's back. However, once the ant develops awareness of the huge elephant's existence, the ant expands its own consciousness, and perceives itself in relation and proper proportion to that giant. The notion of the divine in a person presented here is even more complex, as not only does he manifest in the physical realm, such as the different planetary systems, but he also manifests in the subtle realm where sound is his sense of hearing, and taste or *rasa* is his tongue. It seems that according to this conception, the divine directly shares in the sounds and tastes experienced in this world. Moreover, the divine is taken to be all-encompassing, so much so that one lives in the divine, breathes the divine, tastes the divine and walks on the surface of the earth which is sacred due to its comprising the divine body. As such, this conception serves to spiritualize or divinize one's consciousness, and to evoke a preliminary sense of the divine as a person.

The idea of the attractive illusory *māyā* representing the divine smile is another step aiming at a non-dual worldview. Whereas generally illusion represents *avidyā*, it assumes here a different form, and becomes part not only of the divine plan, but also of the personal manifestation of the divine. Of interest is the notion that the working of the three *guṇas* are the divine's working.[58] Generally, the *Sāṅkhya* system is taken to be atheistic, and even in the *Bg*, which is a rather theistic text, the three *guṇas* do not operate directly under the divine will, but operate independently.[59] Here, however, the working of the three *guṇas* is considered to be the working of the divine. The *Mahat Tattva*, or the aggregate of elements, being the divine's intellectual power represents a similar idea, which may be taken to represent the divine's thinking of the entire world. 'That vision evokes the same feelings of wonder towards the divine's inconceivable greatness; these two points suggest that the *Sāṅkhya* of the *BhP* is theistic.' The divine is depicted here as clearly personal, so much so that his masculine gender can't be mistaken. The explicit mentioning of his private parts not only reveals his gender, but serves as another step towards non-dualism in that it furthers an all-inclusive divinized worldview that transcends commonly accepted social norms. The non-dualism is expressed not by negating the plurality of phenomena, but rather by divinizing the phenomena. Thus the private organs of the universal person are divinized too, and it may follow that the whole of creation is divine, thus offering a kind of pantheistic 'personal non-dualism'.

The notion of the cosmic person seems to be directed towards persons whose worldview is somewhat external. As they hold the physical and subtle world to be of prime significance, and are thrilled at the greatness of the creation, the *BhP* aspires to uplift them by furthering a transformation based upon their appreciation for the gross and subtle components of the universe. The notion of the universal and gigantic, divine person is not devoid of aesthetics. The birds are his artistic expression, and the heavenly residents are the seven musical notes. The social structure of four *varṇas* is part of the divine body; this social structure is one of the foundations of *dharma*, and it follows that in the *BhP*'s version *dharma* is of divine origin. As such, adhering to *dharma* is a form of sacrifice meant to please or worship the divine, and that certainly is in line with the ideas found in the *Bhagavad Gītā*.[60] In other words, the notion of the universal person strengthens social stability and uplifts morality.

In attempting to place the notion of the Universal Person within the *BhP*'s framework, three questions may be presented:

1. What is the balance between *jñāna* and *rasa*?
2. Is language applied here directly or indirectly?
3. Does this section evoke emotions and, if it does, which?

The description of the Universal Person is rather theoretical, as it expands one's mind and intelligence into knowing the world in a different and abstract way. However, it is less abstract than the statement 'I existed before the creation',[61] and therefore it can be said that, although this section uses language directly and aims at presenting knowledge, it is not a very sophisticated type of knowledge. As far as emotional awakening, this section seems to evoke emotions of awe and reverence attained through quiet contemplation, and a desire to serve this gigantic divinity through sacrifice and adherence to *dharma*. Therefore, the emotions evoked could be taken to be a mixture of *śānta rasa* with a tinge of *dāsya* – *śānta* representing the contemplative emotions and *dāsya* representing those emotions which further a service attitude.[62] As far as personhood is concerned, a somewhat obscure notion is presented here. The Universal Person possesses the quality of 'being' and is somewhat specific, as he has some kind of a form composed of the whole world. He is somewhat conscious as he has senses such as eyes, ears, nostrils, a sense of touch and taste, and he is somewhat rational as the *Mahat* is his intellectual power. He expresses himself in an artistic way through the various kinds of birds, and his sense of progress or movement is represented by time. It is not very clear what the nature of his enjoyment is, but it may well be that he is pleased by sacrifices offered to him, a possible sacrifice being the following of *dharma*. This may serve to strengthen the social body of the four *varṇas*, but sacrifice may also be the way of his exchanging relationships with humanity. The nature of his activity is somewhat obscure. The universal activity is indeed part of him, but then it is not clear whether he initiates such activity, aiming to achieve certain purposes, or is comprised by it. The conclusion is that the notion of the Universal Person represents an initial progress from abstraction to divine personhood, and may be considered a first step from which the *purāṇa* unfolds this most central theme.

The *Antaryāmin*: The Divine Person in the Heart

The following section[63] describes a notion more personalized than that of the Universal Person. Similar to the notion of the Universal Person, it is perceived mainly through the state of *śānta rasa*.[64] However, its vision requires introversion and it seems to be a form contemplated in *yogic* meditation. We propose to associate this 'person within the heart' with the term *antaryāmin* and wish to point to its theological significance in developing further personal awareness of the divine. A basic definition of the term *antaryāmin* is given by Klostermaier: '*Antaryāmin* ("the inner ruler"): According to *Vaiṣṇava* theology, the form of the deity that dwells in the human heart and guides it, and accompanies it through the experiences of heaven and hell.'[65] It seems that this notion serves as a kind of personalized providence, who rules, guides and accompanies the *ātman* in its journey through *saṁsāra.* As to this idea's being common to personalist *Vedāntins*, Venkatesachar writes, 'The idea that the Supreme Being exists as the Inner Ruler in every entity, both sentient and insentient is common to all personalist *Vedāntins*.'[66] As such, the *antaryāmin* furthers not only the establishment of relationship between the *jīva* and himself, but evokes a notion of personal identity in the *jīva*, as different and subservient to him.

The second chapter of the second book starts with instructions meant for the aspiring renunciate. From the sixth verse the text turns inwards, the focus being upon the supreme residing in the heart, accepting the role of personal providence:

> 4 When one can simply lie down on the ground, what is the need for a bed? As one naturally has arms, what is the necessity for a pillow? When the palms of one's hands are available for eating, what is the need for cutlery? When open air and tree barks are available, what is the need for garments? 5 Are there no torn cloths lying on the road? Do the trees, which support others no longer give alms? Are the rivers dried up? Are the mountain caves blocked? Does not the unconquered Supreme Lord protect those who seek his refuge? Why, therefore, should the wise flatter those blinded by the pride of their wealth?[67]

This section seems to be addressed to renunciates, or at least to encourage renunciation. For example, in the presence of the earth there is no need for a bed. The notion present here seems to be different from the notion of the cosmic person, which seems to have been addressed to people within the social structure, identifying themselves with one of the four *varṇas*. The text calls for internalization and inner contemplation, which is necessary for contemplating the Divine Person residing within.

> 6 In this way, having realized the truth, one should meditate on the soul existent in the heart who is dear and real, and who is the

> unlimited Supreme Person, by whose worship one gains the
> ultimate gain, which is the permanent extinction of *saṁsāra*.
> 7 Who but the lowest of people will neglect meditation on the
> Supreme and take to the non-permanent, despite seeing the mass
> of people fallen into *saṁsāra* and undergoing different types
> of sufferings as consequences of their past deeds? 8 After
> concentration, some meditate upon the Person residing within
> their own body in the region of the heart, measuring a span, and
> who has four arms holding a lotus, a disc, a conch and a mace.[68]
> 9 He smiles and his eyes resemble lotus petals, his garments are
> yellowish like the *kadamba* flowers, he wears gold bracelets shining
> with precious jewels and his diadem and ear-rings are set with
> radiant precious stones.[69]

By now the text has described the Person in the Heart, who 'measures a span', and who resides in the inner space of the heart. Also, the text has laid emphasis on concentration and meditation as the state of mind suitable for gazing at this form. Now it expands the detailed description of this notion:

> 10 The Lord whose lotus like feet are installed in the hearts of the
> great *yogīs*, on whose chest is the mark called Śrīvatsa, and who
> wears the jewel called Kaustubha around his neck, is beautified by
> a garland of fresh forest flowers. 11 He is adorned with very costly
> anklets, bracelets, girdle, rings and such other ornaments studded
> with precious jewels. His countenance is lovely on account of his
> bluish ringlets of hair, and his face along with his captivating
> smile are very pleasing. 12 The Lord offers unlimited grace by his
> cosmic play, by his smiling face, by his glances and by the
> movement of his eyebrows. One should therefore meditate upon
> him, as long as the mind can remain fixed.[70]

Having described this person, the text goes on to instruct the practitioner on how to meditate on this form; this should be done gradually, proceeding from the feet to the smiling face of the Divine Person within the Heart. However, the text emphasizes, if this form of meditation is too advanced, the practitioner should revert to one step below, and meditate on the previous form offered, which is that of the Universal Person:

> 13 Step by step one should concentrate his mind on the parts of the limbs of the wielder of the mace, from his feet to his smiling face. As one gradually becomes purified and brings his mind under control, he should accordingly give up meditation on the lower limbs and proceed to meditate upon the higher ones. 14 Unless devotion to the Lord of the Universe arises, one should meditate on the huge form of the Cosmic Person after the completion of his daily religious rituals.[71]

Verse 14 reinforces the 'ladder principle', according to which progress is gradual and is made according to one's degree of realization. Hence he for whom this form of meditation is too difficult and evokes no emotional awakening should meditate on the previous form; that is, the Universal Person. Only when he has matured in that practice may he progress to meditate on the 'Person in the Heart'. In articulating Rūpa's theory as appearing in his *BRS*, Haberman further reinforces the 'ladder principle', according to which *śānta rasa* is placed lower on the hierarchical scale, but leads to higher *rasas*:

> All his illustrations (3.1.36–45) involve a tranquil *yogī* who moves beyond the realization of the undifferentiated *Brahman* and the meditative state of objectless consciousness to an encounter with some form of Kṛṣṇa as the object of astonishing love. A cornerstone of *Vaiṣṇava* philosophy is the tenet that the Lord (*Bhagavān* or *Puruṣottama*) represents a higher form of reality than that which is encountered as the undifferentiated *Brahman*. The peaceful devotees may reside in a calm ocean, but finally it must be an ocean stirred up to some degree by the surges of love which indicate an awareness of divine form. And the more motion in the ocean the more intense the waves of emotions, the higher it is ranked on the hierarchical scale. Rūpa, therefore declares the joy of the *yogīs* to be limited or incomplete, whereas that joy related to the Lord is unlimited or complete (3.1.5). The peaceful *rasa* is also placed lowest on the hierarchical scale because it involves only an encounter with the essential form (*svarūpa*) of the Lord, and is not connected in any way with his charming *līlās* or divine play (3.1.6).[72]

Haberman well describes the dynamics of Rupa's theory, which, so we believe, represent the theory underlying the *BhP* too. As such, there is a hierarchy in which *śānta rasa* is placed lowest as it involves only an encounter with the essential form of the Supreme Person, but not with his *līlās*. However, the tranquil *yogī* gradually moves beyond the realization of the undifferentiated *Brahman* and the meditative state of objectless consciousness and begins to encounter the supreme in a somewhat more personal form. The more one becomes aware of the supreme as a person, and the more the supreme is seen through a higher loving mood, the more one progresses in entering deeper into the experience of the Supreme Person's *līlā*.

This notion of the 'Divine Person in the Heart' may be further explored. This is traditionally perceived to be a form of the infinite coming to redeem the finite. Śrīnivasacāri writes:

> The infinite that is the abode of the entire universe has its home in the infinitesimal ether of the heart without being spatialized or conditioned and untainted even by a shadow of evil with a view to infinitize and perfect the self. The transcendental one does not lose its nature when it transforms the self. Likewise, the description of *Brahman* in the *Katavallī* as the Person of the size of the thumb, as the Lord of the past and the future, that resides in the heart of humanity, is of the absolute that has no history, but enters into history to make the mortal immortal. The infinite, therefore, does not lose its infinity by residing in the finite and redeeming it from its evil nature. There is no contradiction in the co-existence of two selves in the same body.[73]

Śrīnivasacāri emphasizes the *antaryāmin*'s maintaining his infinite position and being untouched by evil, despite his residing within the human body. A few *Upaniṣadic* citations may shed further light on this notion. The *Kaṭha Upaniṣad*, fourth chapter, states:

> 12 A person the size of a thumb
> Resides within the body (*ātman*)
> The Lord of what was and what will be –
> From him he does not hide himself.
> So, indeed is that!

> 13 The person the size of a thumb
> Is like a fire free of smoke;
> The Lord of what was and what will be;
> The same today and tomorrow
> So, indeed is that![74]

Here the same idea is conveyed; that of the infinite Lord residing in the heart in a subtle form. His presence is analogous to fire which is all-pervading in a subtle, smoke-free or potential form.

The *Śvetāśvatara Upaniṣad*, third chapter states:

> 11 Who is the face, head, and neck of all, who resides deep in the
> heart of all beings, and who pervades everything – he is the
> Blessed One. Therefore, the Benign One is present everywhere.
> 12 The Person, clearly, is the immense Lord. He is the one who
> sets in motion the real. The Imperishable One rules over the light,
> this totally flawless attainment.[75] 13 The Person the size of a
> thumb abiding within the body (*ātman*) always resides within the
> hearts of people. With the heart, with insight, with thought has he
> been contemplated. Those who know this become immortal.
> 14 The Person had a thousand heads, a thousand eyes, and a
> thousand feet. Having encompassed the earth on all sides, he
> extended ten fingers' breadth beyond it.[76]

This passage adds the notion of the Supreme Soul's hands and feet being everywhere. This is so because he exists in all bodies, and furthermore he encompasses the earth on all sides and rules over the light. In a sense, this notion is an intermediate notion between the Impersonal *Brahman*, and the personal *Bhagavān*. It is more personal than *Brahman*, as it has a form, size, the role of ruler and a mission to deliver the *jīva* from *saṁsāra*. However, it is also somewhat diffused, as it has a thousand heads, eyes and feet, spread everywhere. It may well be that the term *paramātman* mentioned in *BhP* 1.2.11[77] refers to this form.

The *Upaniṣadic* idea of the two birds sitting on the same tree may well refer to the two persons residing in the heart: the infinite and the finite. The *Śvetāśvatara Upaniṣad*, fourth chapter, states:

> 6 Two birds, who are companions and friends, nestle on the very same tree. One of them eats a tasty fig; the other, not eating, looks on. 7 Stuck on the very same tree, one person grieves, deluded by her who is not the Lord. But when he sees the other, the contented Lord – and the Lord's majesty – his grief disappears.[78]

O'Flaherty, in her commentary on this section[79] entitled 'The ultimate reality and the two birds', writes,

> This passage represents another attempt to describe, in metaphor, the relationship between the individual soul and the ultimate reality. It also begins to endow that ultimate reality with specific characteristics that are more theistic than pantheistic, to identify it with the god Rudra, and to address him.[80]

It seems that O'Flaherty takes the two birds to represent the individual soul – *ātman*, and the ultimate reality – *paramātman*. The *paramātman* may well be similar to the *BhP*'s notion of the 'Divine Person in the Heart'. Also, O'Flaherty points at a progress from pantheism to theism, a progress that fits well with our theme of a gradual progress from the impersonal to the personal aspects of the divine. As it is the *Śvetāśvatara Upaniṣad*, which is traditionally associated with *Śaivism*, the personal form of the divine, is that of Rudra. For the *BhP*, which is traditionally associated with *Vaiṣṇavism*, it would naturally be one of Viṣṇu's forms.[81]

Looking back at the passage, one bird is tasting the tree's fruits, while the other is witnessing. When the tasting bird turns to the witnessing bird, apparently giving up the fruits, his grief disappears. A similar idea appears in the *Muṇḍaka Upaniṣad*: 'Two birds that are ever associated and have similar names, cling to the same tree. Of these, one eats the fruit of divergent tastes, and the other looks on without eating.'[82] Does the tree represent the body? Do the two birds represent the soul and the Supreme Soul or *Brahman* residing in one's heart? Śaṅkara's commentary on this verse further reinforces the idea of the two birds being the individual soul and the Supreme Soul, sitting on the tree of the body. Śaṅkara writes:

> Tree means the body because of its being demolished like a tree [. . .] God and the soul – as conditioned by the subtle body which

> holds in itself the tendencies and impressions created by ignorance, desire, and action – cling to it like birds. *Tayoḥ*, of these two who hug this tree; *anyaḥ*, the one (the individual soul), the knower of the field who clings to the tree of the subtle body that is its limiting adjunct; *atti*, eats, enjoys, owing to non-discrimination; *pippalam*, the fruit, consisting of happiness and misery brought about by action [. . .] *anyaḥ*, the other, God who is by nature eternal, pure, wise, and free, who is omniscient and has the totality of *Māyā* as his limiting adjunct – that God does not taste; for merely by his presence as the eternal witness, he is the director of both the enjoyer and the enjoyed.[83]

It is quite clear that, according to Śaṅkara, the two birds seated on the tree of the body are the *jīva*, or the individual soul, and the *paramātman* or the Supreme Soul dwelling in the heart. The *jīva* is not only seated on the tree, but it aspires to enjoy the tree's fruits. The other bird, *Īśvara*, refrains from eating and simply watches. As long as the first bird eats the fruits, it is subjected to enjoyment and suffering under the three *guṇas*. However, when it turns its attention to the other bird, the grief of *saṁsāra* disappears.

In Rāmānuja's theology, this manifestation is called *antaryāmin*, the term taken from the *Pāñcarātra* and translated as the 'inner ruler' or 'inner controller'. This notion represents a further step in the progress from the impersonal towards the personal. If there were hardly any relationships discerned in the previous notion, namely that of the gigantic Universal Person, the present notion involves a progress: here the mystic is invited to contemplate and observe this form closely, and may even feel attraction towards it, seeing the divine person's beauty and his smiling face. Besides a contemplative relationship, there is a slight tinge of friendship, maintenance and even love. The sense of friendship is aroused by the Lord accompanying the *jīva* throughout its journey in *saṁsāra*, and thereby becoming the *jīva*'s companion and friend.[84] The maintenance aspect is more explicitly expressed in the Lord being the *jīva*'s maintainer, while the feeling of love may be invoked by seeing the *antaryāmin*'s beauty. This notion serves also as an intermediate form of divinity, between the Impersonal *Brahman* and the personal *Bhagavān*, in that it reconciles the monistic and pluralistic views. Śrīnivasacāri writes:

> But it is the *Antaryāmīvidyā*, Ch. 3.7 of the *Bṛhadāraṇyakopaniṣad* that reveals explicitly the truth of *śarīra–śarīrī* relation and it is extolled by Rāmānuja as the *ghaṭaka śruti* that reconciles the extremes of pluralism and monism and satisfies the highest demands of life in all its aspects.[85]

The reconciliation of the two extreme positions of monism and pluralism, or, one might suggest, of impersonalism and personalism, provides the reader of the *BhP* with a balanced notion of the divine, which is calm, tranquil, all-pervading, and which, at the same time, exhibits some personal characteristics such as a specific and attractive personal form.

The point is further developed by Śrīnivasacāri:

> The Absolute Substance of the *sad vidyā* is the inner self of the *antaryāmi vidyā* and as the life of life, the seer of all the seers and the love of all loves, He constitutes the *śarīrin* of the universe in the collective and the individual aspects. This view alone reconciles the so-called monistic view of the *Bṛhadāraṇyaka* and the theistic teaching of the *Śvetāśvatara* without torturing any text or twisting its meaning. The crass anthropomorphic idea of the *śarīra–śarīrin* relation as that between the mind and the body is refuted by the text: 'He grasps without limbs, hears without ears, and sees without eyes' (*ŚvUp* 3.19), which contrasts the knowledge of the All self with that of the *jīva* obscured by *karma*.[86]

Śrīnivasacāri, interpreting Rāmānuja, says that in the concept of *śarīra–śarīrin*, the 'Person in the Heart', occupies the position of the *śarīrin*, or the owner of the body which is the world. In other words, the analogy is between the *jīva*–body relations and the *antaryāmin*–world relations. The presence of the *antaryāmin* within the body transforms the body from being a negative connotation, such as a source of bondage to the *jīva*, to its consecration as a temple. Śrīnivasacāri writes:

> The third concrete form of *dayā* is the immanence of *Brahman* in the hearts of all beings as their *antaryāmin* without being affected by their evil. It transforms the perishing body into a living temple of the *Rakṣaka* and is capable of being intuited by the *yogi*.[87]

Here Śrīnivasacāri emphasizes three points central to understanding this notion of the Divine Person residing in the heart: although he resides in the hearts of all beings, he is unaffected by their evil, he consecrates the mortal body and turns it into a temple, and he is capable of being perceived through *yogic* meditation.

Finally, we note a summarizing quote by Śrīnivasacāri regarding the aesthetic growth furthered by the *antaryāmin*:

> The third aspect of divine love is the *antaryāmin* or Beauty that dwells in the lotus heart of all living beings as their inner Enchanter making them pulsate with its creative life and participate in its inner joy. The body is not composed of dust or conceived in sin, but is *Brahmapuri* or the city of *Brahman*, and is a living temple of divine beauty.[88]

Thus the notion of the Divine Person residing in the heart serves to further aesthetic growth in terms of beauty and creativity. This form is still further personalized than the previous one, namely the Universal Person, as it represents a complete person. This person seems to have desires or expectations, as he waits and even longs for the minute person to give up his association with the tree, turn to him and establish relationships with him. He, in return, will deliver the minute person or the soul from *saṁsāra*.

The *Avatāras*: The *Bhāgavata Purāṇa's* Heart

The idea of divine descent known as *avatāra* is no doubt one of the cornerstones of the *BhP*, if not the main theme, and the *Līlā* or sports of the various *avatāras* comprise the heart of the entire text. As to the central position which these manifestations hold in the *BhP*, Sheridan writes:

> The importance of these manifestations (*avatāra*) in *Vaiṣṇavism*, and especially in the *Bhāgavata*, can hardly be stressed enough. The *purāṇa*, as we have seen, begins with the questions of the sages about Kṛṣṇa's manifestations and it also concludes on this note. Thus in Canto twelve Sūta tells the sages: Thus I have answered, O best of the twice-born, what you asked about the sports,

> manifestations, and activities which have been related here in all their details.[89]

The notion of *avatāra* represents an aesthetic progress over the other three notions presented, enables the exhibition of a large variety of personal qualities, and due to its dramatic nature, has the ability of arousing a diversity of emotions. As the text gradually leads the reader into higher stages of emotional understanding of the divine, the stories of the various *avatāras* foster various devotional emotions, based mainly upon *dāsya* or servitude.[90] Concerning the mood of *dāsya* Schweig writes:

> Subservient love (*dāsya rasa*); the soul loves the beloved actively and more closely, as personal servants love and directly serve their king. Here the soul is in a submissive position to the Beloved, who is in a superior position. This love is characterized as obedient service. The distance between the soul and God in reverential love is replaced by dynamic service in subservient love, although the relationship here remains formal.

In characterizing subservient love, Schweig applies the analogy of a servant and his king, the servant representing the soul and the king representing God. This idea is fundamental to theism and is central to the Judeo-Christian tradition as well. This kind of love for the divine is experienced within formal boundaries, and its mood prevails the major part of the *BhP*, up to the tenth book where a further ascension takes place in developing the moods of *sakhya*, *vātsalya* and *mādhurya* or *śṛṅgāra*.

In regard to the mood of *dāsya*, Haberman writes:

> Moving up the hierarchical ladder, the next type of religious experience, or devotional *rasa* is the 'respectful *rasa*'. This *rasa* is divided into two subtypes: politely respectful and relationally respectful. In the first, Kṛṣṇa appears as the awesome master and highest object of worship and the devotees take the form of his servants. It may be of interest to note that the gods, such as Brahmā, Śiva, and Indra are included in this latter category. In the second, Kṛṣṇa appears as a superior and protective elder and the

> devotees take on the forms of his sons and other younger relatives [. . .] Dust from the feet of Kṛṣṇa is listed as an enhancing excitant of the first type, whereas his affectionate smile is listed as an example of an enhancing excitant for the second. Adhering scrupulously to one's assigned task is an indication of the politely respectful *rasa*, and occupying a seat lower than Kṛṣṇa's is an indication of the relationally respectful *rasa* [. . .] The resulting religio-emotional experience is connected with a relationship in which Kṛṣṇa as the Supreme Lord is encountered as the worshiper's own caretaker.[91]

In articulating the progressive order of *rasas* in Rūpa's theory, Haberman uses the analogy of a ladder, meaning that a lower *rasa* leads to a higher one. Haberman calls this *rasa prīta–bhakti-rasa* as well as *dāsya–bhakti-rasa.*[92] In order to experience this *rasa*, one has to consider one's self a servant, the Supreme Person being the master. This mood seems to be prevalent in the *BhP*, and it underlies the *avatāra* stories, which occupy the main part of the text. A slightly different version is considering Kṛṣṇa to be one's elder and as such offering him respect within a social setting such as sitting on a lower seat in front of him and so forth. At any rate, it is clear that in this relationship the Supreme Person is the supreme master and caretaker, whereas the soul is the subordinate servant and dependent.[93] One of the first topics to be discussed in the *BhP* is the list of the *avatāras* and their functions. The topic is a fundamental one within the *purāṇa*, and it traces back to the dawn of history; that is, the creation.

> 1 Sūta said: In the beginning, desirous of creating the world, the Supreme Person assumed the form of a Universal Person, and manifested the sixteen elements. 2 The Universal Person was lying in the water of the universal ocean, and sleeping in a *yogic* state. There was a lake in His navel, and from that lake a lotus flower sprouted; from that lotus was born Brahmā, the chief universal progenitor. 3 The various planetary systems are resting on this universal form, which is comprised of a state of unadulterated purity. 4 Seers visualize this wonderful form along with its thousands of legs, thighs, arms, faces, heads, ears, eyes, and noses, shining with thousands of garlands, garments and earrings. 5 This

> form is the imperishable seed of the various *avatāras*, and from its parts and fragments, beings such as gods, humans and animals are created.[94]

This section lays the foundation for the *avatāra* doctrine in describing how the Lord assumed the form of a person,[95] how Brahmā took birth from his navel and how the original form of the Supreme Being[96] became the seed and resting place of the various incarnations. Through the fragments of his fragments, the supreme creates not only the gods, animals and men, but also different qualities, attributes, doctrines and ideas that will be henceforth stated.

Now the text goes on to describe the various *avatāras*, one by one. As the text is rather long, only the stories of eight *avatāras* are cited:[97]

> 6 At first, that Divine Person manifested himself as the four celibate sons of Brahmā known as the Kumāras, and as a brahmin, practised the very difficult vow of unbroken celibacy. 7 Second, the Lord of sacrifices assumed the body of a boar and for the welfare of the earth, raised it from the lower regions where it had fallen to, and re-established it in its place. 8 Third, in the seer-creation, he appeared as seer among the gods, Nārada, and propounded a devotional treatise which has the power of freeing one from the bondage of actions. 9 In the fourth incarnation, he appeared as the twin sages Nara and Nārāyaṇa born of Dharma's wife, and performed severe austerities with a fully pacified mind. 10 The fifth incarnation named Kapila, the foremost among the perfected beings, taught the brahmin Āsuri the doctrine of *Sāṅkhya* which is engaged with the fundamental elements, as this knowledge was lost in the course of time. 11 Being invited through the penances of Anasūyā, in the sixth incarnation her and Atri's son, and taught metaphysics to Alarka, Prahlāda and others. 12 The seventh incarnation was Yajña, the son of Ruci and Ākuti, and with the help of Yāma and other gods, he protected Svāyambhuva Manu's reign. 13 In the eighth incarnation Viṣṇu appeared as the son of King Nābhi and Queen Merudevī, and paved the path of perfection for those who are resolute and firm, a path which is honoured by all social classes.[98]

Altogether the *avatāra* section[99] contains a list of 22 *avatāras*, listed as follows:

1. The four Kumāras, the child sages who practised unbroken celibacy.
2. The Boar, Varāha, raised the earth and placed it back in place after it had sunk to the lower regions of the universe.
3. Nārada, the divine sage, who taught knowledge which releases one from *karma*.
4. Nara and Nārāyaṇa, two saints who performed severe penance.
5. Kapila, founder of the *Sāṅkhya* school of philosophy.
6. Dattātreya, a saint who taught knowledge of the soul.
7. Yajña, who protected the universe during Svāyambhuva Manu's regime.
8. Ṛṣabha, who taught the path of *sannyāsa* to the strong-minded.
9. Prithu, a king who milked the earth for the various goods she was withdrawing from the population.
10. The Fish, Mātsya, who protected the *Vedas* during the universal flood.
11. The Tortoise, Kūrma, who supported the *Mandara* mountain on his back while gods and demons were churning the ocean.
12. Dhanvantari, the divine physician.
13. Mohinī, who enchanted the demons, thus alluring them to give her the nectar, which she then gave to the gods.
14. Narasiṁha, the lion man, who saved his devotee Prahlāda from his demonic father Hiraṇyakaśipu.
15. Vāmana, the dwarf brāhmaṇa who reclaimed the three worlds by covering them with three steps.
16. Paraśu-Rāma, who extirpated the warrior class from the earth 21 times.
17. Veda-Vyāsa, who divided the one *Veda* into branches for the benefit of the less intelligent people of *kali yuga*.
18. Rāma, the heroic king who helped the gods by killing the demonic king Rāvaṇa.
19. Balarāma, elder brother of Kṛṣṇa.
20. Kṛṣṇa. The two brothers relieved the burden of the earth from the many armies marching on its surface.
21. Buddha will appear in the *kali yuga* to delude the enemies of the gods.[100]
22. Kalkin will appear at the twilight of the Kali age, when kings will be as good as robbers.

The last two *avatāras*, Buddha and Kalkin, are spoken of in the future tense, as if the *BhP* predicts their future coming. The text considers this list a sample only, and states that there are unlimited *avatāras*.[101]

So far we have articulated three consecutive notions of divinity, the *avatāta* being the fourth. It seems that in order to further develop our central argument pertaining to the *BhP*'s structure, mere engagement with the emotional moods will not suffice. It may well be that what is needed here is a philosophical look into the *BhP*'s doctrine, and an attempt to decipher its underlying concept of personhood. The idea of *avatāra* no doubt presents a philosophical challenge, as it appears to stand in contrast to the *Vedāntic* principle of non-duality. The question of reconciling the notion of *avatāra* with the principle of non-duality should therefore be addressed. Having addressed this issue, not only the idea of the *avatāra*, but also the relationship between the *BhP*'s underlying notion of personhood and its structure will become evident. It may be helpful to first look closer at the relations between non-dual ideology and the idea of *avatāra*. As to the apparent problem, Parrinder writes:

> It has seemed to some Indian writers, past and present, that the concept of Avatars is an unnecessary complication, if not a betrayal of the non-dualism of the Upanishads. If the cardinal assertion of monism, 'thou art that', is true then all men are divine. It is hard to see a difference between an Avatar and other people. At most, it appears that the Avatar knows his identity with *Brahman*, whereas others are yet unaware of it, though potentially they are the same as he is.[102]

Parrinder raises the question: In what essential way is the *avatāra* unique? If the *avatāra* is to be considered at all unique, Parrinder argues, it is due to his possessing true knowledge of his identity with *Brahman*.

However, one may assert that this kind of knowledge is open for every *jīva* who undergoes the process of self-realization, and as such doesn't really highlight the *avatāra*'s specification. Parrinder goes on further to shed light on the tension between monism and the *avatāra* doctrine:

> The appeal that monism still has comes from its apparent unity, simplicity and refinement. It does away with mythology and

> crude theological symbols. In place of a transcendental deity, a God 'up there', it teaches a universal Mind, with which the human mind is one. The universe appears to be informed by intelligence, indeed to be all mind, and man is that mind. Religion and worship disappear along with superstition. It goes without saying that there is no room for incarnation. Nor indeed is there room for revelation, prayer, or anything that suggests a transcendent Deity.

It seems that the idea of *avatāra* stands in sheer contradiction to this unity, simplicity and refinement. This deep tension between non-dual theorists and the *avatāra* doctrine is expressed in traditional commentaries. Sometimes reservations are directly expressed while sometimes they are conspicuous by their absence. Parrinder comments, 'Since thorough-going non-dualists have tried all down Indian history to maintain belief in the undifferentiated unity of divine and human, their comments on the Avatar doctrine of the *Gītā*, however respectful, have been weak.'[103] Parrinder gives the example of Śaṅkara and contrasts his approach with that of Rāmānuja:

> It is significant that in his commentary on the *Gītā* Śaṅkara wrote only short notes on the critical verses that deal with the coming of Avatar, though he went to considerable length in exposition of anything that could be turned to the service of non-dualism [. . .] In contrast, his successor and critic Rāmānuja wrote pages of comment on these crucial verses.[104]

It seems that Rāmānuja's *Viśiṣṭādvaita* is indeed compatible with the *purāṇic* genre, in which the idea of *avatāra* is common.

Regarding Rāmānuja, Klostermaier notes:

> His *viśiṣṭa* theory enables him to incorporate into the philosophical system of *Vedānta* all the traditional Hindu notions of *bhagavān* from the *Epic-Purāṇic-Āgamic* tradition.[105]

Sheridan holds the view that the doctrine of *avatāra* does not contradict the non-dual doctrine of the *BhP*, and hints that his position on the question of the *BhP*'s doctrine may be somewhat close to *Viśiṣṭādvaita*:

'The *avatāra*, however, is a particular immanent form of the Supreme Deity within his non-duality, the transcendent becoming immanent within the phenomenal which is ultimately not other than the Deity.'[106] This raises a question as to Sheridan's own view of the *BhP*'s doctrine, which he indicates by the name of his book *The Advaitic Theism of the Bhāgavata Purāṇa*. Sheridan addresses this in the book's concluding words:

> For the *Bhāgavata* non-dualism functions within a religion of devotion which maximizes the personhood of the Deity. Although each tradition of devotion characteristically maximizes the personhood of the Supreme Deity, and thus distinguishes the Deity from the person of the devotee, the *Bhāgavata* introduces this distinction within the person of the Supreme Deity. Perhaps a homologue to the nature of this distinction is the Christian doctrine of the Trinity wherein otherness does not imply separation. Rather the perfection of the Deity requires a Triune difference within the identity of the Godhead. In a homologous manner the *Bhāgavata* proposes a vision of a God who by his own power creates distinctions within himself. These distinctions derive reality from the Godhead without diminishing his reality. To separate devotion from non-dualism as has often been done is therefore to trivialize the *Bhāgavata*'s vision of the devotee's love for Kṛṣṇa. Devotion is primarily an ontological rather than a moral phenomenon.[107]

Sheridan's analysis soundly represents the doctrine of the *BhP*, and he is right in stating that 'a religion of devotion maximises the personhood of the Deity'. Personal devotion concentrates indeed on the specific attributes of the deity, it magnifies and maximizes them, and experiences them through tasting various related *rasas*. Moreover, we agree with the idea 'of a God who by his own power creates distinctions within himself, distinctions that derive reality from the Godhead without diminishing his reality', as representative of the *BhP*'s doctrine of non-dualism. The *avatāras* exemplify this principle, as the divine creates distinctions within himself by appearing or manifesting in various personal *avatāra* forms. These *avatāras* represent divinity and infinity, and the existence of one doesn't diminish the divinity of the other. We also agree that devotion is an ontological phenomenon rather than a moral one, and, as argued earlier, devotional emotions indeed have an ontological value. In other words, being devoted and experiencing devotional sentiments is not only a state of mind, but it seems to represent the ontological status of the *jīva*, according to the *BhP*, and that implies the essential personhood of the *jīva*, too. What does this have to do with the *BhP*'s *Vedāntic* doctrine? A doctrine in which 'God who by his own power creates distinctions within himself', 'a religion of devotion which maximizes the personhood of the Deity', and in which 'devotion is primarily an ontological rather than a moral phenomenon', seems to be close to Rāmānuja's *Viśiṣṭādvaita*. Moreover, the idea of 'a God who by his own power creates distinctions within himself' no doubt resembles Rāmānuja's doctrine where *Brahman* creates distinctions within himself to form *Īśvara*, *cit* and *acit*.

The distinctions within divinity are manifested, inter alia, through the *avatāras* who exhibit various personal distinctions yet simultaneously keep a unified divine identity. The religion of devotion, which maximizes the personhood of the deity, points to the emotional religion following the *avatāra* doctrine – every *avatāra* evokes a different aesthetic and emotional mood, and through that mood the personal characteristics of the deity are magnified. Devotion as an ontological category corresponds to the *jīva*'s nature in *Viśiṣṭādvaita Vedānta*, as being essentially devoted to the supreme, even at the state of *mokṣa*. As such, it may well be that the type of *Vedānta* underlying the *BhP* resembles in some ways *Viśiṣṭādvaita Vedānta*. Sheridan's conclusion as to the nature of the *BhP*'s doctrine is basically acceptable, but is still in need of some refinement. In what sense is devotion ontological? Is the tendency to express devotional relationships an essential and ontological quality of a person? Is this devotion reciprocal; that is, does the deity return this expression of devotional relationships? If the deity does respond, does this response emanate from the deity's essential nature, or is it a lower, lesser or external expression of the deity's personhood? As far as Sheridan's mentioning the homologue for the Christian doctrine of the Trinity, does that imply that the *BhP* holds the same notion of personhood as the Christian tradition? In order to focus further on the point under discussion, which is the reconciliation of the essential personhood of both the deity and the devotee with the doctrine of non-duality, we shall refer to Sheridan once more on this issue:

> But what is this non-differenced, non-dual reality? In certain passages the *Bhāgavata* says that it is knowledge or consciousness itself. Thus in the first canto, where the program for the *Bhāgavata* is laid out, Sūta replies to the questions of the sages by pointing out that 'the aim of life is inquiry into the Truth and not (desire for enjoyment in heaven) by performing religious rites. Those who possess the knowledge of the Truth call the knowledge of non-duality as the Truth; it is called *Brahman*, the Highest Self, and Bhagavān' (*BhP* 1.2.10b–11). The non-duality of Truth or the reality (*tattva*) is such that no ultimate distinction between knower and knowledge can be made, though by giving the absolute reality different names, the *Bhāgavata* affirms that the richness of absolute reality cannot be exhausted by considering it from one angle only. With admitting any distinction within the absolute reality, the *Bhāgavata* draws on various traditions to aid the understanding. The terms '*Brahman*' and 'Highest Self' are drawn from the *Vedānta*, while '*Bhagavān*' is dear to the *Vaiṣṇavas*. The final position given to *Bhagavān* seems to raise it above the other two in importance, and this is borne out by the *Purāṇa* as a whole. Thus non-dual knowledge, which is the essence of the absolute reality, is, according to the *Bhāgavata*, ultimately personal.[108]

Sheridan undoubtedly offers a deep doctrinal analysis of the *BhP*, but is still unable to fully remove obscurity from the question. At first Sheridan points to knowledge and consciousness as comprising the non-dual reality. He then quotes verse 1.2.11, which no doubt is engaged with this very question. He explains the non-duality of the Truth by concluding that no ultimate distinction between knower and knowledge can be made, though he expresses a reservation, and claims the *BhP*'s reality to be rich and many-angled. He then expresses a counter-reservation by saying that this richness does not necessitate any distinction within the absolute reality, yet he doesn't reconcile the two seemingly contradicting views. He then points to the *BhP*'s eclectic nature by saying that *Brahman* and the 'Highest Self'[109] are of a *Vedāntic* source, whereas the term *Bhagavān* is of a *Vaiṣṇavite* source, as if there is a contradiction between *Vaiṣṇavism* and *Vedānta*. However, Sheridan does not actually reconcile the problem under discussion, but rather concludes that 'non-dual knowledge, which is the essence of the absolute reality, is, according to the *Bhāgavata*, ultimately personal'. So the question still remains: How can non-dual knowledge be personal? Or phrasing it differently: How can the reality of *Bhagavān* be non-dual? In order to shed further light on this question, we propose to look closer at the definition of personhood, which we consider to be underlying the *BhP*. This definition intertwines the components of rationality, enjoyment, creativity and exchange of relationships in a way that is perhaps more natural for the *BhP*: 'A specific individual, conscious and rational being, whose nature is enjoyment, desires, creativity and reciprocal relationships with other similar beings.' This definition seems to be balanced and holistic, in that it perceives personhood through a variety of qualities, rationality being but one of them. It not only represents a balanced view of the knowledge and aesthetic paradigms, but expresses specific qualities such as rationality, enjoyment, creativity and so forth without having to compromise its essential position. This definition of personhood may better reconcile non-dualism with the person of *Bhagavān*, as manifested through the various *avatāras*. Based on this notion, the *avatāra* may be seen as manifesting a deeper amount of personhood than the previous notions. In other words, the *avatāra* is more specific; that is, his qualities are particular, whether he is a boar, lion or dwarf. His consciousness is manifested to a wider degree through his activities and speech. His emotional state is clearer and it is evident when he is pleased, enjoying or displeased. His desires and aims are also clearer, and so his creativity is manifested in the way he does things – the boar *avatāra* dives into the cosmic ocean to rescue the earth, the tortoise *avatāra* has the *devas* and the *āsuras* scratch his back with a mountain, the dwarf *avatāra* begs for three steps of land and then expands to cover the entire world and so forth. The *avatāra* exhibits a wide variety of relationships with various other persons. With some he fights, others are saved by him, to some he relates as a king to his subject or a master to his servant, whereas to others he acts as an obedient son, a friend or a lover.

Having offered a definition of personhood which, so we believe, represents the *BhP*'s underlying notion of personhood, we may now attempt to differentiate it from a classical notion of personhood, which is somewhat more knowledge-oriented. For this purpose we may offer a critique of Geoffrey Parrinder's important work *Avatar and Incarnation*. We do not know what definition of personhood underlies this work, but we will take liberty and presume that it is a Western definition. Again, there are various Western definitions, but just to give some idea, we may choose a very central and basic one, of Boethius, according to which, a person is an 'individual substance of a rational nature': *naturae rationabilis individua substantia.*[110] This definition emphasizes rationality as the essence of personhood, and as such places rationality above aesthetics or the emotional realm. It seems to us that a similar definition underlies Parrinder's ideas as articulated in the book under discussion. Parrinder analyses 12 characteristics of the *avatāra* doctrine.[111] In general his points are sound and rigorous, and thoroughly cover the theology of *avatāra*. He effectively emphasizes the *avatāras*, reinforcing the personal aspects of God and points out the difficulty this imposes on the monists. The *avatāras* reinforce a realist worldview as opposed to an idealistic one and they reinforce the sense of God as a person, able to exchange relationships, reciprocate prayers and show grace. The *avatāras* also serve as role models to be practically followed by people, and thus to sublimate and enhance the quality of human action and life in the world. However, Parrinder's view of the *avatāras* is somewhat alien to the *BhP* in that his worldview seems to be either oriented towards the *Bg*, Western thought or both. He writes:

> The divine descent has a purpose, it is not mere 'play'. These purposes range from slaying demons and delivering earth, men and gods, to showing the divine nature and love. The great purpose is to establish *dharma*, to restore right and put down wrong.[112]

The world 'play' refers most probably to the term *līlā*. Parrinder considers it to be on a lower level than the serious business of restoring *dharma*, and that is exemplified by applying to it the adjective 'mere'. Although this may fit well with the mood of the *Bhagavad Gītā* in which the reinstatement of *dharma* is much valued, it may not necessarily best represent the mood of the *BhP*, in which dramatic and aesthetic expressions occupy a central place. Also,

> the character of Kṛṣṇa is many-sided, and both [his] character and history are very different from those of Christ. It is easy to smile at the infant prodigies of the child Kṛṣṇa in the *Purāṇas*, or perhaps lament enviously his adventures with the milkmaids, and frown at

> the ecstasies of the Rādhā-Kṛṣṇa cult. Yet in considering the character of Kṛṣṇa the dominance of the *Bhagavad-gītā* must be remembered, and here Kṛṣṇa is noble, moral, active and compassionate.[113]

Here Parrinder resorts to the *Bg*, and stresses nobility and morality as representing higher values than smiling at the infant prodigies of Kṛṣṇa or frowning at the ecstasies of the Rādhā-Kṛṣṇa cult.

In considering the question of whether nobility and morality are higher values than emotional exchange, we may return to the *BhP*'s idea of a person. According to that definition, expressing emotions is not a lesser expression of personhood than acting nobly and morally, or teaching a philosophical treatise such as the *Bhagavad Gītā*. Also, a dramatic expression of creativity, such as appearing as a boar or half-man half-lion, is not taken by the tradition to be inferior to appearing in a human *avatāra*. It seems that Parrinder's statements are underlain by a concept of personhood that may not fit the *BhP*, in that they consider emotional expression to be inferior to moral and noble deeds. In maintaining this concept, one has to somewhat apologetically restore to Kṛṣṇa's noble and moral deeds, as if to compensate for one's rather lower deeds expressed through infant prodigies or frowning at the ecstasies of the Rādhā-Kṛṣṇa cult. Parrinder's citing the *Bg* as a reference is somewhat problematic for our purpose too. The *Bg* does not have the same dominant personal flavour as the *BhP* does, rather it is dominated mainly by the *jñāna* trend,[114] and therefore much larger sections tend to be interpreted impersonally, that is considering the supreme to be ultimately impersonal. As an example to the common tendency to interpret the *Bg* in this way, or at least to question its personal interpretation, we may quote Keith Ward:

> Within the *Gītā* itself, atheistic forms of *Sāṅkhya* are revised so that the eternal souls become creations of one Supreme Lord. But it is not entirely clear that this Lord is finally adequately characterized as a loving person. For much of the *Gītā*, it seems that the Supreme Self is pure consciousness and bliss, without purpose and unaffected by anything in the material realm. Śaṅkara [. . .] might be prepared to accept Viṣṇu as Īśvara (the Supreme Lord), and Kṛṣṇa as one of the main *avatāras*, or earthly

> embodiments of Viṣṇu. But he would insist that beyond the personal form of Viśṇu lies the impersonal or supra-personal *nirguṇa Brahman*, which is in itself without qualities and so is indeed beyond action and enjoyment as we understand them.[115]

Ward questions whether the personal notion of the Lord as the supreme is not imposed on the *Bg*, and refers to Śaṅkara, who 'would insist that beyond the personal form of Viṣṇu lies the impersonal or supra-personal *nirguṇa Brahman*, which is in itself without qualities'.

The *Bg* is one of the triple foundations of *Vedānta*, and as such it is generally a philosophical text, using language in quite a direct way. Therefore it can be relatively easily interpreted in an impersonal way, and, indeed, this was done by Śaṅkara, as Ward points out. The *BhP*, however, is differently composed, and contains not only a direct philosophical mode of expression, but an indirect one too. That is why the *BhP* is much more congenial than the *Bg* for expressions of personhood, and it is the *BhP* and not the *Bg* in which the *Vaiṣṇava* idea of God being a person is expressed so clearly. Therefore, in order to state that the *avatāra*'s aspect of being a moral agent in establishing *dharma* is higher than his *līlā* aspect, Parrinder has to resort to the *Bhagavad Gītā*, leaving his ideas to be somewhat at odds with the *Bhāgavata Purāṇa*. In conclusion, I believe that in order to look into the *BhP*'s structure, one has to avoid imposing a notion of personhood that emphasizes knowledge over aesthetics, as this is somewhat alien to the spirit of the *Bhāgavata Purāṇa*. I hope and believe that the alternative notion suggested here actually represents the *BhP*'s underlying ideas and as such has the potential of shedding further light on the structure of this great treatise.

The natural outcome of the integration of *Vedānta* and Indian aesthetics is a doctrine that, on the one hand, maintains the *ātman*'s striving to achieve *mokṣa* through the attainment of *Brahman* and, on the other hand, is an aesthetic construction of reality. As *Vedānta* awards the *ātman* with the qualities of existence, consciousness and bliss, and as Indian aesthetics enhance the unique, variegated and specific as opposed to the abstract and impersonal, the outcome is a specific, conscious and unique personal *ātman* which aspires to establish relationships with *Brahman* in person through constantly sublimating emotional experiences. Thus a notion of an 'aesthetic self' is created.

As the worldly self of *Mīmāṁsā* expresses itself through refining the act of sacrifice, as the solitary self of *Sāṅkhya* expresses itself through involution and, as the transcendental self of *Vedānta* expresses itself through striving to attain *Brahman*, similarly this aesthetic self expresses itself through a constant emotional refinement. As this is the *BhP*'s major theme, the text leads its devoted reader or spectator from the experience of *śānta rasa* all the way to the experience of *śṛṅgāra rasa*, thus exhibiting the full emotional spectrum and the dynamics of emotional growth.

We may also rise to Kohak's challenge and attempt to construct reality out of a personal point of view, considering that: 'In the beginning there was a person.' Following this trend of thought, we may assume that there exists such a person, who is 'a specific individual, conscious and rational being, whose nature is enjoyment, desires, creativity and reciprocal relationships with other similar beings'. As he desires to reciprocate relationships with other persons, he expands and generates many other persons with whom he can reciprocate relationships and these are the minute persons, the souls or *jīvas*. As he wants to enjoy various types of relationships, he appears in various personal forms, such as those of the *avatāras*, each evoking a different *rasa* or mood, which he enjoys. The minute persons want to exchange relationships with him, and in this way a complete doctrine or worldview may be formed, attempting to explain the entire range of existence in these terms. This approach takes into consideration many points discussed in this work.

It takes into account the *rasa*'s potential for universality and the ontological status emotions may hold in Indian thought, and as such its ability for constructing a parallel paradigm for articulating reality in the same manner that knowledge does. The idea of the *jīva*'s personhood has already been discussed as representative of Bhoja's aesthetic doctrine, and may be natural to a universal aesthetic worldview.[116] Thus the idea of two worldviews, the personal and the impersonal, corresponds to Kohak who considers that one can either see the world impersonally or personally. In this way the problem of reconciling non-duality with a personal worldview characterized by *avatāras* is reconciled. On the one hand, the truth is non-dual, as there really is only one such person who naturally is the Supreme Person, one without a second. On the other hand, it follows from his essential nature that he desires to expand into a variety of other persons who are naturally secondary persons with whom he can reciprocate relationships. Some of these minute persons sometimes desire to leave his company and therefore fall into the material world where repeated birth and death takes place. However, the Supreme Person appears there in his various *avatāra* forms in order to attract them back to his loving company. Looking into the *BhP*'s underlying doctrine, one may assert that: the worldly condition is *saṁsāra*, and this is a result of the soul's falling from the spiritual world of *Vaikuṇṭha*;[117] the goal of freedom is to return to that eternal and perfect world of *Vaikuṇṭha* and re-unite with the Supreme Person through an exchange of various *rasas*; the mode of revelation is the *BhP* itself;[118] and the process of redemption is hearing the *BhP* along with the *avatāra* stories depicted in it. This, I believe, represents the doctrine of the *BhP* in a nutshell, and it may be considered to be the doctrine of 'Aesthetic Non-Dualism'. However, if a person is defined through a knowledge paradigm as a 'rational individual', how could his desires for enjoyment, creativity and reciprocal relationships be justified? It must pose a theological problem and obscure the *BhP*'s doctrine, as indeed it does.

Having discussed some of the theological implications of the *avatāra* doctrine, we may now look briefly on the literary implications of the *avatāra* idea. The question may be raised: How should the *BhP* be read? Or, what literary genre does the *BhP* represent? Is it philosophy, epic, poetry or something else? Freda Matchett sheds further light on the notion of *avatāra* as distinct from the notion of 'Incarnation', and emphasizes that the *avatāra* is 'God appearing upon the world's stage'. She writes:

> Although its primary meaning is 'descent', the word *avatāra* is often translated into English as 'incarnation'. This is misleading because it suggests too strong a resemblance to the Incarnation of Christian theology. The Latin *incarnatio*, like the Greek *ensarkosis* which it translates, implies that what is important in the Christian concept is that the divine personage should be 'in the flesh', that is, totally real in human terms, all of a piece with the rest of human history. Whereas Christians have been reluctant to use words like 'appearance' or 'manifestation' of their incarnate Lord, such ideas are implicit in the term *avatāra*, since it has associations with the theatre (*raṅgāvataraṇa*, 'entering on the stage', is a word for the acting profession; *raṅgāvatāraka* is an actor). The *avatāra* is God

> appearing upon the world's stage, having descended from the highest level of reality to that of the *trailokya* (the triple world of *devas*, *asuras* and human beings) in order to perform some beneficial action, notably the restoration of the socio-cosmic order (*dharma*).[119]

Matchett highlights the nature of *avatāra* as 'appearing' or 'manifesting' while not necessarily being 'in the flesh'. She also highlights the way in which the divine descends from the highest reality, to appear on the world's stage, by associating the term *avatāra* with theatre and the acting profession. Having argued for the important and central role occupied by the *avatāra* theme in the *BhP*, we may proceed to articulate the next notion, moving up the ladder from *dāsya* to *sakhya.*

The Supreme Person as a Friend

The *BhP*'s main corpus is engaged with the stories of the various *avatāra*'s in the mood of servitude or *dāsya*. However, the tenth book takes a dramatic turn and offers a glimpse into three higher *rasas*, that is *sakhya*, *vātsalya* and *śṛṅgāra*. The *sakhya* mood is different than the mood prevailing the *avatāras*' stories. The superiority of the supreme diminishes and is exchanged by feelings of fraternity and equality. First, a textual encounter:

> 1 Śrī Śuka said: Once upon a time, intending to enjoy his meal in the forest, Hari rose up early in the morning and woke up his cowherd boyfriends by blowing his bugle melodiously, and they all proceeded from *Vraja* towards the forest with the calves walking in front. 2 Thousands of young and beautiful boys affectionate to each other, equipping themselves with slings, sticks, horns and flutes, each joyfully driving his own herd of thousands of calves. 3 Joining their own herds with Kṛṣṇa's innumerable calves and grazing them, they diverted themselves to playfully enjoy children's games around the forest. 4 Although they were already adorned[120] with glass-beads, *Guñja* seeds, precious stones and gold ornaments, they decorated themselves with fruits, tender foliage, bunches of flowers, feathers and minerals. 5 They stole the slings, packages of food and other

> objects from one another, and when detected, threw them at a distance to other boys, who in turn threw them still further laughing all the while, before returning them. 6 When Kṛṣṇa had gone further away to observe the forest's beauty, the boys competed with each other in touching Kṛṣṇa, and enjoyed themselves by calling 'I will touch Kṛṣṇa first' or 'I will touch Kṛṣṇa even before'. 7 Some played their flutes, some blew their horns, some sang in tune with bumble-bees, while others imitated the sweet notes of the cuckoo. 8 Some ran after the shadows of the flying birds, some walked beautifully like the swans, some sat down with the cranes, while others danced with the peacocks. 9 Some pulled the young monkey's tails dangling down from branches of trees, others climbed trees imitating the monkeys, others made faces with them while others were jumping like monkeys from one branch to another. 10 Some boys entered the stream and jumped with the frogs, others were laughing at their shadows, while others cursed their own echoes. 11 In this way, the cowherd boys who had previously amassed a vast amount of merits, played with Kṛṣṇa, who to the transcendentalists was the Supreme *Brahman*, to the devotees who dedicated themselves to his service was the supreme worshipful deity, to those who are under the influence of *Māyā* or ignorance was a human child. 12 The dust of the Supreme Person's feet cannot be obtained even by self-controlled *yogīs* who have performed austerities for many lives. Is it possible to describe the good fortune of the inhabitants of *Vraja* unto whom he has personally appeared, face to face?[121]

This scene depicts a group of young boys enjoying the company of each other in the forest and especially the company of their friend Kṛṣṇa. As such they play, blow their horns, imitate the birds' voices and follow their shadows, or compete over who will touch Kṛṣṇa first. This lovely scene could seem to be mere folklore and devoid of theological significance had not the text included verses 11 and 12. These verses take a step back and examine the scene from a distance. As such, they offer a commentary by considering the large amount of past good deeds the boys had to perform in order to attain this situation, and they further evaluate the great fortune Kṛṣṇa's companions have gained.

A deeper insight into the text will reveal that it conveys the *rasa* of friendship or *sakhya*. Schweig writes:

> Mutual love (*sakhya-rasa*); the soul loves the beloved more intimately in mutuality and equality, as a friend loves a companion. The endearing love of close friendship is now experienced with the supreme beloved, who places himself on an equal level with the soul. This love is characterized by confidential, even playful and affectionate exchanges. Mutual love constitutes a greater level of intimacy with the divine, since the superior position of the beloved is no longer acknowledged.[122]

We have stated earlier that *śānta rasa* is characterized by knowledge and detachment, and is devoid of affection. *Dāsya* includes the characteristics of *śānta*, but service is added and the affection is that of a servant towards his master. In *sakhya* there is knowledge of the friend, and as Kṛṣṇa's friends are aware of his various qualities, their love for him is excited by that knowledge. Furthermore, confidence and fraternity are added, whereas the hierarchical, formal and distant relationships exchanged between master and servant are replaced by egalitarian feelings. Haberman writes:

> The third type of devotional *rasa* is that of companionship. Here Kṛṣṇa appears as the devotee's friend, and the devotee assumes the position of Kṛṣṇa's friend, equal to Kṛṣṇa in form, dress and qualities. The devotees who experience this *rasa* are completely unrestrained and enjoy confident familiarity with Kṛṣṇa. Here we begin to see the positive effects of the increasing presence of the 'sweetness' (*mādhurya*) and 'myness' (*mamatā*) perspectives [...] and the concomitant fading of the 'majestic' (*aiśvarya*) that was dominant in the previous *rasa*.[123]

It seems that as one progresses higher on the ladder of intimacy with the supreme, one leaves behind the *rasa* of servitude, along with the majestic sense of the supreme, which evokes awe and reverence. One allows one's self to maintain a sense of ego indicated by the term *mamatā*, and this sense of ego comprises the foundation upon which a sense of equality and, following that, fraternity, are evoked. Hence one experiences a sweet taste that is absent in a more distant relationship such as the two lower *rasas*.[124]

In regard to the corresponding foundational emotion, Rūpa Gosvāmin writes:

> 105 The Foundational Emotion of this *rasa* is that love called
> 'friendship' (*sakhya*) which exists between two persons of
> approximately equal status; it consists of confident familiarity
> and lacks a sense of awesome respect. 106 Confident familiarity
> (*viśrambha*) is a special kind of deep trust that is devoid of any
> hesitation.[125]

In general, equality may yield either friendship or rivalry. Underlying *sakhya rasa* is a deep sense of friendship generated by a sense of equality. This is accompanied by feelings of fraternity, love, confidence and familiarity. Haberman writes:

> Confident familiarity (*viśrambha*) is defined as a special kind of deep trust that is devoid of any hesitations. This is the important quality of friendship that allows one to approach Kṛṣna as an equal. The commentators point out that this is what differentiates this relationship from the 'respectful *rasa*', wherein Kṛṣṇa is viewed as an elder, and the 'parentally affectionate *rasa*', wherein Kṛṣṇa is viewed as a youth in need of care.[126]

The deep sense of trust among friends seems to be unique to this *rasa*. Kṛṣṇa's friends are of two types: the rural friends from *Vraja*, and the urban friends from *Dvārakā*. The former group includes Balabhadra (Balarāma), Maṇḍalībhadra, Devaprastha and Stokakṛṣṇa, whereas the latter group includes Arjuna, Bhīmasena, Draupadī and Śrīdāmā. The friends in *Vraja* are of four types: the allies,[127] the assistants,[128] the dear friends[129] and the dear playful friends.[130] An illustration of Kṛṣṇa's friends in *Vraja* may be expressed by their addressing him during his lifting of Mount Govardhana:

> Friend, you have remained standing for seven continuous days without any sleep. Ah, you must be exhausted! Hand that mountain over to Śrīdāmā. Our minds are greatly distressed by

> this! At least switch the mountain over to your right hand for a few moments so that we can massage your left hand.[131]

This statement expresses deep love and care, devoid of any recognition of Kṛṣṇa's divinity or his supra-human powers enabling him to lift a mountain. The foremost of the urban friends is Arjuna; his sitting on Kṛṣṇa's throne along with Kṛṣṇa, sprawled lovingly on Kṛṣṇa's lap telling jokes, may illustrate their mutual friendship. Becoming a friend of Kṛṣṇa is a desirable state. Some may achieve it through lifetimes of practice and these are the *sādhakas*. Others are former gods who become friends and these are the *suracaras* class of friends. The third class is composed of friends who are eternally serving Kṛṣṇa in that capacity, and these are called *nityapriyas*. The friends themselves are of various types. Rūpa writes that,

> some are frivolous and entertain Kṛṣṇa as clowns, some are honest and serve Kṛṣṇa with sincerity, some are cunning and astonish Kṛṣṇa with their crooked ways, some are arrogant and engage Kṛṣṇa in senseless arguments, and other are gentle and delight Kṛṣṇa with pleasant words. In this way, the great variety of the sweet natures of all his friends enhances the diverse beauty of pure friendship with Kṛṣṇa.[132]

The various enhancing excitants in the *rasa* are Kṛṣṇa's age, form, horn, flute, conch; his qualities such as playfulness, humour and bravery; his beloved people; and his dramatic actions such as imitating of kings, gods and *avatāras*. Rūpa writes:

> 6–7 In this *rasa* Hari's qualities are such that he has a beautiful attire, possesses all good characteristics, is most powerful, knows many wonderful languages, is eloquent, extremely learned, very wise, capable, compassionate, the best of the heroes, skilled in the arts, intelligent, forgiving, the charmer of all people, successful, happy, and the dearest of all. 8 His friends are said to be equal to him in form, dress, and qualities; they are completely unrestrained and enjoy confident familiarity.[133]

It seems that Kṛṣṇa's attractive qualities such as his beautiful attire, bodily power, knowledge of many languages and so forth incite and evoke feelings of comradeship experienced and exchanged between him and his friends. These loving feelings are also graded from lower to higher. Rūpa writes: 'Love as friendship advances through five increasingly higher stages: from love as friendship (*sākya rati*), to attachment (*praṇaya*), to supreme love (*prema*), to tenderness (*sneha*), and finally passion (*rāga*).'[134] Although there are different stages of love in friendship, it is always love that underlies the relationships, and it is based on a sense of a permanent ego or a firm identity, which allows the sense of equality to arise.

The Supreme Person as a Child

Still higher than the mood of friendship with the Supreme Person is the mood of relating to him in parental affection. This mood is best exemplified by Yaśodā, the cowherd woman and Kṛṣṇa's foster mother:

> 1 One day, when the maidservants were engaged in some other
> work, Yaśodā, the wife of Nanda, began to personally churn sour-
> milk. 2 While churning, she was thinking of her child's playful
> activities in *Vraja*, and sang to herself about them. 3 Wearing
> round her abundant waist a silk garment fastened with a belt, and
> with her pair of shaking breasts that were overflowing with milk
> from maternal affection for her son, with her ear-rings set
> swinging as well as her bangles moving about her forearms,
> fatigued with pulling the churning rope to and fro and her face
> bedewed with drops of perspiration, the handsome lady went on
> churning while *mālātī* flowers continued to drop from the braids of
> her hair. 4 Desiring to suck her breasts, Hari approached his
> mother who was engaged in churning. As he tried to stop her from
> churning, he caught hold of the churning rod, thus awakening her
> maternal affection for him. 5 As her child climbed upon her lap,
> she, who was affectionately overflowing with milk, began to suckle
> him while gazing at his smiling face. But when the milk placed on
> the oven was about to overflow, she hastily put him aside and left
> him alone, still unsatisfied. 6 He angrily bit his quivering reddish
> lips with his teeth and smashed the pot for churning sour-milk
> with a piece of stone. Shedding false tears, he entered the interior
> of the house and began to secretly eat freshly churned butter.

> 7 After getting down the boiled milk, Yaśodā returned and found the smashed pot of sour-milk. Knowing that to be the act of her child who was not there and failing to see him there, she just laughed. 8 Kṛṣṇa was sitting on top of an overturned grinding mortar, freely distributing to a monkey the butter kept on a swing, and looking about with his eyes through caution and fear, lest somebody should detect the theft. Observing this scene, Yaśodā quietly approached him from behind. 9 Seeing his mother with a stick in her hand, Kṛṣṇa quickly got down from the mortar and ran away as if very much afraid. The *gopī* pursued him, but failed to overtake him whom cannot be captured even by *yogīs'* power of meditation, penance and austerities. 10 Running after him, the thin-wasted mother who was impeded by her abundant, quivering hips, and from whose hair flowers were dropping due to its being loosened by running, ultimately caught hold of him. 11 Catching the child by the hand, she threatened him with a stick and rebuked him who was crying for having committed that offence, who was rubbing his eyes with his hand whereby the black ointment around his eyes got smeared all over, and who was looking up with eyes bewildered and agitated with fear. 12 As her son was terrified, Yaśodā, who was very affectionate to her child, threw away the stick. Being unable to comprehend the prowess of Kṛṣṇa, Yaśodā tried to bind him with a rope. 13–14 He is neither inside nor outside, neither in the past nor in the future; but he is outside and inside the universe, and he is the universe itself. Considering the unmanifest who has assumed a human form, to be her child, the *gopī* tried to bind him with a rope to the grinding mortar, just as one would tie down an ordinary child.[135]

This story carries the mood of maternal affection mother Yaśodā felt towards her beloved child, Kṛṣṇa. While attending to her household duties she sang about the activities of her child, and her breasts overflowed with milk out of affection for him. She fed him for a while, but then placed him down, rushing to take care of a boiling pot of milk. Being neglected, Kṛṣṇa angrily smashed the melting pot and not only ate the butter in secret, but also mischievously shared it with a monkey. When she learnt of her boy's naughty behaviour, she laughed lovingly, and when she finally caught hold of him, desiring to punish the misbehaving child, she realized how fearful he was and therefore threw away the stick she held in her hand. The narrator reflects upon the situation, and remarks how inconceivable it is to attempt to catch 'him who cannot be reached by the minds of the *yogins*, and how ludicrous is the attempt to bind him who has neither inside neither outside'.

The *rasa* of *vātsalya* is referred to by Schweig as 'nurturing love', he writes:

> The soul loves the beloved even more deeply and tenderly, as a parent loves a child. The soul's love for the beloved is from a higher or superior 'parental' position as the soul cares for and protects the Beloved, who in turn exhibits dependency upon the soul. This love is characterized by adoration and nurturing affection; here, the carefree and casual familiarity of mutual love is replaced by a constant mindfulness and a sense of responsibility for the well-being of the Beloved.[136]

Schweig highlights this *rasa*'s theological implications by indicating that it is the soul who is the lover, and implicitly, the Supreme Person who is the beloved. It seems that one of the unique features of this *rasa* is the Supreme Person's reciprocation to the parental feelings by becoming dependent upon his devotee. About foundational emotion Rūpa Gosvāmin writes, 'The Foundational Emotion called "Parental Affection" (*vātsalya*) consists of a love that is devoid of deferential respect and belongs to one who shows kindness to Kṛṣṇa as a needy recipient of kindness.'[137] According to Rūpa, this *rasa* is experienced by one who perceives Kṛṣṇa as needy or helpless and, as such, naturally dependent. This state of helplessness attracts feelings of kindness and tenderness. The feelings of respect, which no doubt reach their peak with the *rasa* of servitude, gradually diminish in friendship, and disappear completely at the state of parental affection. Haberman analyses this *rasa*, which is considered to be the second most intense:

> The second most intense *rasa* according to Rūpa is the *rasa* of 'parental affection' (*vatsala-bhakti rasa*). Here Kṛṣṇa (*viṣaya*) appears as a child in need of nurturing protection and the devotee (as the *āśraya*) assumes the position of an elder who cares for young Kṛṣṇa. These are opposite to the conditions of the 'respectful *rasa*'.

> Moreover, Rūpa states that since Kṛṣṇa is here the recipient of kindness and protection, his majestic power is not manifest (3.4.5). Again, the absence of any sense of Kṛṣṇa's majestic power and the presence of the sense of his sweetness is the measure of the intensity and value of a *rasa*.[138]

Haberman, too, emphasizes the lack of any sense of majestic power, and it seems that this lack is replaced by the sweetness of parental affection. In regard to the dramatic elements including the characters, the enhancing excitants, indications and responses, Haberman writes:

> Kṛṣṇa's foster parents Yaśodā and Nanda are ranked the highest among this type of devotee (3.4.10–16). The enhancing excitants are the sweet, charming, and mischievous ways of the child Kṛṣṇa. The indications include such acts on the part of Kṛṣṇa's parents as smelling his head and giving him baths. A ninth and unique response is added to the standard list of eight responses for women in this *rasa*: the flowing of breast milk (3.3.45).[139]

Whereas the *rasas* of servitude, friendship and amorous love are all characterized by reciprocal relations, a unique feature of this *rasa* is the lack of expectation for reciprocation, Haberman writes:

> This *rasa* too has a unique feature: it will not diminish when not reciprocated (3.4.79). When mutual friendship is not returned it disappears, whereas there is no expectation of mutual friendship from a tiny baby. Rūpa therefore, recognizes a unique strength in this kind of love.[140]

There are various illustrations of emotional states expressing parental affection, and these include tenderness, passion, separation, anxiety, grief, indifference, mental inertia, depression, carelessness, madness, confusion, and satisfaction upon union.[141] These emotional states exist, no doubt, in other *rasas* as well, but they manifest in a unique, parental form when expressed through *vātsalya rasa.* An illustration of parental separation is given by Rūpa, quoting the *BhP*: 'While Yaśodā was listening to Uddhava's description of her son's activities (after Kṛṣṇa had left *Vraja*), tears flowed from her eyes and milk dripped from her breasts out of affection for him.'[142] This may serve as an example of an emotional expression, of *vātsalya rasa.* The same emotional state of separation may be expressed through other *rasas* as well, and its famous example is the *gopīs*' feelings of separation from Kṛṣṇa through *śṛṅgāra rasa*, the *rasa* which is the topic of the next section.

The Supreme Person as a Lover

The *BhP* reaches its aesthetic peak in the *rāsa līlā* episode.[143] Schweig points to the central and unique position this episode holds in Indian thought:

> The *Rāsa Līlā* is considered the ultimate message of one of India's most treasured scriptures, the *Bhāgavata Purāṇa*. The narrator of this story tells us that the highest devotional love for God is attained when hearing or reciting the *Rāsa Līlā.*[144]

Schweig seems to think that the *rāsa līlā* episode carries a deep theological meaning, apparently representing the love between the soul and the supreme; but first, a textual reference:

> 1 Having heard these most charming words from the Supreme Person, the *gopīs* forgot the distress caused by his separation, and by touching him they became completely satisfied. 2 At that place[145] Govinda inaugurated the *Rāsa* Dance with those jewel-like and faithful damsels who all formed a circle with their arms interlocked with each other. 3 At that time the festive *rāsa* dance commenced with the beautifully decorated *gopīs* arrayed in a circle. In a display of his supreme mystic power, Kṛṣṇa expanded himself and entered between each pair of *gopīs*. As he embraced them, each girl thought that she alone was in his proximity. 4 At that time hundreds of heavenly airplanes crowded in the sky, all carrying celestial gods along with their wives, their minds being attracted to the wonderful scene. 5 Kettle-drums then resounded and flowers fell from the sky like rain, while the Gandharva chiefs along with their consorts sang the Lord's immaculate glories. 6 The jingling sound of the *gopīs*' arm-bells, ankle bells and girdle bells arose as they danced with their beloved Kṛṣṇa in

> the circle of the *rāsa* dance. 7 The Supreme Person, the son of Devakī, appeared exceedingly beautiful in the midst of those dancing *gopīs*, just like a highly precious emerald among golden ornaments. 8 Kṛṣṇa's consorts praised him though singing; with their measured dancing steps and their hand gestures, with their smiles and playful movements of their eyebrows, with their waists bending, their breasts shaking and their garments slackening, with ear-rings swinging on their cheeks, with drops of perspiration rolling down their faces, with their braids of hair and girdles loosening, the *gopīs* appeared beautiful like flashes of lightening illuminating a mass of clouds. 9 Overwhelmed by conjugal love for Kṛṣṇa and excited by his touch, the dancing *gopīs*, with their decorated throats, sang at the pitch of their voices thus filling the entire universe with their songs. 10 One *gopī* joined Mukunda in singing, and together they sang a pure and melodious tone; when her tone rose to a higher gamut than his, Kṛṣṇa was pleased and applauded her with the words 'well-done, well done'; as she proceeded to reach her highest pitch according to the Dhruva[146] beat, Kṛṣṇa, even more so praised her performance.[147]

This scene carries the conjugal mood of *śṛṅgāra*, expressed through the romantic *rāsa* dance. The *gopīs* are affectionate and devoted to Kṛṣṇa or (Govinda), but this devotion and affection is different from the parental or fraternal devotion and affection, as it is expressed through the mood of conjugal love. The dance itself is meticulously performed according to artistic and dramatic conventions, such as singing specific musical *rāgas* or expressing feelings through certain artistic hand gestures. There seems to be a certain neglect of formalities on the part of the *gopīs*, hinting at a deeper emotional state of the participants – for example, in allowing their braids of hair and girdles to get loose, or in singing disharmoniously. Kṛṣṇa seems to enjoy these expressions, whether meticulously or loosely expressed, and to reciprocate the loving feelings expressed. The *rasa* of *śṛṅgāra* is referred to by Schweig as 'passionate love':

> The soul loves the beloved in the most intimate way, as a lover loves a beloved in a conjugal, premarital, or extramarital

> relationship. It is the most confidential form of love, and the intensity of amorous feelings exchanged represents the greatest attainable intimacy in *rasa*. This love is characterized by total self surrender of the lover in an exclusive passionate union with the divine, often heightened by periods of intense separation. Essential elements of all four previous *rasas* are present within this highest *rasa*.[148]

Schweig highlights the unique characteristics of this *rasa*, which he considers the highest of all *rasas*. These are the breaking of social conventions expressed through premarital or extramarital conjugal relationships, through feelings of intense separation from the beloved and a deep passion for union with him. Schweig also mentions that the essential elements of all four previous *rasas* are present within this one.[149]

In regard to the foundational emotion Rūpa Gosvāmin writes, 'the foundational emotion for this *rasa* is Amorous Love (*madhurā-rati*), which has already been mentioned.'[150] The previous mentioned verse referred to reads as follows:

> That love, which is the primary cause of the mutual sensual pleasure of Hari and the doe-eyed women, is called 'Amorous Love' (*priyatā*); it is also known as 'Sweet Love' (*madhurā*). It produces such acts as sidelong-glances, raising the eyebrows, love-talk, and smiles.[151]

In general, amorous love is the sentiment expressed between young men and women and is characterized by its sweetness. The topmost example for this *rasa* is expressed in the *BhP* through the amorous relations of Kṛṣṇa and the cowherd maidens and married women of *Vraja*. This *rasa* is divided into two types, which are separation (*vipralambha*) and union (*sambhoga*).[152] Out of the two states, the state of separation is considered to be the more intense and emotionally deeper. This *rasa* is unique in that it does not diminish under any circumstances, not even competing or incompatible emotions: 'This love of Rādhā and Mādhava is never diminished under any circumstances by either compatible or incompatible competing emotions.'[153] Haberman further analyses this *rasa* according to the *BRS*:

> The erotically charming Kṛṣṇa represented in the *Gītagovinda* is the object (*viṣaya*) of this *rasa* (3.5.5), and the *gopīs* of *Vraja* are its vessels (*āśrayas*, 3.5.6). The most exalted of all the women – of all vessels or devotees for that matter – is Rādhā, daughter of Vṛṣabhānu (3.5.7). The 'enhancing excitants' are exemplified by the sound of Kṛṣṇa's flute, and the indications include such acts as smiles and side-long glances.[154]

Apparently, this *rasa* is not only very intense but is very complex as well. Since Rūpa has written another book devoted entirely to this *rasa*, the *Ujjvalanīlamaṇi*, he doesn't expand the discussion about it much in the *BRS*. However, it is clear from his previous statements that this *rasa* encompasses the strengths of all the other forms of love, making it the *rasa* par excellence.[155] This may raise a question as to why Kṛṣṇa is considered the supreme, as opposed to Viṣṇu or Nārāyaṇa.

It seems that the choice of Kṛṣṇa as representing the highest form of aesthetic personhood is not circumstantial, but rather is a natural derivative of the *BhP*'s underlying aesthetic theory. Rūpa comments, 'Even though from a philosophical perspective there is no difference in the essential nature of the Lord of Śrī and Kṛṣṇa, the disposition of *rasa* is such that it reveals the form of Kṛṣṇa to be the most excellent.'[156] Although both the Lord of Śrī, that is Nārāyaṇa and Kṛṣṇa, are philosophically the same Supreme Person, they differ from the aesthetic point of view, as Kṛṣṇa's personality is aesthetically richer. Haberman comments on this verse:

> Jīva explains that here *rasa* means *prema-rasa*, or love, the highest of all *rasas* – hence the capitalized designation [. . .] Only Kṛṣṇa contains all the necessary qualities for the experience of the highest *rasa* experience, the 'great emotional experience' called *mahābhāva*. Verse 2.1.43 indicates that only Govinda is complete with all sixty-four qualities necessary for the highest experience. Specifically Nārāyaṇa lacks the important qualities of divine love sports, supreme love, the sweet flute, and the sweet form, whereas Govinda fully possesses these. Nārāyaṇa can grant worldly pleasures and liberation, but only Kṛṣṇa-Gopāla of *Vraja* can give the highest bliss. In other words, only Kṛṣṇa-Gopāla contains all *rasas*, as was proclaimed in the opening verse (1.1.1).[157]

It is apparent that the form of Kṛṣṇa as the supreme is not circumstantial, but rather it is the only form representing fully all 64 qualities.[158] Other forms of the Supreme Person, such as Nārāyaṇa or Viṣṇu, possess a lesser amount of these qualities, and are therefore suitable for the experience of other *rasas* only. Haberman points to the conjunction of aesthetics and theology clearly manifesting in this *rasa*:

> The most supreme devotional *rasa* and the highest type of religious experience possible is the amorous *rasa* (*madhura-bhakti-rasa*) [. . .] Nonetheless, it is clearly the highest *rasa* for him and he presents it in the familiar terms of the classical *rasa* theory.[159]

The *rāsa līlā* episode has since long occupied a major place in Indian religious thought and culture, and this is one of the main reasons why the *BhP*'s tenth book is considered a literary gem.

As the *BhP* leads the reader deeper and deeper into the personal realm of divinity through hearing and meditating upon the Supreme Person, and as the mood of *śṛṅgāra* or *mādhurya* is considered the highest according to the *BhP*'s underlying aesthetic theory, it is no surprise that this mood is considered to be the 'queen of all moods of meditation'. As Norvin Hein comments,

> the content of Kṛṣṇaite introspection became, now, something extraordinary. In the older and central *yoga*, one of the very first demands, asked of any beginner, was to root out every vestige of erotic thought. With the meditators on Kṛṣṇa, to the contrary, the queen of all the moods of meditation became the *madhura*, the romantic mood, that hopes for experience of the deity in an erotic relationship. The revered saints of these spiritual seekers were not ascetics but the very nubile *gopīs*, the cowherd women of *Vraja*.[160]

The *rāsa līlā* no doubt presented a challenge to *yogic* ethics of renunciation and to normative *dharmic* moral codes. How could seekers of *mokṣa* meditate upon such seemingly immoral and sensually exciting topics? How could the followers of *dharma* consent to the enacting of such a play? Again it is dramatic theory, which considers the pure emotional experience enacted through drama, that has an edifying and purifying effect. As the basic framework of the *rāsa līlā* is dramatic, it allows the experience of conjugal feelings and the tasting of *śṛṅgāra rasa* without arousing lust in the spectators or hearers. Instead it evokes a sense of inner purification and religious excitement. Hein describes the effect of the *rāsa līlā*:

> The story of Kṛṣṇa and the cowherd women became the prime literature of meditation. Writers fulfilled a great demand for the story, told in innumerable Sanskrit manuscripts, in vernacular translations and retellings. The erotic aspects of the stories were no longer resisted but deliberately evoked and dwelt on in the mind. Even devotees' conception of salvation was eroticized: the ancient paradises – *Kailāsa*, even *Vaikuṇṭha* – lost their charm. Devotees aspired now to reach the cow-world *Goloka*, highest heaven of all, the heaven of Kṛṣṇa, were the blessed *gopīs* are assembled, and Kṛṣṇa in his eternal sporting place calls departed devotees to savor eternally the blameless deeds described in scripture.[161]

As such, the *BhP* had reached its climax with the *rāsa līlā* episode, which epitomized the integration of *Vedānta* with *rasa* theory, as articulated by theorists carrying ideas similar to Bhoja's and preceding him.

This chapter has attempted to display the effect of reading the *BhP* as a theological treatise intertwining the *Vedānta* and *rasa* traditions. We aimed at demonstrating the development of divine notions in terms of complexity and intensity, and how these dynamics underlie the *BhP*'s structure. From the point of view of aesthetic personhood, the concept of Impersonal *Brahman* represents the peak of the knowledge paradigm and, at the same time, the departure point for the aesthetic paradigm. The concept of Impersonal *Brahman* was argued to be different, however, from Śaṅkara's: whereas in Śaṅkara's system awareness of personal manifestations of the deity represents a state of incorrect understanding of identity from which one is encouraged to progress still further to true knowledge, in the *BhP* the emphasis is not epistemological but aesthetic. Here one who has developed an awareness of Impersonal *Brahman* is considered to have experienced the supreme through *śānta rasa*, and is encouraged to progress still further to a higher ontological state by learning to experience the supreme through higher and higher *rasas*. The notion of the Universal Person is a stage further, relying on the universe in its physical, aesthetic and social aspects for developing awareness of the divine. From this notion, which is more external, the text progresses to a more internal one, which is the Divine Person in the Heart, a notion based on inner contemplation. The text then progresses to the major theme of the *BhP* – *avatāra*. Here we have pointed out the dramatic character of the text and, as far as theory, have built upon the works of Sheridan and Parrinder, offered a concept of personhood suitable for the *BhP* and demonstrated how the application of this definition helps to reconcile personal and aesthetic expressions with non-duality. From this stage we have pointed to the three higher moods culminating in *śṛṅgāra* and expressed in the *rāsa līlā* episode.

Adopting a wider perspective, it may become evident that the process of integration apparently begun around the second half of the first millennium gradually developed during some 800 years or so, and it may well be that Rūpa and Jīva Gosvāmīs' conceptualizing of the structure of the *BhP*'s *bhakti* is the fruit and culmination of a long historical process. This is supported by Hardy, who writes:

> We may sense behind the history of these philosophical schools[162] a progressive harmony and interaction between religious thought and practice. While *Viśiṣṭādvaita* theology had little resemblance to *Ālvār bhakti*, Rūpa and Jīva Gosvāmī's theology was in fact the conceptual interpretation of their *bhakti*.[163]

The historical process through which the *Vedānta* tradition has gradually adopted itself in the face of the challenge presented by the *BhP* is no doubt interesting and, as such, the concluding chapter of this book will be engaged with this subject matter.

Having shed some light on the role Rūpa and Jīva played in summarizing the conceptual interpretation of *bhakti* for the entire tradition, it may be conducive to quote Haberman on the special contribution of Rūpa Gosvāmin:

> In summary, Rūpa has created a typology of religious experience that ranks the various types of ultimate relationships in terms of intimacy with the divine and intensity of emotion. Within this typology Rūpa is able to place both the Peaceful (*śānta*) experience

> of the ascetic *yoga* traditions, which often defines the ultimate state as the absence of all emotions, and the Amorous (*śṛṅgāra*) experience of passionate devotion, which seeks to utilize the power of all emotions to establish a solid connection with the divine as beloved. These two impulses represent polar tensions that have defined and enlivened much creative debate within Hindu philosophy, and Rūpa's presentation provides yet another important way of viewing their relationship.[164]

This chapter has therefore attempted to shed light on the structure of the *Bhāgavata Purāṇa*, as moving between these two polar tensions of the peaceful and the amorous.

CHAPTER 4

A TEXTUAL ENCOUNTER

Having presented various theoretical arguments as to the *BhP*'s structure, this chapter aims at reinforcing the same idea through a textual encounter. Also, I felt that although this work is of a theoretic nature, it will be lacking without a textual encounter of some form, an encounter that will convey to some extent the flavour of the *BhP* itself. We shall proceed then and offer two textual examples for each *rasa*[1] in a paraphrased form. As such, *śānta rasa* would be exemplified through the teachings of the *Sāṅkhya* doctrine by Kapila to his mother Devahūtī and the story of Nārada's revelation, while the examples for *dāsya* would be the story of Dhruva worshiping Viṣṇu and Prahlāda's devotion to Hari. As examples of *sakhya*, Kṛṣṇa's friendship with the brahmin Śrīdāman would be highlighted, and so will Arjuna's friendship with Kṛṣṇa as well as the story of Kṛṣṇa's cowherd friends in Vraja. *Vātsalya* would be demonstrated by Vasudeva's devotion to baby Kṛṣṇa, and of Yaśodā's love for her child. As far as *śṛṅgāra*, two types would be analyzed: *svakīyā* as represented by Rukminī's devotion to Kṛṣṇa, and *parakīyā*, represented by the *rāsa līlā*, or Kṛṣṇa's love affairs with the *gopīs*. The picture emerging is that the *BhP* begins with knowledge or impersonal versions of *śānta*, then progresses to more personalized forms of *śānta* in the second book and, following that, books 3–9 offer by and large various mixtures of *śānta* with *dāsya*. The tenth book, which is the largest book and comprises about one-third of the entire *BhP,* is the richest as far as aesthetic expressions, as it offers *vātsalya*, *sakhya* and *śṛṅgāra*. The eleventh book returns to a mixture of *dāsya* with *śānta* and so does the twelfth book. It may be noted that episodes in the moods of *śānta* and *dāsya* occupy the *BhP*'s main textual corpus, whereas the other higher three categories appear as a relatively small portion of the text within the tenth book. As such, some distance and theory is required in order to see how these relatively simple folk stories actually represent a mature theological concept of divinity.

Śānta: Kapila Explaining *Sāṅkhya* Philosophy to Devahūti (*BhP* 3.26.1–20)

Kapila declares that he is going to explain to his mother the fundamental principles of *Sāṅkhya*, by which one can liberate himself from the bonds of *prakṛti*, characterized by the three *guṇas*. The knowledge he is about to give has the quality of cutting the knot of egoism existing within one's heart known as *ahaṅkāra*, thus leading one to the final release. Kapila proceeds to describe the *puruṣa* who is the beginningless and eternal soul, who is devoid of qualities, is superior to *prakṛti* and is self-luminous. This pure spirit has entered *prakṛti* consisting of the three *guṇas* out of his own free will in the mood of play or *līlā*. Having entered the sphere of *prakṛti*, which obscures knowledge and creates the variegated phenomenal world, the *puruṣa* begins considering himself to be the performer of activities, which are in actuality carried out by the three *guṇas* alone. Though by nature the *puruṣa* is the blissful and uninvolved witness, the condition of *saṁsāra* reduces him to a state of bondage and dependence. The wise can see that *prakṛti* is the cause of the body, the sense organs and actions, whereas the *puruṣa* is the experiencing agent of pleasure and pain due to his identification with *prakṛti*.

At this point Devahūti asks her son to speak further about the *puruṣa* and *prakṛti*. Kapila then describes the *pradhāna*, the chief principle that consists of the three *guṇas*. In itself, *pradhāna* is unmanifested, eternal and undifferentiated, but it is nevertheless the basis of attributes and variegatedness. *Brahman*[2] is comprised of *pradhāna*'s effects which are the 24 principles: these are the five *mahābhūtas* or gross elements, the five *tanmātrās*, sense objects or subtle elements, the four internal organs,[3] and the ten senses. The five gross elements are earth, water, fire, air and sky,[4] and the subtle elements are smell, taste, form, touch and sound. The ten sense organs are the ear, skin, eye, tongue and nose,[5] and the speech organ, hands, feet, genitals and anus.[6] The internal organ is composed of four components, which are the mind,[7] intelligence,[8] ego[9] and consciousness.[10] This enumeration delineates the qualities of *Brahman* as conditioned by the three *guṇas*, and the 25th principle is time.[11] It is said that time represents the Supreme Person as it evokes fear of death in those deluded by the ego due to their association with *prakṛti*. This divine power of the Supreme Person[12] sets in motion the agitation of the *guṇas*, which are otherwise in a neutral and undifferentiated state. The same Supreme Person who controls externally through time also dwells within all beings as the inner controller. The Supreme Person has impregnated *prakṛti*, which was agitated by the unseen destinies carried by the conditioned souls, and as such *prakṛti* gave birth to the aggregate of principles known as the *mahat*, which seemed resplendent as gold. Considering the above, it seems that the eternal cause of the universe wished to manifest and actualize the universe which was existing within it in a subtle potential form, and thus the *mahat* dispelled the darkness covering it.

Discussion

This section conveys an exposition of classical *Sāṅkhya*, and as such follows the standard description of the *puruṣa* becoming entangled in the bonds of *prakṛti*, which is composed of 24 elements and governed by the three *guṇas*. As such, the text articulates the *Sāṅkhya* doctrine. It deconstructs reality into the two basic components, which are the *puruṣa* and *prakṛti*, and it describes the state of the *puruṣa* identifying with the 24 elements. This exposition is overtly theistic, as opposed to the common atheistic version of *Sāṅkhya*. As such, the 24 elements are actually *Brahman*, or some kind of a modification of *Brahman*, presumably in a *Viśiṣṭādvaitic* manner where the world comprises the body of *Brahman*. This clearly adds a theistic and *Vedāntic* dimension to the serene exposition of knowledge. Moreover, having mentioned *Brahman*, the text goes on and mentions the Supreme Person, using the term *Bhagavān*,[13] which in the *BhP*'s opening verse denotes Kṛṣṇa or Vāsudeva. The Supreme Person can be perceived externally through time, and internally through the inner ruler, or the Supreme Person in the heart. Moreover, it is the Supreme Person who has impregnated *prakṛti*, thus causing the evolution of the elements comprising this world. It seems that this section is dominated by knowledge and, as such, evokes a universal vision accompanied by feelings of serenity. The text then develops very carefully a universal notion of *Brahman* or the

Supreme Person, whose body comprises the universe perceived through the 24 elements, who controls all externally in the form of time, and internally as the inner ruler.[14] In that, the text directs these serene emotions of *śānta* towards constructing a notion of the divine experienced through the emotional state of *śānta*. As far as the emotional state evoked in this passage towards the Supreme Person, Schweig's characterization of this mood as 'quiet veneration and admiration' evoking a 'passive and contemplative' mood seems to fit well this notion of divinity.[15]

Śānta: Vyāsa Enquires about Nārada's Past Life (*BhP* 1.5.23–1.6.42)

The chapter opens with a conversation between Nārada and his disciple Vyāsa. Nārada has just told Vyāsa how in a previous life he had been the son of a maidservant, and how he encountered a group of mendicants who spent a few months with him and his mother. The mendicants, who were associated with a *Vedic* branch, initiated the child and imparted their knowledge unto him during the period of his attending them. Following that, the child became purified of sins, his mind and heart became cleansed and he developed a taste to hear about topics related to self-realization and spirituality. He gained control over his senses and realized he was different from the mental and bodily coverings in which he was encaged. The young Nārada lived with his mother in poor conditions, but was internally satisfied and awaiting the grace of the supreme. When his poor mother died, he took it as an opportunity to get released from all attachments and went on his own to seek the supreme, in whom he had already acquired faith. Although a mere child, Nārada left home to become like a *sannyāsī* travelling on his own, relying on nothing but divine protection. The journey must have been troublesome, but purifying as well. At last he was all alone in a jungle, bathing in a river lake, and it was in those surroundings that he was to encounter a divine revelation.

In that solitary place, the young Nārada began practising a type of meditation he had learnt from his teachers. That particular meditation focused on the *Paramātman*, or the Lord within the heart, and it seems that he had reached a depth he had never encountered before, and thus experienced various ecstatic emotions. The experience became deeper and deeper, and gradually he attained a vision or some kind of a direct experience of the divine[16] within the heart. Having attained that extraordinary vision and experience, Nārada was engulfed by deep bliss and satisfaction, and underwent a kind of bodily transformation, in which his limbs appeared to be separated from his body and his hair stood on end. In that state Nārada lost sight of the supreme. Upon directly envisioning the supreme, Nārada was delighted and his grief dispelled. However, having lost sight of that most cherished divine form, Nārada was despondent and repeated his attempts through further meditation in order to attain once more that extraordinary vision. He again concentrated and fixed his mind on his heart, but his attempts remained futile and he was aggrieved. At that point, the supreme who is beyond the range of the senses spoke to Nārada in a grave and pleasing voice, thus mitigating Nārada's grief. The Lord said that unfortunately Nārada would not be able to see him anymore during this lifetime, as he is not visible to those who have not become free from desires or purified of their passions, nor have attained success in *yoga*. However, the Lord explained that he still bestowed this revelation upon Nārada despite his lack of qualifications in order to invoke in the child a desire to attain him, as this desire gradually cleanses the heart of all material desires.

Discussion

This story relates the events in Nārada's previous life leading up to his encounter with the divine person in the heart. Various events, such as his receiving initiation from the *Vedic* ascetics, his mother's untimely death and his wondering through the forests, evoked in young Nārada an attitude of detachment, austerity, and a sense of dependence upon the supreme. At last, he sat under a tree and meditated upon the Supreme Person within, and surprisingly, the Supreme Person appeared to him within his heart. During the revelation, relationships were established between Nārada and the Supreme Person, presumably Viṣṇu. On the one hand, Nārada was searching for Viṣṇu through meditation and, on the other hand, Viṣṇu appeared and disappeared out of his own will, having a purpose to fulfil, which was to reciprocate Nārada's desire for proximity with himself,[17] and to evoke in Nārada an attachment for himself. That was certainly achieved as Nārada was deeply moved by the revelation and as a result of it had experienced strong feelings and a deep attachment towards Viṣṇu. As opposed to other revelations, this one did not involve the exposition of a doctrine or a sermon conveying knowledge, rather it mainly evoked in Nārada, an emotional excitement and an intense attachment towards the divine. Even after the revelation, the supreme remained mysterious and mainly unknown. As such the overall features of this revelation lead to its categorization as a revelation evoking emotions in *śānta rasa*. Nārada did not identify himself as a servant of the Supreme Person, having some active task or role to play, rather he aspired to gain a view of the supreme through meditation. It seems that characterizing this mood as the relation of a subordinate to a 'great and powerful emperor' and 'awareness of his or her finite existence in relation to the overwhelming majesty and omnipresence' of the supreme, well fits this episode.[18]

Dāsya: The Story of Dhruva (*BhP* 4.8–9)

King Uttānapāda who was Brahmā's grandson had two wives and among them he preferred Suruci over Sunīti.[19] One day the king was holding Suruci's son, Uttama, on his lap, while Sunīti's son, Dhruva, wished to climb on his father's lap too. The king rejected Dhruva, and the proud Sunīti spoke to the child in the king's presence and said:

> Although you are the king's son, you do not deserve to ascend the royal throne as you were not born from my womb. However, if you do wish to ascend the throne, you should worship the Supreme Person by penance, and by his grace you may then take birth from my womb.

Being extremely hurt and angry by these harsh words and leaving his father who listened silently and without protest, the child went crying to his mother, who became greatly afflicted as she heard the news. The mother encouraged her angry son to give up his anguish and propitiate Viṣṇu, as by this, he will attain the throne, earthly and celestial happiness, and ultimately liberation too. She advised him to adore Viṣṇu by firmly fixing the mind on him, by being exclusively devoted to him and by purifying himself through the performance of his duties. Dhruva bathed in the river *Yamunā*, fasted for the first night with a concentrated mind and worshiped the Supreme Person according to the instructions he had received from his *guru*, Nārada. Accordingly, during the first month he worshiped Hari, eating a little fruit every third day, in the second month he continued his worship, eating some grass and leaves every sixth day, and on the third, he further concentrated his mind and continued his worship drinking water every ninth day. In the fourth month he controlled his breath, by breathing every twelfth day, and in the fifth month he controlled his life air, and stood motionless meditating upon *Brahman*. As he performed *dhāraṇā*[20] and fixed his mind on the Supreme Person within, the three worlds began to shake. At that point, the earth was getting out of balance due to his intense practice. When he controlled his life breath and meditated upon Hari as being non-different than himself, the worlds experienced a feeling of suffocation and the gods resorted to Hari, the Supreme Person, for shelter. Hari said to the gods, 'Do not be afraid, this feeling of suffocation is due to Dhruva's identifying his self with me. I shall dissuade the child from this austere penance.' Having said that, he mounted his eagle carrier Garuḍa and went to meet his devotee.

Dhruva suddenly lost sight of the Lord within, and as such he opened his eyes and saw that very person standing in front of him. Awed by his presence, the child fell down on the ground like a stick, offering his respects to the Supreme Person. The child was as if drinking Viṣṇu with his eyes, as if kissing him with his mouth and as if embracing him with his hands. Dhruva wanted to praise the Lord but was unable to express himself. Viṣṇu touched the child's cheek with his conch thus inspiring Dhruva with divine speech, and being full of devotion and love, Dhruva began to praise the Supreme Person and said:

> I bow to you who is the *antaryāmin* of all. Having entered into me, you have reactivated the power of my speech which was lying dormant, and enlivened my sense organs. You are a wish-fulfilling tree capable of liberating persons from the cycle of births and deaths. Your *māyā* has deluded the intelligence of those who worship you for other purposes, such as pleasures enjoyable in this body which is as good as a corpse. Oh my Lord, bless me with the intimate companionship of those great persons who bear constant devotion to you and are of a pure heart. Thereby, being intoxicated with drinking the nectar in the form of stories about your excellent attributes, I will easily be able to cross the ocean of *saṁsāra*. You

> are eager to confer your grace like a mother-cow which nourishes and protects its newly born calf.

In reply, Viṣṇu said:

> O prince, I know the desire cherished in your heart, and will bestow upon you your cherished object even though it is unattainable by others; upon your father's retirement, you will ascend to the throne and rule the earth for thirty six thousand years. Your brother will loose his life in a forest expedition, and his mother will loose her life in search of him; you will later attain the highest star, the pole star, which is bowed to by all the worlds – a place from which there is no return.

The Supreme Person left for his abode, and Dhruva returned to the city, with a displeased heart, thinking to himself: In a short period I have attained what others attain only in many lifetimes, namely the shelter of the Supreme Person. However, all I desired was ephemeral. My judgement was deluded and hence I did not follow the advise of Nārada. When I met with the soul of the universe who alone can grant the terminating of *saṁsāra*, all I asked for was *saṁsāra*. I am like a penniless man who begs unhusked grains from the emperor.

Discussion

The story of Dhruva appears elsewhere, too.[21] Seen from Dhruva's point of view, Viṣṇu was rather distant at the beginning. Dhruva first heard of him from his mother, and later, Nārada described his qualities. When Dhruva practised austerities, his awareness of Viṣṇu gradually increased until he reached the point where he was able to meditate on Viṣṇu as non-different than himself. At that point Viṣṇu actually appeared, but it was not before his touching the boy that Dhruva attained the peak of the revelation and was able to praise the Supreme Person according to his understanding. While praising the Lord, Dhruva indicated that he saw him as a mother-cow protecting her new-born calf. This exemplifies a developmental change in his view, as at first Dhruva understood Viṣṇu as he who would satisfy his desires for revenge and power, as opposed to a loving mother-cow. At the peak of the story he faced the Lord, who in turn touched his cheek with his conch. That invoked a supreme aesthetic experience in Dhruva whose senses became all enlivened, who experienced a kind of divine reality and whose reaction to that revelation was the praise of the Lord. After the Lord had granted Dhruva his original desire, power, fame and revenge, Dhruva felt frustrated for having desired such unimportant boons.

This passage's structure represents the *BhP* in a nutshell. Dhruva approaches the Lord out of some utilitarian purpose, the narrative then gradually attracts the reader to absorb him in descriptions of the divine, one's aesthetic awareness of the Supreme Person is then expanded and widened, an instruction to practise this kind of contemplation follows, and the reward of attaining *mokṣa*, apparently an aesthetic form of *mokṣa*, is promised. In transformational terms, it can be said that the text is aiming to gradually take the reader from the finite towards the infinite, and that one transcends one's own petty desires and gradually replaces them with some form of an encounter with the Supreme Person. The encounter itself takes the form of some definite relationships. In this case the Lord is like a cow and Dhruva is like the calf. It may well be that Dhruva's disappointment after encountering the Lord follows these relationships. Dhruva may have wanted to serve his Lord rather than take service from him. The reading of the text is a kind of ritual or even a sacrificial practice, resulting in a *Vedāntic*-aesthetic experience. The *Vedāntic* experience is the liberation from *saṁsāra*, or the gradual purification of *karma* which ultimately leads to *mokṣa*, and the aesthetic experience is a widening of one's horizons, from the lower states of existence or the *guṇas* to the beauty of the Lord and his variegated world. It may well be that the reader of this story is inclined to identify with Dhruva, feel the anger he felt having been rejected by his father, have some experience of his concentration of mind and austerities, and then share Dhruva's excitement in meeting the Lord. Later the reader may share Dhruva's regret for having begged Viṣṇu for 'unhusked grains' and in this way the reader participates in Dhruva's emotions while reading or hearing. That places the text closer to drama than to philosophy, and as portrayed earlier in this work, it may apply language indirectly, as triggering emotions rather than merely denoting information.

The dominant *rasa* of this story is *dāsya*, as Dhruva envisions his Lord as a master or sovereign. As such, when he is awarded with a personal revelation, he experiences feelings of servitude and devotion, and he wants to praise the Lord, as a servant praises his master. Apparently, he does not meditate on the Lord in quiet contemplation, he does not consider himself a friend of the Lord, yet alone a parent or a lover. It seems that characterizing the mood expressed here as 'loving the beloved actively and more closely, as personal servants love and directly serve their king', applies well here.[22]

Dāsya: The Story of Prahlāda (*BHP* 7.8–9)

Prahlāda, who was the son of the great universal king Hiraṇyakaśipu, was a devotee of Viṣṇu. That very much irritated his demonic father. Despite his father's objection, Prahlāda talked to his playmates and persuaded them to become devotees of Viṣṇu, too. Prahlāda propounded devotion to Viṣṇu, saying that it consists of nine limbs: hearing the names and episodes of Viṣṇu, singing his names and glories, remembering him, rendering service unto him, worshiping him, dedicating all one's actions to him, confiding him as a friend and offering one's body and belongings to his service and care.[23] After Prahlāda completed his talk, it became evident that the boys accepted his message, thereby rejecting the teachings of their preceptors, who became disturbed and reported the incident to Hiraṇyakaśipu. Hearing the upsetting news, Hiraṇyakaśipu was extremely enraged, and decided to kill his own son. Reprimanding Prahlāda in harsh words, Hiraṇyakaśipu asked him on whose power did he rely while violating his commands. Prahlāda replied that the source of his power was the Lord, who controls the entire creation. To this, Hiraṇyakaśipu asked:

> Where is the Lord of the universe, if at all there is a controller above me? If indeed he is all pervading as you say, how is it that he is not present in this very pillar? I shall now sever your head from your body. Let us see whether Hari will actually come to protect you.

Repeatedly reproaching his son with harsh words, the powerful *asura* got up and struck the pillar with his own fist with great power.

From within the pillar there arose a terrific roar, so dreadful that it seemed to be crashing the cosmic shell. Hiraṇyakaśipu, who was about to kill his son, was unable to detect the source of that mysterious sound. At that time, in order to prove true the words of his devotee, as well as to demonstrate his omnipresence, the Lord appeared from within that very same pillar. He appeared in a form, neither human nor beastly, rather as a half-man and half-lion. The king gazed at the strange creature standing in front of him, and tried to ascertain what he actually was. His eyes were fierce, his mane shining, his teeth were terrible and his tongue was sharp. His stature touched the sky, his neck was short and thick, his chest broad and his waist slender. Hiraṇyakaśipu thought that whomever that fearful personality may be, it must be an expedient for his death planned by Viṣṇu. Nevertheless, the king was assured of his victory in the combat soon to come, and thus attacked the creature with his mace in great force. The divine Man-Lion Nṛsiṁhadeva caught the demon just as Viṣṇu's eagle Garuḍa seized a serpent, and played with him. The king, however, slipped away from the Lord's hands, much to the concern of the gods who concealed themselves behind the clouds, and thought the Lord to be afraid of his great powers. The *asura* took up his sword and shield and attacked the Lord, moving around him with great speed. Hari roared terrifically and seized Hiraṇyakaśipu and held him tightly. Being situated at the door of the assembly hall, the Lord laid the demon on his thighs and tore him apart with his nails. Nṛsiṁhadeva's eyes were so indignant and fierce that they were impossible to look at, his mane and face were reddish due to the demon's drops of blood, and the king's intestines were surrounding his neck like a garland. The Lord, having uprooted the demon's heart, threw his body aside and turned to fight the thousands of the king's soldiers who attacked him from all directions and struck them down with various weapons. The clouds were scattered away by the Lord's mane, the oceans became turbulent by his breath and the earth was heavily pressed by his feet. His indignation not abated, he sat down on Hiraṇyakaśipu's throne appearing so angry that no one dared approach him. At that time, being jubilant upon the demon's death, the various gods and heavenly residents came from all directions and assembled around the Man-Lion *Avatāra*.

Brahmā said, 'I bow down to the unlimited Lord of inconceivable and various powers, who creates, maintains and destroys the universe through the instrumentality of the *guṇas* out of his own *Līlā*, while remaining changeless.' Śiva said, 'The termination of the one thousand *yugas* cycles is the proper time for the exhibition of your wrath. O Lord who is affectionate to his devotees, please protect your devotee Prahlāda who has now approached you.' Indra said, 'O Lord, of what avail is this sovereignty of the three worlds which is to be devoured by time; to those who wish to serve you, even liberation from *saṁsāra* is of little importance, what to speak of the four aims of life?' The seers said, 'O Original Person, you taught us the supreme form of penance by which you evolved the universe; however, our practice was obstructed by the demon, and by assuming this form you have permitted us to perform it again.' The ancestors said, 'This *asura* has forcibly deprived us of the offering offered to us in order to enjoy them himself; O Lord, you have restored our offerings. The perfected beings[24] said, 'The demon robbed us of our mystic powers, by his own power of penance; we now offer our obeisance unto you.' The Manus said, 'O Lord, the bonds of the social order given by us under your order, have been violated by Diti's son; now that the demon is killed, please command us again.'

Although having offered eloquent prayers to the Lord, the gods still dared not come closer to him, as he was still extremely angry. An attempt was made to send his beloved goddess Lakṣmī to appease him, but even she was afraid to approach Nṛsiṁhadeva while he was in such a furious mood. Then Brahmā requested Prahlāda to go and pacify the Lord. The devoted child then slowly approached the Lord with folded hands, and prostrated himself at his feet. The Lord, being overwhelmed with affection, raised the child up and touched his head with his lotus-like hand. Being touched by the Nṛsiṁhadeva's hand, all inauspiciousness in Prahlāda was washed away. At that time he gained a vision of the supreme, his eyes were full of tears and, being delighted at heart, he was filled with deep devotional emotions. Prahlāda said:

> As the great gods were not able to satisfy the Lord with their prayers, how would I, a mere descendant of a demoniac family, be able to do so? As the Lord was pleased with the elephant king[25] due to his deep devotion, I presume that opulence, noble lineage, beauty, austerity, intelligence and *yogic* perfection are of little avail in propitiating the Supreme Person. A *cāṇḍāla* of low birth is in a superior position to a brahmin endowed with the twelve brahminical qualities[26] but who is averse to Lord Viṣṇu, for a devoted *cāṇḍāla* sanctifies his whole race, whereas a brahmin although he may be very qualified, is unable to do so. O Supreme Person, you appear as various *avatāras* in order to protect *dharma* and to uplift the ignorant from *saṁsāra*.

Discussion

The story of Prahlāda exemplifies well the *rasa* of *dāsya* or servitude. It is evident that when Prahlāda explains devotion unto Viṣṇu to his playmates, he considers himself to be the servant, whereas he considers Viṣṇu to be his Lord and master. As such he propounds rendering service unto Viṣṇu, worshipping him, dedicating all one's actions to him and offering one's body and belongings to his service and care. It seems that hearing about his names and episodes, singing his names and glories, remembering him, are all done in that service mood, and even the idea of confiding in him as a friend, which seems to express but a tinge of friendship, still does not go beyond the general mood of servitude. Prahlāda's ninefold expression of devotion exemplifies well the subtleties of the mood of servitude as it combines direct service, surrender, dependence, remembrance, glorification and friendship.

The personality of Nṛsiṁhadeva fully displays the qualities of Lordship or *aiśvarya*. He is therefore fierce and victorious in battle, careful to adhere to Brahmā's boon, and protective of his devoted servant. As the episode ends, he justly occupies Hiraṇyakaśipu's throne, and accepts the prayers of the various gods present.

Nṛsiṁhadeva's manifestation of divine anger was indeed extraordinary, so much so that the gods did not dare approach him. However, Nṛsiṁhadeva displayed a soft side too. The expression of simple and pure devotion touched the Lord's heart, and it was only then that he was appeased. His being pleased was noted by his touching the boy's head with his hand, who at the touch of the Lord's hand gained immediate purification, and a subsequent vision of the supreme, and his devotional ecstasy increased even further. In his prayers Prahlāda eulogizes the Lord as appearing in many *avatāra* forms, and indeed, Viṣṇu's appearance as Nṛsiṁhadeva exemplifies well the major dynamics of the *BhP*. Accordingly, most *avatāras* generally exhibit *aiśvarya* to some extent, and the devotees identify themselves as their servants. Considering *dāsya* or obedient service to be 'in a submissive position to the beloved, who is in a superior position', fits well here as Prahlāda considers Nṛsiṁha to be superior and approaches him submissively. Such also is the understanding of *dāsya* as an expression of 'dynamic service in subservient love, although the relationship here remains formal'.[27] This formality can be perceived in the way Prahlāda approaches Nṛsiṁha; Prahlāda carefully approaching while Nṛsiṁha occupying the royal throne.

Sakhya: Śrīdāman, Kṛṣṇa's Brahmin Friend (*BhP* 10.80–1)

There was a certain brahmin friend of Kṛṣṇa named Śrīdāman, who was learned, pure and austere. Although he and his wife lived in poverty, he was still satisfied with whatever came his way without striving for it. However, when poverty became unbearable his wife asked him to approach his childhood friend, Kṛṣṇa, who was a great king ruling over Dvārakā, and ask him for some help. The brahmin was not inclined to go but, at last, having been pleaded at over and over again by his wife, he got inspired by the idea of personally meeting Kṛṣṇa, and decided to go. The brahmin asked his wife for something to present to Kṛṣṇa and she gave him some fried rice for that purpose. He travelled to Dvārakā and entered one of Kṛṣṇa's palaces, where the Lord was residing with his queen Rukminī. Having noticed a brahmin approaching, Kṛṣṇa rose from his seat and with tears in his eyes happily embraced his beloved friend. He then seated the brahmin on his own seat and personally washed his feet, sprinkling the water from Śrīdāman's feet on his own head, and smearing the brahmin with perfumes and pastes. At the same time, Rukminī fanned the brahmin, and the assembled were surprised to see the amount of affection and worship offered to the poor brahmin by Kṛṣṇa, who turned to his friend and said:

> Please tell me of the events occurring to you after the completion of our education. Do you remember how we lived together at the home of our *guru*? Do you remember the incident, in which our *guru* had sent us to collect wood for fuel? As we entered the thick forest, there was an unexpected outbreak of a violent storm, a heavy shower of rain and a terrible roaring of thunders. Meanwhile, the sun had set and we had lost our way in the forest. Holding our hands, we wandered in all directions searching the path back home. After the sun had risen, our *guru* Sāndīpani had realized that we were lost, and accompanied by the other disciples, he had found us in a bewildered state. Our *guru* was touched by our devotion to his instructions, and blessed us by saying that all our knowledge of the *Veda* will never fail.

Having conversed with his friend, Kṛṣna turned to him and asked in a joking mood as to what he had brought him. Considering his humble offering, the brahmin felt bashful and did not hand over his offering of fried rice. Kṛṣna understood that his friend had come on his wife's request and that the brahmin was not motivated by a desire to attain any kind of wealth from him. Having decided to bestow immense wealth upon his devoted friend, Kṛṣṇa snatched the parcel of rice and ate a handful of it. The next morning the brahmin left for his home, happy at heart for meeting his beloved friend, although abashed for not having requested any riches from him. He was reflecting upon the warm reception he had received, how he sat on the same sofa with Kṛṣṇa, just like a brother, and how Kṛṣṇa showed his respect and love for the brahmins by washing his feet. Śrīdāman had considered Kṛṣṇa to be very merciful by not having bestowed any wealth upon him, as to keep him humble and austere. As he returned home, the brahmin realized that a marvellous palace had appeared on the site, surrounded by pleasure gardens, exotic birds, water ponds and lotus flowers. A crew of servants were ready to attend him, and his wife, being dressed opulently, had happily received him. At that time he reflected upon the generosity of his friend, Kṛṣṇa, who had given him so much, despite the humble offering brought to him by the brahmin. Reflecting on the whole affair, Śrīdāman prayed to be blessed with Kṛṣṇa's friendship in future births, and to always associate with his devotees.

Discussion

This story exemplifies the mood of friendship mixed with servitude. On the one hand, the brahmin is Kṛṣṇa's friend, but his feelings of friendship are mixed, so to speak, with servitude and devotion. In his present state, the brahmin belonged to a different class than Kṛṣṇa, as he was a brahmin, while Kṛṣṇa was a king. This difference in class evoked some formalities, as the brahmin paid Kṛṣṇa the respect due to a king, while Kṛṣna paid the brahmin the respect due to brahmins. However, despite these formalities the two friends did share a common experience, which served as a basis for fraternity and friendship, and this is the experience of living in the same *gurukula*, and serving the same preceptor. Especially meaningful was the night in which they were both lost in the frightening forest, while trying to serve their *guru* by fetching wood. That experience of the two young boys holding hands in the dark forest while searching for their way out, and the great satisfaction their guru experienced realizing their devotion unto him, became a deeply unifying experience and established strong bonds between them, a bond which remained for years to come. Although the brahmin realized Kṛṣṇa's divine lordship, this sense of friendship still remained vital enough as to be expressed many years later.

Sakhya: Arjuna Remembering His Friendship with Kṛṣṇa (*BhP* 1.15.1–21)

Having returned from Dvārakā and realizing that the Yadu clan had been annihilated by a fratricidal war, Arjuna's eyes teared up on account of his affection for his dear friend Śrī Kṛṣṇa, and he expressed his deep feelings of separation from his comrade. Remembering their companionship Arjuna said:

> O Yudhiṣṭhira, I have been deceived by the Supreme Person who assumed the form of my kinsmen, by separation from whom the world becomes empty and deprived of life. It was by Kṛṣṇa's power that I was able to hit the fish target and defeat all the assembled kings at Draupadī's *svayaṁvara* ceremony. Kṛṣna who had come to visit us while in the forest had eaten a remnant of a vegetable preparation, thereby saving us from the curse of Durvāsas who came to dine with us along with his ten thousand disciples. As Kṛṣṇa ate from that preparation, Durvāsas and his entourage all became satiated thereby giving up the idea of dining with us, and thus were we saved from Durvāsas' curse, which would have come upon us had we failed to feed that huge crowd. Kṛṣṇa had become my charioteer, and led me through the Kuru army consisting of Bhīṣma, Karṇa, Droṇa and Śalya. By his glance, all these warriors were deprived of their strength, skills and life. Just as the missiles of the *asuras* aimed at Prahlāda did not hurt him, being protected by Govinda, similarly missiles aimed at me by the *Kuru* generals did not hurt me as I was protected by Kṛṣṇa. The Lord of the universe was employed by such a vicious-minded person like me, as a charioteer, though his lotus-like feet were sought after by those desirous of *mokṣa*. Protected by his powers my enemies did not assail me while I was standing on the ground, my horses being exhausted from the battle. It breaks my heart to remember Mādhava's jokes accompanied by his sweet smile and his heart

touching speech, addressing me as 'O Arjuna my friend.' Being close associates, we have been sleeping, eating, sitting, wandering, prattling, and even boasting together. He used to tease me, and at the same time tolerated my faults in a friendly manner. I am the same Arjuna, I have the same bow, arrows, chariot and horses, but in the absence of Śrī Kṛṣṇa all these seem to be bereft of reality and void, just like offering butter into ashes, or sowing seeds in barren land.

Discussion

After Kṛṣṇa had left the planet, Arjuna recalled their sweet relationship, which was clearly in the mood of *sakhya* or friendship. Underlying these fraternal relations was a sense of equality, furthered by their sharing a similarity of age, a common family, and a similar royal class. Kṛṣṇa has shown his fraternal love for Arjuna by saving him and his family from various dangerous situations, and giving him the ability to achieve victory during the royal competition over Draupadī. However, their relationship was not only chivalrous, but rather intimate as well. As such they slept together, ate, sat, wandered about, conversed, joked and boasted, as close friends do. In doing so, Arjuna was not aware of Kṛṣṇa's divinity and of his being the Supreme Person. The sense of awe and reverence accompanying this realization did not enter their relationship. However, as Arjuna recalls the past, he reflects upon Kṛṣṇa's supremacy too and, realizing that, his emotions intensify even further, contemplating how the Supreme Person became his charioteer. It seems that characterizing *sakhya-rasa* as intimate in mutuality and equality 'as a friend loves a companion'[28] fits well Arjuna's relationship with his friend Kṛṣṇa.

Sakhya: Kṛṣṇa and His Playmates in *Vraja* (*BhP* 10.12.1–12)

One morning, Kṛṣṇa got up early and woke up his fellow cowherd boys by blowing his horn. Many affectionate and joyful young boys gathered to Kṛṣṇa's call, each leading his own herd of calves and, together with Kṛṣṇa's herd, they all proceeded to the forest. The boys were equipped with slings, horns and flutes, and decorated with precious stones and golden ornaments, as well as flowers and feathers. Having reached the forest, they let their calves graze around and started playing among themselves. As such, they stole each other's slings and the like, and laughingly threw them from one boy to another. When Kṛṣṇa had gone to a distance observing the beauty of the forest, the boys competed over who would touch him first. Some played their flutes, some blew their horns, some hummed, imitating the bees, and some imitated the sweet notes of the cuckoo bird. Some ran after the shadows of the flying birds, some imitated the swans, some sat down near the cranes while others danced with the peacocks. Some pulled the monkeys' tails, some made wry faces at the monkeys while others climbed on the trees and jumped from branch to branch with the monkeys. Hopping with the frogs, some became drenched with the waters of the streams and the waterfalls, while others were looking into their own reflection in the water. In this way, the cowherd boys who have accumulated a vast amount of good deeds in previous lives were able to play with Kṛṣṇa who was the Supreme Person himself.

Discussion

This lovely passage describes a scene that later develops into the episodes of the 'Slaying of the Agha demon', 'Brahmā's steeling away the boys and the calves', 'The slaying of Dhenuka' and the 'Expulsion of the Kāliya serpent', all exemplifying the deep friendship and fraternity exchanged between Kṛṣṇa and his friends in *sakhya rasa*. In those lovely scenes Kṛṣṇa is part of a group of young cowherd boys who love him and enjoy his association as their beloved peer or pal. Schweig writes:

> The endearing love of close friendship is now experienced with the supreme beloved, who places himself on an equal level with the soul. This love is characterized by confidential, even playful and affectionate exchanges. Mutual love constitutes a greater level of intimacy with the divine, since the superior position of the beloved is no longer acknowledged.[29]

This description seems to befit well the relationships of the cowherd boy with Kṛṣṇa, as their jolly, affectionate and playful mood is devoid of formalities and based on a notion of equality, that is that they are all boys of the same age, community and occupation. This passage undoubtedly serves as one of the *BhP*'s emotional peaks.

Vātsalya: The Birth of Śrī Kṛṣṇa *(BhP* 10.3.199)

As a favourable constellation of the stars came about, the world became full of all kinds of auspicious signs. As such, despite the rainy seasons, all directions became clear and the sky was illumined with shining stars. The waters of the rivers became crystal clear, the lakes were blooming with lotuses, and the forest trees were laden with beautiful flowers. Various kinds of bird chirped sweetly, and the Brahmins' domestic fires burst into flames. The Gandharvas[30] sang beautiful melodies, and the gods showered flowers from the sky. At midnight, Viṣṇu, who dwells in everyone's heart, manifested himself in his own complete divine form through Devakī, just as the full moon rises in the eastern horizon. Vasudeva saw that wonderful child of lotus - like eyes, endowed with four arms, holding a conch, a mace, a discus and a lotus.[31] He was gorgeously dressed with yellow garments and decorated with valuable ornaments. Realizing that their son is no other than the Supreme Person himself, Vasudeva and Devakī began to praise him with folded hands. Vasudeva said:

> You are the Supreme Person, transcendental to and distinct from *prakṛti*; how blessed am I for having seen you directly in person. You have incarnated in my own house, or rather prison cell, with a desire to protect the world, and annihilate the hordes of demonaic forces appearing as *kṣatriyas*.

Devakī said:

> Please protect us, who are your devotees, from the wicked Kaṁsa. But also, let not this divine form of yours manifest to the general public, because as soon as Kaṁsa hears of your appearance, he will try to harm you. It is certainly wonderful that the Supreme Person got accommodated in my womb, but may you now withdraw this superhuman four-armed form in favour of a normal human baby form:

Answering his devoted parents, Kṛṣṇa spoke:

> In your previous life you were Pṛśni and Sutapas, and you had performed severe austerities together, while at the same time

> fixing the mind and heart on me. As I was pleased with your devotion and austerities, I had manifested before you and offered you a boon, to which you responded by requesting to have a son like me. As nobody else is comparable to me, I myself was born as your son and known as Pṛṣṇi-garbha. In a future life you appeared as Aditi and Kaśyapa, and I was born as your son Upendra known also as Vāmana, and now, I am appearing for the third time as your son. By constantly thinking of me as your son, and by loving me affectionately, both of you will attain the highest state in relation to me. If you are still afraid of Kaṁsa, please take me to *Gokula* and replace me with the baby girl just born to Yaśodā.

Having spoken thus, the Supreme Person assumed the form of an ordinary baby. By divine illusion, the prison gate keepers all fell asleep, Vasudeva's chains were open, and so were the prison gates. Vasudeva took baby Kṛṣṇa and walked towards Gokula, and when he had reached the banks of the stormy river Yamunā the river had miraculously afforded passage to Vasudeva and Kṛṣṇa. Arriving at Nanda's house in *Vraja*, Vasudeva found all the family members absorbed in deep sleep. Nanda's wife, Yaśodā, had just delivered a baby but, due to being exhausted, she fell into deep sleep without noticing that it was a girl she gave birth to. Vasudeva exchanged the two babies and returned with the baby girl to the prison.

Discussion

The story begins with a description of the various auspicious signs preceding the birth of the divine child, thus evoking a festive mood. As Kṛṣṇa had first appeared in the form of Viṣṇu, his parents praised him in a manner befitting the Supreme Lord, in a rather formal way. However, Devakī's speech exemplifies the shift from the reverential mood into the parental or maternal, as at first she asks Kṛṣṇa to protect them, but soon wants to protect Kṛṣṇa herself. She therefore asks Kṛṣṇa to withdraw this superhuman four-armed form in favour of a normal human baby form, so that Kaṁsa would not recognize him and consequently harm him. This shows the tension or even contradiction between the *vātsalya* mood and knowledge. When Kṛṣṇa's parents know him to be the Supreme Person, they treat him in awe and reverence, and ask for his protection. However, only when this knowledge is lost in favour of some delusion or even ignorance of his supreme position can they enter into the parental mood, treat him like a child, try to protect him and so forth. As such, knowledge prevents entering into the emotional mood of *vātsalya*.

In his speech, Kṛṣṇa explains the circumstances and reasons by which he had become Vasudeva and Devakī's son. Reciprocating their austerities and devotion, he had appeared as their son three times in three different life periods. Kṛṣṇa tells his devotees that by entering the parental mood, that is loving him affectionately as their son, they will attain the highest state in relation to him, presumably a devotional version of *mokṣa* in which the devotees attain to Kṛṣṇa's planet named *Gokula* or a similar state. This means that the parental form of devotion is considered at least equal to the more common type of devotion, that is, devotion in the mood of servitude, in that it results in liberation from *saṁsāra* and the attainment of the highest state. As the story continues, Kṛṣṇa assumes an ordinary baby form. Vasudeva assumes the role of a caring father and, helped by miraculous powers, carries baby Kṛṣṇa to *Gokula* and exchanges him with Yaśodā's baby girl, for the sake protecting him from the evil Kaṁsa. Sweig's characterization of this relationship as caring and protective certainly applies to the mood of Vasudeva and Devakī, both of whom were ready to give up the company of their wonderful baby for the sake of caring for him and protecting him by transferring him to *Gokula*. Kṛṣṇa's seeming dependency on his parents serves to further enhance and deepen the relationships.

Vātsalya: Baby Kṛṣṇa's Sports in Vraja (*BhP* 10.8.21–52.201)

A short while after Kṛṣṇa and Balarāma had gone through the name-giving ceremony, they began to creep on their hands and knees around *Gokula*. Their crawling around *Vraja* evoked a sweet tinkling sound from their tiny ankle bells. They followed the passers-by for a few steps and then hurried back to their mothers, as if bewildered and frightened. Due to motherly affection, milk flowed from their mothers' breasts, while they embraced their baby sons in their arms. The mothers experienced great delight observing their sons' countenances and infant smiles, and were moved by realizing that the babies' first and tender teeth started to grow. When the boys grew up further, they played by holding the tails of the calves, being dragged hither and thither. Forgetting their household duties, the women of *Vraja* burst out laughing and were overwhelmed with joy at the sight. The mothers experienced not merely delight, but anxiety as well. As the playful boys were so active, it was difficult to restrain them and therefore the mothers were constantly striving to protect them from all sorts of dangers, such as horned beasts, fire, dangerous birds, water, weapons, thorns and such like.

When the boys grew up further and began walking, they started playing with boys of their age. Kṛṣṇa sometimes behaved naughtily, performing all kinds of mischievous activities. He had therefore let the calves loose untimely, thus allowing them to drink the cows' milk just before the milking was completed. Sometimes he stole curd and ate it, and sometimes he even distributed that to the monkeys. When the pots of curd were hanged up high, Kṛṣṇa managed to reach them by climbing on a chair or a wooden mortar, breaking the clay pot for the purpose of getting the curd. When the room was dark, Kṛṣṇa used his own shining person and bright jewels as a source of light, and found that which he was after. Sometimes he even passed urine in neat and clean houses and, after all these mischievous deeds, behaved as if he was an innocent boy of a good behaviour. All these naughty activities of Kṛṣṇa, made Yaśodā smile with motherly affection, and she did not punish Kṛṣṇa at all.

One day, the cowherd boys headed by Balarāma, who were all playing together, came to Kṛṣṇa's mother, Yaśodā, and complained that Kṛṣṇa had eaten earth. Yaśodā rebuked her boy for having secretly eaten mud, but Kṛṣṇa in reply denied that it was the case. Yaśodā then asked Kṛṣṇa to open his mouth so she could see for herself, and Kṛṣṇa opened his mouth as requested. When Yaśodā looked into the child's widely open mouth, she was struck to see the entire universe. As such, she saw the gross and subtle elements, the whole planetary system along with the presiding deities, time, nature, the souls, the earth along with mountains, the oceans and continents, as well as the whole of *Vraja* including herself looking into her child's open mouth. Yaśodā was struck with wonder and was not able to ascertain whether this was a dream or illusion, or a manifestation of her child's divinity. For a moment she rose above the illusion of identifying herself with her earthly figure of a cowherd woman in *Vraja*, but then she was again covered by divine illusion and continued to experience motherly affection towards her son. Forgetting the wonderful revelation she had just encountered, Yaśodā placed her son Kṛṣṇa on her lap and continued to experience intense motherly affection towards him as before.

At this point, the text raises the question: How were Nanda and Yaśodā so fortunate, as to become the parents of The Supreme? The answer given is that both Nanda and Yaśodā had served the god Brahmā in a previous life and, in answer to their request, had received the boon of giving birth on earth as devotees of the Supreme Lord Hari. As such, they had become Nanda and Yaśodā, and served the Supreme Lord, who had become their son, with utmost devotion.

Discussion

These episodes offer an insight into the mood of parental or rather maternal affection, as both mothers of Kṛṣṇa and Balarāma enjoy deep motherly feelings of affection towards their special children. As such, they derive great pleasure from hearing the sweet sounds of their babies' ankle bells, and from protecting their babies when they are bewildered and frightened. Similarly, the mothers are excited to see the growing of the babies' tender teeth, and later watch their playing with the calves. It seems that not only do the mothers experience these maternal emotions, but that the other cowherd women of *Vraja* share in these emotions, too. Even Kṛṣṇa's naughty behaviour serves the purpose of inciting further loving emotions in his mother, and presumably in the other women involved. The whole scene therefore exemplifies the emotional state of maternal affection. The story then takes an interesting turn and describes the supernatural incident in which Yaśodā had encountered a revelation through looking into the mouth of her child.

This incident highlights the inherent conflict between the motherly experience of *vātsalya rasa* and knowledge. As soon as she became aware of her child's supreme position, her maternal affection was lost and replaced by a mood of awe and reverence, which emotionally represents *śānta*. Only when she fell again under the illusion that Kṛṣṇa is nothing but her child could she again experience her maternal mood. By this, the text supports an insight into her emotional mood, and emphasizes that the parental and maternal affection are in need of some delusion, or a lack of true knowledge. As such, when Yaśodā received true knowledge of her son's supreme position, she was not able to maintain her motherly affection and mood any longer, and only when she fell under illusion again was she able to express herself as a mother. Having supplied some insight into the nature of *vātsalya*, the text raises the question: How was it possible for Nanda and Yaśodā to attain such a supreme position, of becoming the Supreme Person's parents? The answer is that it was a boon granted to them in previous life, when they desired to become devotees of the supreme and practise the highest form of devotion. This supreme form of devotion achieved by them was in the mood of *vātsalya*. Schweig's characterization of this mood of a parent loving a child as 'deep and tender', involving 'nurturing affection', certainly applies here. Similarly, 'a constant mindfulness and a sense of responsibility for the well-being of the beloved' are major components of Yaśodā's love for her child, Kṛṣṇa.[32]

Śṛṅgāra: Rukminī and Kṛṣṇa (*BhP* 10.52.21ff., 10.53, 54, 60, 204)

Rukminī was the daughter of the celebrated Bhīṣmaka, the *Vidarbha* king, and as she heard about the beauty, prowess, excellent virtues and affluence of Kṛṣṇa from travelling bards who used to visit her father's palace, she made up her mind to marry him. Kṛṣṇa on his part heard about Rukminī's intelligence, auspicious characteristics, nobility of heart, beauty and high character, and desired to marry her too. In spite of all her brothers supporting her marriage to Kṛṣṇa, her eldest brother, Rukmi, who disliked Kṛṣṇa, tried to prevent the marriage and arranged for her marriage to Kṛṣṇa's enemy, Prince Śiśupāla. Understanding the situation, Rukminī wrote Kṛṣṇa a letter and sent it to Dvārakā with a loyal brahmin messenger. Rukminī wrote:

> Oh Kṛṣṇa, lion among men! What girl of noble descent will not seek you as a husband? You are most beautiful, and excel in family, character, personal charm, knowledge youthfulness, affluence and splendour. I have therefore chosen you as my husband and submit myself unto you. Please take me as your wife! As my brother has arranged my marriage to Śiśupāla, please come and snatch me away by force before the marriage takes place. Oh Lord, great souls perform severe austerities in order to attain the dust of your feet. If I do not receive your mercy and become your wife, I shall starve myself to death and observe other vows, so that at least after a hundred births I will be favoured by your grace.

Hearing Rukminī's message, Kṛṣṇa said to the brahmin messenger, 'Just as Rukminī has fixed her mind on me, similarly did I fix my mind on her. I will vanquish Rukmi and his royal friends in battle and take away Rukminī by force.'

Mounting his chariot drawn by his four famous swift horses and driven by Dāruka, his charioteer, Kṛṣṇa speedily travelled to the city of Vidarbha. As the marriage ceremony was soon to commence, the city was gorgeously decorated with banners, and the residents were decorated with fragrant flower garlands and dressed with immaculate clothes. The king had worshipped the brahmins, and they were performing various auspicious *Vedic* ceremonies. King Damaghoṣa, Śiśupāla's father, entered the city accompanied by regiments of elephants, chariots, cavalry and infantry, and was formally received by Bhīṣmaka, king of Vidarbha. Many prominent and powerful kings who were Śiśupāla's allies, such as Śālva, Jarāsandha and Dantavakra, accompanied by their powerful armies, entered the city, too. As they were aware of the possibility of Kṛṣṇa trying to forcefully kidnap Rukminī, they made plans to prevent this from happening by arraying their phalanx in a protective manner around the princess. Hearing that Kṛṣṇa had gone on his own to kidnap Rukminī, his brother Balarāma followed him, heading a big army. Meanwhile, the time for the marriage celebration was approaching, and the bride was becoming more anxious and nervous, fearing that Kṛṣṇa would not appear in time. At that time the brahmin messenger had reached the harem, and she was delighted and overjoyed to hear that not only was Kṛṣṇa nearby, but that he had promised to take her away. Hearing that Kṛṣṇa and Balarāma had arrived, Bhīṣmaka happily received them respectfully as honoured guests, and offered them luxurious accommodation. The town residents came to see Kṛṣṇa and Balarāma, and all felt that it was Kṛṣṇa whom Rukminī should marry.

As the ceremony began, Rukminī, protected by the royal guards and deeply absorbed in thinking about Kṛṣṇa, proceeded towards the temple of the goddess in order to worship her and beg her blessings for the marriage. As Rukminī, surrounded by her consorts, approached the goddess, she prayed to have Kṛṣṇa as her husband. As Rukminī exited the temple, the assembled kings and their forces were struck by the wonder of her beauty. They unconsciously laid down their weapons and stared at the exquisite young princess, who was excited to recognize Kṛṣṇa present in the crowd. At that moment and in the midst of all the assembled kings and barons, Kṛṣṇa snatched Rukminī and seated her on his chariot, and fearlessly departed towards Dvārakā accompanied by Balarāma and his army. The humiliated kings headed by Jarasāndha could not tolerate the insult and rose up to attack Kṛṣṇa. The Yādava army counter-attacked and a fierce battle took place. Rukminī turned to her Lord fearfully, but Kṛṣṇa assured her of their victory thus laughing away her fear. As the battle went on, the Yādavas overcame the army headed by Jarāsandha and soon hordes of slain soldiers and animals lay dead on the battlefield, while Jarāsandha and his followers turned back and fled away. They all approached Śiśupāla who was lamenting and grieving, and offered their condolences, then departed for their respective cities. Having reached Dvārakā, the whole city along with many noble guests celebrated the marriage of Kṛṣṇa and Rukminī.

One day, Rukminī was waiting upon her beloved husband while he was comfortably relaxing on an excellent white cushion, and she started fanning him with a golden handle fan. At that time, desiring to remove a tinge of pride from Rukminī's heart due to her being so close to him, and wanting to test her love, Kṛṣṇa spoke to her as follows:

> Oh princess, you were sought after by the leading rulers of the earth who were endowed with beauty, wealth, magnanimity and might, and whose affluence and power equalled those of the gods. Why did you reject the noble Śiśupāla to whom you were given by your father and brother, and select me, who am in no way a match to these great monarchs? It is advisable that marriage and friendship take place between those who are equal in wealth, heredity, power, beauty and the like, and not between inferiors and superiors. As I am inferior to you in every respect, you may still choose a hero of your stature such as Śiśupāla, Śālva, Jarāsandha and the like, and give up my company, for I at any rate do not have much interest in worldly affairs.

Upon hearing this surprising speech, Rukminī began to tremble and shed tears. Scratching the floor with her foot, her face cast down, her voice choked with excessive grief. The fan dropped from her hand, she lost her consciousness, fainted and fell down like an uprooted tree. It had occurred to Kṛṣṇa that due to her deep love and attachment for him, his beloved could not understand the subtle significance of his joking words, and that evoked in his heart loving feelings towards her. He quickly lifted her up, gently wiped her face with his hand, wiped away the tears from her eyes and hugged his beloved and faithful wife. He offered her consolation and comforted her with gentle words, thus relieving his broken-hearted queen from the anxiety caused by his misunderstood joking words, which really, she did not deserve. Kṛṣṇa begged Rukminī to not be displeased with him, and said that he was hoping to only slightly agitate her so that he could behold her beauty being intensified by anger. Rukminī said:

> It is true that we are not equals in any way, but the real reason is that being the Supreme Person, you are much superior to me. Although there are indeed women who although married, have their minds dwell on another, I pray that my love to you be everlasting.

To this Kṛṣṇa replied:

> My joking words were meant to make you speak these words, which I desired to hear. Your deep love for me as your husband has been proven, and I am very much indebted to your devotion. Such attachment and devotion as you have shown towards me liberates one from *saṁsāra*, and is indeed difficult to practise for a wife who is not as faithful to me as you are. Although I have many wives, I have no other such loving wife, who has sacrificed so much for my sake. You rejected great monarchs in order to marry me, although you have never before met me in person. You have sent me a brahmin messenger, and were ready to give up your life in case I didn't come, thus proving your supreme love to me which is impossible for me to repay.

Discussion

The story of Rukminī exemplifies the amorous sentiment experienced between a married couple, Kṛṣṇa accepting the role of the husband, while his devotee accepting the role of his religiously married wife. The husband and wife relationship takes place within the social arena and within the framework of *dharma*. Kṛṣṇa's opulence and supreme position is also known here, and serves as an incitement for further loving him, and is one of his attractive features. Rukminī's devotion is expressed here as the devotion of a bride to her bridegroom, or later, as the devotion of a loving wife to her husband. Thus, the various difficulties undergone by her in the course of her service to her husband, Kṛṣṇa, are considered to release her from the state of *saṁsāra*, just as other forms of devotion and service to the supreme award liberation. The characterization of this mood as 'most intimate'[33] certainly applies here as in many respects, Kṛṣṇa and Rukminī exemplify the ideal couple, compared only to Sītā and Rāma.

Śṛṅgāra: The *Rāsa Līlā* Episode (*BhP* 10. 29–33.208)

As the autumn was approaching, Kṛṣṇa realized how beautiful the *Vraja* area had become, and made up his mind to engage in amorous affairs with the *gopīs*. Beholding the beautiful moon, Kṛṣṇa started to play melodious music on his flute to capture the minds of the lovely cowherd damsels and housewives. The *gopīs*, who were captivated by the sounds of the flute, were so eager to join Kṛṣṇa and left their various engagements hastily. Some who were milking cows left the milking half done, some left in the middle of serving food to their family members, some who were suckling their babies just put them down and left, and others who were waiting upon their husbands just stopped and departed to meet Kṛṣṇa. So eager were the *gopīs* to meet Kṛṣṇa that they even neglected their own appearance. As such some went in a disorderly fashion, while others who started to apply make up left it unfinished and rushed to the forest. Although prevented by their relatives, and even forbidden by their husbands, fathers and brothers from going, the *gopīs* acted as if hypnotized, and ignoring any consequences rushed to meet their beloved Kṛṣṇa. The desire to unite with their beloved Kṛṣṇa and their agony over unbearable separation from him served to wash away their inauspicious *karma* and posit them above the three *guṇas*. Although the *gopīs* didn't know Kṛṣṇa to be the Supreme *Brahman* but considered him to be their lover only, and although they were attracted to him through desires that are ordinarily within the realm of the *guṇas*, they still rose to a position above the *guṇas* due to their love for him.[34]

Seeing the damsels of *Vraja* approaching him, Kṛṣṇa addressed them with fascinating expressions and said:

> My dear beautiful ladies, what is the cause of your hasty arrival here? This fearful forest is not a proper place for a woman to stay at night, and your relatives must be searching for you. Therefore please return home. Perhaps you have come as your heart is attached to me and as you feel deep affection for me, and want to be with me in this beautiful forest illuminated by the full moon, but it is the duty of a woman to render service to her husband with a sincere heart, even though he may sometimes be ill-natured or quarrelsome, and resorting to illicit relations with a paramour is an obstacle to the attainment of heaven. Devotion to me is engendered by hearing of me, looking at me, thinking of me and so forth, and not necessarily by physical proximity. Therefore, please return home.

Having heard Kṛṣṇa's words, the *gopīs* grew despondent and frustrated. Their beautiful faces cast down in disappointment, scratching the ground with their toe-nails, they stood silently, heavily burdened with distress. Having discarded their cherished for Kṛṣṇa's sake, being deeply attached to him, and being offended by his rejecting them, they spoke to him as follows:

> It does not befit you to speak to us, your devotees who have sacrificed so much for being here with you, in this way. As far as our *dharma*, by serving you who is the soul of the universe, we serve everyone else and fulfil our duties, and besides, being attracted to you we have lost all interest in engaging with our household duties. Please, therefore, extinguish with the nectar of your lips the passion in our hearts, set aflame by your smiles, furtive glances and melodious music.

Having thus spoken the *gopīs* surrounded Kṛṣṇa who looked like the full moon surrounded by stars. Exciting amorous sentiments in the beautiful damsels of *Vraja* by embracing them, touching their hands, hair, thighs, waists and bosoms, Kṛṣṇa gave them great delight.

At that point Kṛṣṇa disappeared from their sight, and the *gopīs*, missing Kṛṣṇa greatly and experiencing intense separation, began imitating him and playing Kṛṣṇa's role, as if they were in a dramatic performance. As such, two *gopīs* played the role of Kṛṣṇa and Balarāma, while others played the role of the cowherd boys. One *gopī* emulated him by acting as she was playing a flute, while another *gopī* embraced another *gopī* and called, 'Look, I am Kṛṣṇa'. They started wandering around the forest in search of Kṛṣṇa, while addressing various trees and asking them whether they had seen their beloved. At a certain point they recognized Kṛṣṇa's footprints on the ground, and started following them. However, they were disappointed to realize that beside Kṛṣṇa's footprints were another set of footprints that apparently belonged to a young woman.

Then the maid's footprints disappeared and, as Kṛṣṇa's footprints became deeper, the *gopīs* realized that Kṛṣṇa had carried her on his shoulders, and apparently kissed her in a secret place. Soon, the *gopīs* found Kṛṣṇa's beloved *gopī* alone in the forest. It occurred to them that she felt somewhat proud to occupy the position of Kṛṣṇa's beloved *gopī*, and, as such, he had left her alone and disappeared from her sight.

The *gopīs* started praying to Kṛṣṇa and begging him to return. They said:

> Dear Kṛṣṇa, your hearty laughs, your loving ogling, your lovely sports, your enchanting jokes and acts in privacy have all deeply entered our hearts and agitated them. Oh beloved, when you go out of *Vraja* to graze the cattle, our hearts get agitated thinking that your lotus-like feet will be pricked and pained by blades of grass. Oh delightful enchanter, be pleased to place your feet on our bosom, and please grant us the nectar of your lips which enchants the charm of amorous enjoyment and destroys all grief, a nectar which is fully enjoyed by your flute. We long to see you all day, when you are away in the forest. When you return, however, we complain that the creator has created our eyelids which while blinking, deprive us from a moment's joy of looking at you. Remembering your secret amorous promises and beholding your smiling face and your broad chest, passion is provoked in our hearts and we get excited with an excessive desire to be in your proximity. Who would abandon poor women like us, who have left husbands, children and relatives for your sake?

Kṛṣṇa then appeared surprisingly in their midst, with his lotus-like face beaming with a smile, wearing a yellow garment and adorned with a garland of beautiful flowers. Seeing their beloved, the *gopīs* at once rose to their feet delighted and, once again, gained their vitality. In their ecstasy, they all surrounded him in great love. As such, one *gopī* clasped Kṛṣṇa's lotus hand with her palms while another *gopī* placed his lotus feet on her bosom. One *gopī* meditated on Kṛṣṇa as established in her heart. She first closed her eyes as to prevent his exit, and then mentally embraced him being immersed in bliss. With their anguish completely dissipated by extreme joy, the *gopīs* accomplished their desires to their heart's content. With their upper garments coloured with saffron spots applied to their breasts, they prepared a seat for Kṛṣṇa who spoke to them as follows:

> Seeing your intensity and the constancy of your devotion to me, I remained with you invisibly, enjoying your devotion to me. It is not possible for me to adequately repay your devoted service, expressed through pure and faultless relationships. Sacrificing your ties to your kith and kin, you have resorted to me and served me with love. May your loving service unto me be your reward.

Hearing the soft words of their lord, the *gopīs* gave up all agony caused by separation from him. There, at the banks of the *Yamunā*, Govinda inaugurated his *Rāsa Līla* with the beautiful and devoted *gopīs* of *Vraja*. They all formed a large circle, and Kṛṣṇa miraculously expanded himself and assumed as many forms as the *gopīs* so that he could personally enter between every two *gopīs* and embrace them. At that time kettle drums sounded and showers of flowers fell from the sky, as the gods came to observe this wonderful scene. With their artistic movements, their smiles and amorous glances, with bending waists and shaking breasts, with their braids of hair and girdle getting loosened in the course of dancing, the *gopīs* glorified Kṛṣṇa in songs, singing at the pitch of their voices sweet songs. Seeing that the *gopīs* were becoming tired, Kṛṣṇa affectionately wiped the sweat off their faces, and in their company entered the waters of the *Yamunā*, where they all continued to sport together, the *gopīs* sprinkling water on him from all sides, while heartily laughing and casting amorous glances at him.

Discussion

This beautiful and romantic episode is no doubt a world classic. With regards to the *Rāsa Līlā* Schweig writes:

> It is a dramatic poem about young maidens joining with their ideal beloved to perform the wondrous 'circle dance of love', or *Rāsa* [. . .] Undeniably, its charming poetic imagery, combined with deeply resonating devotional motifs, expresses to any reader much about the nature of love. Narrated in eloquently rich and flowing Sanskrit verse, it has been recognized as one of the most beautiful love poems ever written.[35]

The beautiful rural scene serves as a background to this unique love story. As opposed to the love of Rukminī and Kṛṣṇa, which falls under the category of *svakīyā* or the relations between a husband and his religiously married wife, the present story falls under the category of *parakīyā*, or amorous relations between a man and another's wife, relations that due to their being illicit and socially unacceptable, become more intense. The story seems to consider the *gopīs*' desires and attraction towards Kṛṣṇa to be an expression of pure devotion, and this seems to indicate the *pariṇāma* nature of the text already discussed extensively in this work. As such, ordinary emotions can undergo sublimation and be transformed into pure *rasas* to be exchanged with Kṛṣṇa.

The text applies indirect speech in a suggestive and provocative way, and this characterizes Kṛṣṇa's speech, where he preaches to the *gopīs* a sermon on *dharma* and duty, explicitly sending them back home but implicitly urging them to stay with him. The *gopīs*' mood of separation expressed after Kṛṣṇa had disappeared from their sight exemplifies the depth of love in separation, which was expressed, inter alia, in their imitating him and acting his person in his absence. Then, Kṛṣṇa's return fills them with great joy, and being united with him, they enjoy his company to their hearts' content. Kṛṣṇa, on his part, considers them to not only be his lovers but his devotees as well, reinforcing the idea that loving him in an amorous fashion is not only a legitimate expression of devotion, but its highest form. Finally, the *rāsa* dance itself no doubt occupies the peak of the entire *BhP*, and that is reinforced by the gods attending the scene with astonishment and showering flowers from the sky on the participants.

Characterizing the amorous *rasa* of *śṛṅgāra* as 'loving the beloved in the most intimate way, as a lover loves a beloved in a conjugal, premarital, or extramarital relationship', certainly applies to this episode. His pointing at the 'intensity of amorous feelings exchanged', which represents the greatest attainable intimacy in *rasa*, and the 'total self-surrender of the lover in an exclusive passionate union with the divine', fits well here, especially since the *gopīs* have abandoned and surrendered their families and social position for the sake of union with Kṛṣṇa. The feelings of intense separation expressed in Kṛṣṇa's absence are another intensifying agent, and as such, and in compatibility with both Bhoja's and Rūpa's aesthetic theories, it is no surprise that Schweig considers this to be the 'highest *rasa*',[36] containing the essential elements of all four other *rasas*.

GLOSSARY

Abhinavagupta:	eleventh-century Kashmiri theorist of aesthetics, author of *Abhinavabhāratī*
ācārya:	teacher, preceptor
adharma:	that which is contrary to *dharma*, improper, immoral, unlawful
Advaita Vedānta:	a non-dual *Vedānta* school whose famous exponent is Śaṅkara
ahaṅkāra:	lit. 'I am the doer'; ego, self-consciousness, the eighth element
ajñāna:	ignorance, absence of knowledge
ānanda:	bliss, one of the three qualities of *Brahman*
anitya:	finite, temporary, non-eternal
anubhāva:	the aesthetic component in a play, comprised of words and gestures, enabling the drama's emotional experience
apauruṣeya:	knowledge received from non-human sources: *śruti* or the *Veda*
āśrama:	one of the two categories of *dharma*, which defines one's personal stage of life in terms of *brahmācarya*, *gṛhastha*, *vānaprastha* and *sannyāsa*
aṣṭāṅga yoga:	a ladder-like *yoga* system of eight limbs or stages
āstika:	traditions conforming to *śruti* or the *Veda* such as the six orthodox *darśanas*

asuras:	demons, the opponents of the *devas*, the demonic enemies of the gods
ātman:	the conscious and eternal self, the spiritual soul
avatāra:	divine descent, the Supreme Person appearing in this world in a human or a non-human form
avidyā:	absence of knowledge, ignorance
avyakta:	undifferentiated *prakṛti* in a primordial state prior to the creation
bandha:	bondage to repeated births and deaths
Bhagavad Gītā:	lit. 'the Supreme Person's sacred poetical treatise', the classic Hindu treatise sometimes considered to be the 'Indian Bible'
bhagavān:	the Supreme Person who possess all personal opulence
bhakta:	devotee
bhakti:	devotion in a religious context
bhakti yoga:	a path leading to *mokṣa* wherein the devotional practices become *yogīc* practices
Bhaktirasāmṛtasindhu:	a sixteenth-century text compiled by Rūpa Gosvāmin, in which devotion is articulated in terms of Bharata rasa theory
Bharata:	the legendary author of the *Nāṭyaśāstra*
bhāva:	emotion or feeling, the foundation of *rasa*
Bhoja of *Dhārā*:	an eleventh-century Rajasthani king, theorist of aesthetics and author of *Sarasvatī-kaṇṭhābharaṇa* and *Śṛṅgāra-prakāśa*
Brahmā:	a *Vedic* god, the creator of the universe whose planet is the highest in the universe
brahmacārī:	a celibate student who studies under the *guru* and practices various types of austerities
brahmacarya:	the first stage in the *āśrama* system, wherein the celibate student studies under the *guru*
brahma jñāna:	knowledge of *Brahman*
Brahman:	the Supreme, either impersonal or personal
Brahma Sūtra:	also called *Vedānta Sūtra*; one of the three founding texts of the *Vedānta* tradition, along with the *Upaniṣads* and the *Bhagavad Gītā*;

comprised of 550 aphorisms summarizing the contents of the *Upaniṣads*

brahmin: (Skt: *brāhmaṇa*) the priestly and intellectual class, the highest of the four *varṇas*

buddhi: intellect, one of the 24 elements of *prakṛti*

Caitanya-caritāmṛta: the seventeenth-century biography of the Bengali saint Caitanya

cit: knowledge, consciousness; one of the three qualities of *Brahman*

darśana: a vision of the truth, one of the six orthodox philosophical schools

dāsya: the mood of servitude

deha: the physical body

dharma: a universal principle representing religion, law, order, duty, justice and morality; *it* upholds the world by categorizing human society into *varṇas* and *āśramas*

dvija: twice-born, a term referring to the members of the three upper *varṇas*, who are considered to be born for the second time through the *upanayana* or initiation rite

gopīs: the cowherd damsels of Vraja, lovers of Kṛṣṇa

gṛhastha: the second stage in the *āśrama* system, wherein the celibate student becomes a householder

guṇas: the three subtle qualities of *prakṛti* or material nature; these are *sattva* or goodness, *rajas* or passion and *tamas* or ignorance

guru: a teacher or *ācārya* who transmits spiritual wisdom

īśvara: the Supreme Lord, the personal form of God

itihāsa: 'so has it been', a traditional term for history denoting the two great epics, the *Mahābhārata* and the *Rāmāyaṇa*

jīva: the spiritual, individual soul, in many ways synonymous with the *ātman*

jñāna: knowledge and specifically spiritual knowledge

jñāna yoga: a path leading to *mokṣa* wherein philosophizing and intellectual engagement with the scriptures become *yogīc* practices

kali yuga:	according to *purāṇic* accounts, it is the present age of quarrel where *dharma* declines and also the good qualities of the human being
kāma:	sensual pleasures, one of the four goals of human life known as *puruṣārthas*
Kapila:	an *avatāra* of Viṣṇu, born to Kardama and Devahūti, who propounded the knowledge of Sāṅkhya
karma:	action and its various implications in future lives
karma yoga:	a path leading to *mokṣa* wherein action according to *dharma* becomes a *yogīc* practice
Kṛṣṇa:	the speaker of the *Bhagavad Gītā*, the Supreme Person appearing in this world to uphold *dharma*, whose personality is perhaps the main topic of the *Bhāgavata Purāṇa*
Kṛṣṇadāsa Kavirāja:	author of the *Caitanya-caritāmṛta*
kṣatriya:	the warrior and ruling class comprised of nobles and royals
līlā:	divine play, a spiritual mode of action free from any utilitarian purpose
mādhurya:	synonymous with *śṛṅgāra*, the mood of romantic love
manas:	mind
māyā:	illusion
mokṣa:	liberation from the cycle of rebirth
mūrti:	divine embodiment, the physical form worshipped in the temple
nāstika:	traditions not conforming to *śruti* or the *Veda* such as Buddhism and Jainism
Nāṭyaśāstra:	the canonical text on Indian dramaturgy attributed to Bharata Muni, probably composed between the second century BCE to the second century CE
nirguṇa:	devoid of attributes
nirvāṇa:	extinction of material existence
niṣkāma karma:	acting while disinterested in action's fruits, a central teaching of the *Bhagavad Gītā*

paramārtha:	the highest, absolute reality
Prahlāda:	the son of the demonaic king Hiraṇyakaśipu; although born in a demonic family, he was one of the greatest devotees of Viṣṇu, so much so, that Viṣṇu appeared as the Lion-Man *avatāra* to rescue him from his demonaic father
prakṛti:	material nature consisting of the three *guṇas*
pralaya:	the universal destruction
pramāṇa:	means of valid knowledge
prasāda:	divine grace
prasthānatraya:	the three foundations of the *Vedānta* tradition: the *Bhagavad Gītā*, the *Brahma Sūtras* and the *Upaniṣads*
puṇya:	meritorious *karma*
puruṣa:	the conscious principle as opposed to material nature, also 'person'
puruṣārthas:	the four goals of human life; *dharma*, *artha*, *kāma* and *mokṣa*
rajas:	one of the three *guṇas* representing passion, desire, attachment to the fruits of action and excessive endeavors
rasa:	pure emotion, aesthetic rapture
saguṇa:	with attributes
sakhya:	the mood of friendship
samādhi:	the peak of the *yoga* practice, an introverted state of spiritual realization
saṁsāra:	the chain of repeated births and deaths, the state of worldly existence
sāṅkhya:	one of the six orthodox philosophical traditions, propounding the differentiation of *prakṛti* from the *puruṣa*
sannyāsa:	the fourth and last stage of the *āśrama* system, the stage of renunciation
sannyāsī:	the fourth and highest stage of the *āśrama* system, a renounced celibate and generally wandering ascetic
śānta:	the peaceful mood
śāstra:	the traditional authoritative teachings

sattva:	one of the three *guṇas* representing purity, serenity, goodness and knowledge
Śiva:	the great god, one of the three main universal deities along with Brahmā and Viṣṇu and who is considered the Supreme according to Śaivism; he is in charge of the *tamo guṇa*, and is therefore endowed with the task of destroying the universe when the time for annihilation comes; is an ascetic and lives in Mount Kailāsa
smṛti:	a category of canonical texts such as the epics and the *purānas* regarded as 'humanly authored'
soteriology:	doctrines of salvation
śṛṅgāra:	synonymous with *mādhurya*, the mood of romantic love
sthāyi-bhāva:	a foundational or dominant emotion comprising the basis of *rasa*
śūdra:	the serving class comprised of serfs, menial workers and artisans
sūtra:	a short and condensed aphorism, conveying knowledge
svarga:	heaven, eden
tamas:	one of the three *guṇas* representing darkness, ignorance, illusion and indolence
Upaniṣads:	late *Vedic* philosophical texts propounding the unity of *ātman* and *Brahman*
vaikuṇṭha:	the abode of Viṣṇu which is eternal, spiritual, pure and beyond the influence of the three *guṇas*
vaiṣṇava:	a devotee of Viṣṇu
vaiśya:	the merchant and agricultural class
vānaprastha:	the third stage of the *āśrama* system, a forest dweller
varṇa:	class system, category; refers to the four social classes of *brāhmaṇas*, *kṣatriyas*, *vaiṣyas* and *śūdras*
varṇāśrama dharma:	duty according to one's specific *varṇa* and *āśrama*, the basic *Vedic* social structure
Vāsudeva:	Kṛṣṇa, the speaker of the *Bhagavad Gītā*, son of Vasudeva and Devakī

vātsalya:	the mood of parenthood
Vedānta:	'the end of knowledge', the orthodox school of philosophy derived from the *Bhagavad Gītā*, *Brahma Sūtras* and the *Upaniṣads*
Viṣṇu:	Supreme Person according to *Vaiṣṇavism*; appears in his *avatāra* form whenever and wherever there is a decline of *dharma* and a rise of *adharma*
vyabhicāri-bhāva:	secondary accompanying emotions supporting and fostering the dominant emotion
yajña:	sacrifice, and in particular a *Vedic* sacrifice
Yoga:	one of the six orthodox *darśanas*, offering a disciplined path aiming at the state of *samādhi*
Yoga-sūtra:	a classical text ascribed to Patañjali, propounding the *aṣṭāṅga yoga* system
yugas:	universal ages; *kṛta*, *tretā*, *dvāpara* and *kali*

NOTES

Introduction

1. Presumably dated ninth century CE.
2. The exact number varies according to the edition.
3. Klostermaier, *A Survey of Hinduism*, p. 70.
4. Rukmani, *A Critical Study of the Bhāgavata Purāṇa*, p. xiii.
5. Ibid., p. 4.
6. Bryant, *Krishna*, pp. xli–xlii.
7. Sanskrit poetry.
8. Shulman, 'Remarking a Purāṇa', p. 126.
9. Bryant, 'Kṛṣṇa in the Tenth Book of the *Bhāgavata Purāṇa*', p. 118.
10. Ibid., p. 125.
11. Rukmani, *A Critical Study of the Bhāgavata Purāṇa*, p. 5.
12. Nelson, 'The Ontology of *Bhakti*', p. 347.
13. *Paro dharmaḥ*, *BhP* 1.2.6.
14. Hopkins, 'The Social Teaching of the *Bhāgavata Purāṇa*', p. 6.
15. Ibid., p. 7.
16. Ibid., p. 6.
17. Hopkins, *The Hindu Religious Tradition*, p. 119.
18. *Bg* 3.1–3. My translation.
19. *Prasthāna trayī.*
20. Klostermaier, *A Survey of Hinduism*, p. 156.
21. Hardy, *Viraha Bhakti*, p. 13.
22. Van Buitenen, 'On the Archaism of the Bhāgavata Purāṇa', p. 35.
23. Ibid., p. 24.
24. Ibid.
25. Van Buitenen, 'On the Archaism of the Bhāgavata Purāṇa', pp. 24–5.
26. Ibid., pp. 33–4.

27. Despite the fact that I accept Van Buitenen's view as a point of departure, I am well aware of the complexity of the subject matter of the *BhP*'s circumstances of compilation. For a detailed discussion, see Bryant, 'The Date and Provenance of the *Bhāgavata Purāṇa*'.
28. I.e. later than the *Vedic* period.
29. Hardy, *Viraha Bhakti*, p. 13.
30. Ibid.
31. Kohak, *The Embers and the Stars*, p. 125.

Chapter 1 Associating the *Bhāgavata Purāṇa* with *Rasa* Theory

1. De Smet, 'Towards an Indian View of the Person', pp. 52–3.
2. See Mauss, 'A Category of the Human Mind', pp. 14–20.
3. Approximately 475–525 CE.
4. De Smet, 'Towards an Indian View of the Person', p. 53.
5. Ibid., p. 54.
6. Sacrificer, the patron of the sacrifice.
7. Raju, 'The Concept of Man in Indian Thought', p. 207.
8. Sharma, *Human Personality in Ancient Indian Thought*, p. 59.
9. Fourth century BCE.
10. First century BCE.
11. Both seventh century CE.
12. Hymns and ritualistic texts.
13. Raju, 'The Concept of Man in Indian Thought', p. 208.
14. Jaimini, *The Mīmāṁsā Sūtra*, 1.1.1–2.
15. An unseen force.
16. Radhakrishnan and Moore, *A Sourcebook in Indian Philosophy*, p. 486.
17. Sharma, *Human Personality in Ancient Indian Thought*, p. 61.
18. Raju, 'The Concept of Man in Indian Thought', p. 220.
19. The conscious subject.
20. The unconscious object generally translated as 'nature'.
21. Radhakrishnan and Moore, *A Sourcebook in Indian Philosophy*, p. 424.
22. Lit. 'The great' or 'The great one'.
23. The individual's intelligence.
24. Lit. 'I am the doer', the sense of self.
25. Quality of goodness or tranquillity.
26. Mind.
27. *Jñānendriya* – lit. the knowledge senses.
28. *Karmendriya* – lit. the action senses.
29. Quality of darkness or ignorance.
30. Smell, taste, sight, touch and sound.
31. Earth, water, fire, air and ether.
32. Quality of passion or energy.

33. *Sthūla śarira.*
34. *Liṅga śarira.*
35. *Antaḥkarana.*
36. *Vṛttis.*
37. Dasgupta, *A History of Indian Philosophy*, vol. I, p. 243.
38. Citta.
39. De Smet, 'Towards an Indian View of the Person', pp. 62–3.
40. Probably seventh century BCE.
41. Third century CE.
42. Translation by Suryanarayana Śastri, in Radhakrishnan and Moore, *A Sourcebook in Indian Philosophy*, p. 426.
43. Sharma, *Human Personality in Ancient Indian Thought*, p. 41.
44. Regarding theistic *Sāṅkhya* in the *Bhagavad Gītā*, see for example, De Smet, 'Towards an Indian View of the Person', p. 66.
45. *Sat*, *cit*, *ānānda*.
46. *Avidyā.*
47. Radhakrishnan and Moore, *A Sourcebook in Indian Philosophy*, p. 507.
48. *Īśvara.*
49. Radhakrishnan and Moore, *A Sourcebook in Indian Philosophy*, p. 508.
50. Sharma, *The Philosophy of Śrī Madhvācārya*, p. 253.
51. Ibid., p. 448.
52. Zaehner, *Hinduism*, p. 127.
53. Sheridan, *The Advaitic Theism of the Bhāgavata Purāṇa*, p. 57.
54. The Sanskrit terminology offers various terms such as *puruṣa*, *bhagavān*, *paramātman* and others. However, these would need further interpretation to substantiate their personal nature.
55. As its name denotes: *The Purāṇa of the Supreme Person.*
56. See *BhP* 1.8.18 – pervading all beings, thus representing existence.
57. See *BhP* 8.19.2–27 – Vāmana holds a conversation with Bali, c.2 ch. 7, appearing in different *avatāras*, c.10, ch. 44 – fighting Kaṁsa, c.10, ch. 21 – tempting and attracting the *gopīs*.
58. See *BhP*, book 11, chs 6–29 – where Kṛṣṇa speaks the *Uddhava gītā.*
59. See *BhP* 1.8.21 – Kṛṣṇa, who is Vāsudeva, the son of Devakī, the child of the cowherd Nanda and Govinda.
60. See *BhP* 1.8.18 – pervading all beings, thus representing existence.
61. See *BhP* 2.7.13 and 8.7.10 – Kūrma *avatāra* enjoys a nap while his back is being scratched.
62. See *BhP* 1.8.13–17 – Kṛṣṇa protects Parīkṣit in the womb of Uttarā, and book 10 ch. 6 – Pūtanā emancipated.
63. See *BhP* book 1 ch. 3 and book 2 ch. 7 – the description of the various *avatāras* and their contributions to the world order. 1.3.2 – a specific example is that of Brahmā being born of a lotus growing in the lake situated in Viṣṇu's navel, which is a rather creative way of creating the world.
64. Larson and Bhattacharya (eds), *Encyclopedia of Indian Philosophies*, p. 29.

65. Ibid.
66. See pp. 4–5 of this volume.
67. Minor, 'The *Gītā*'s Way as the Only Way', p. 340.
68. Zimmer, *Philosophies of India*, p. 605.
69. Dasgupta, *A History of Indian Philosophy*, vol. III, p. 471.
70. *Tiruvāymoli*; composed by Śaṭakopan, known also as Nammālvār.
71. Hardy, *Viraha Bhakti*, p. 483.
72. Ibid., p. 489.
73. Parthasarathi, 'The Drāvida Veda-Vedāṅga', p. 50.
74. Raghavan, '*Āḷvārs*', p. 25.
75. Hopkins, *The Hindu Religious Tradition*, p. 117–18.
76. The language.
77. Periyāḷvār Tirumoḷi 5.1.6.
78. The divine light of the meaning of *Vedānta*: Periyāḷvār Tirumoḷi 4.3.11.
79. Sanskrit: *Chandoga*, *Taittirīya*, *Sāma-vedī*.
80. *Periya Tirumoli* 5.5.9, 7.7.2.
81. Narayanan, *The Way and the Goal*, pp. 10–11.
82. Hopkins, *The Hindu Religious Tradition*, p. 117.
83. *Tiruvāymoli* 10.3.5, cited from Narayanan, *The Way and the Goal*, pp. 41–2.
84. Gonda, 'Vedic Literature', p. 65.
85. Swami Gambhirānanda (trs), *Eight Upaniṣads*, p. 360.
86. Kane, *History of Sanskrit Poetics*, p. 356.
87. All *BhP* translations in this work are mine unless indicated otherwise.
88. *BS* 1.1.2.
89. 1.1.3b.
90. From whom emanates the creation and so forth, of the universe.
91. Oh connoisseurs of *rasa*... For full translation see above.
92. Swami Gambhirananda (translator), *Eight Upaniṣads*, vol I. p. 391.
93. *BS* 1.1.1. The translations and connections between phrases made in footnotes 74–90 are based on Joshi, 'The First Verse of the *Bhāgavata-Mahāpurāṇa*', p. 388.
94. *BS* 1.1.2.
95. *BS* 1.1.3.
96. *BS* 1.1.4.
97. *BS* 1.1.5.
98. *BS* 1.1.1.
99. *BS* 1.1.1.
100. *BS* 1.1.1
101. *BS* 1.1.2.
102. Joshi, 'The First Verse of the *Bhāgavata-Mahāpurāṇa*', pp. 388–90.
103. *Anta.*
104. *Veda.*
105. Dandekar, '*Vedānta*', p. 207.
106. After 800 BCE.

107. *Prāṇa*.
108. *Ātman*.
109. *Brahman*.
110. Clooney, *Seeing through Texts*, p. 27.
111. Klostermaier, *A Survey of Hinduism*, p. 69.
112. Matilal, '*Jñāna*', p. 94.
113. Knowledge of reality as it is.
114. Ibid., pp. 94–5.
115. *The New Oxford Dictionary*, p. 1395.
116. Hamilton, *Indian Philosophy*, p. 9.
117. Or perhaps mystical.
118. *The New Oxford Dictionary*, p. 1018.
119. *BhP*, 1.1.3b. For translation see above p. 28, footnote.
120. The opening and concluding statements are traditionally considered to indicate the meaning of a treatise. Ravi gupta quotes Jīva Gosvāmī's *Paramātma-sandarbha* 105 and writes, 'Jīva (Gosvāmī) sets out to determine the overall purport of the *Bhāgavata Purāṇa* by examining the six indicators of meaning (*tātparya-liṅga*): "This *mahāpurāṇa* has the name Śrī *Bhāgavata* because it teaches about him (*Bhagavān*). As it is said, 'This *Purāṇa*, called *Bhāgavata*, is equal to the *Veda*.'" The chief meaning of the *Bhāgavata* will be considered from different angles according to the six indicators of meaning (*tātparya-liṇga*): "The opening and concluding statements (*upakrama-upasaṁhāra*), repetition (*abhyāsa*), novelty (*apūrvatā*), result (*phala*), subordinate statements of commendation or praise (*arthavāda*), and reasoning (*upapatti*) are the indicators which are used to determine the purport."' Gupta, *The Caitanya Vaiṣṇava Vedānta of Jīva Gosvāmī*, p. 93.
121. *BhP* 12.13.15.
122. Haberman, *Acting as a Way of Salvation*, p.13.
123. Kapoor, *Literary Theory*, p. 15.
124. Shulman, *Lectures on Indian Poetry*, pp. 46–8 (my translation).
125. Gerow, *A Glossary of Indian Figures of Speech*, p. 219. The quote is from Rudraṭa, author of *Kāvyālaṅkāra*, ninth century.
126. See Tagare (trs), *The Bhāgavata Purāṇa*, p. 208, footnote.
127. Due to their pre-existence as the material cause of the universe.
128. As the Supreme Person existed before them and created them all.
129. *BhP* 2.9.33–6.
130. II 9.30–3. Joshi refers here to verses 30–3, whereas Tagare and Sheridan refer to verses 32–5, while all of them number the verses the same. However, as far as we are concerned, both groups of verses serve the same purpose.
131. Joshi, '*Catuḥślokī* or *Saptaślokī Bhāgavata*', p. 26.
132. Apparently receiving the *darśana* or vision of the deity in the temple.
133. *BhP*, 10.29.18–27.
134. Gerow, '*Rasa* as a Category of Literary Criticism', p. 226.

135. Some association could be made with the terms *sāmānya* (generality) and *viśeṣa* (particularity), which are two of the six *padārthas* (categories) of which the world is made up, according to the *nyāya-vaiśeṣika* school.
136. *The New Oxford Dictionary*, p. 301.
137. Haberman, *Acting as a Way of Salvation*, p. 4.
138. Shakespeare, 'Romeo and Juliet', 2.2.19–25, in Clark, *The Complete Works of William Shakespeare*, p. 719.
139. Gerow, '*Rasa* as a Category of Literary Criticism', p. 226.
140. Sharma, *Classical Hindu Thought*, p. 123.
141. Mishra, *Devotional Poetics and the Indian Sublime*, p. 15.
142. Lott, *Vedantic Approaches to God*, p. 121.
143. Ibid.
144. *Sat*, *cit*, *ānanda*.
145. Introduction, p. 7.
146. Sharma, *Classical Hindu Thought*, p. 43.
147. Ibid., p. 62.
148. *BhP* 1.2.11.
149. The Divine Person within the heart.
150. The Supreme Person.
151. Chapter 3, p. 123–128.
152. Sheridan, *The Advaitic Theism of the Bhāgavata Purāṇa*, pp. 23–4.
153. The term 'Universe of Feelings' is noted by Klostermaier.
154. Gerow, '*Rasa* as a Category of Literary Criticism', p. 227.
155. Ibid.
156. Approximately 1400 CE.
157. Sinha, *Indian Psychology, Emotion and Will*, p. 164.
158. Gerow, '*Rasa* as a Category of Literary Criticism', p. 227.
159. Klostermaier, 'A Universe of Feelings', p. 123.
160. Ibid.
161. Gerow, '*Rasa* as a Category of Literary Criticism', p. 236.
162. Ibid., pp. 240–1.
163. Klostermaier, 'A Universe of Feelings' p. 124.
164. Ibid.
165. Ward, *Concepts of God*, p. 3.

Chapter 2 The Aesthetic Doctrine of the *Bhāgavata Purāṇa*

1. Sheth, *The Divinity of Krishna*, p. 108.
2. Ibid., p. 115.
3. Ibid.
4. Ibid., p. 116.
5. Ibid., p. 118.
6. *BhP* Book 10, chs 29–33.

7. Flood, *An Introduction to Hinduism*, p. 140.
8. Haberman, *Acting as a Way of Salvation*, p. 14.
9. *Anukṛti*.
10. Haberman, *Acting as a Way of Salvation*, p. 12.
11. Ibid.
12. Wulff, *Drama as a Mode of Religious Realization*, p. 7.
13. Ibid.
14. Hein, *The Miracle Plays of Mathurā*, p. 259.
15. Ibid., p. 240.
16. Wulff, *Drama as a Mode of Religious Realization*, p. 8.
17. Matchett, 'The Purāṇas', p. 129.
18. *V.P.* 5.10. 46–7.
19. Wulff, *Drama as a Mode of Religious Realization*, p. 10.
20. E.g. *BhP* 10.10.42.
21. Wulff, *Drama as a Mode of Religious Realization*, p. 10.
22. *Bg* 4.5–9.
23. Wulff, *Drama as a Mode of Religious Realization*, p. 9.
24. Ibid., pp. 9–10. The three *purāṇic* passages are: *HV* 2.21.26, *VP* 5.13.28, *BhP* 10.30.14.
25. E.g. 1.1.2.
26. *Raso vai saḥ rasaṁ hyevāyaṁ labdhvānandī bhavati*, *Taittirīya Up*. 2.7.
27. Delmonico, *Sacred Rapture*, p. 34.
28. Kulke and Rothermund, *A History of India*, p. 68.
29. Seventh to eighth century.
30. Eighth century.
31. Ninth century.
32. Ninth century.
33. *Abhidhā*.
34. Tenth century.
35. *Abhinava-bhāratī*.
36. *Dhvanyāloka-locana*.
37. *Sarasvatī-kaṇṭhābharaṇa and Śṛṅgāra-prakāśa*.
38. Chs 337–47.
39. Thirteenth century.
40. Twelfth century.
41. Seventeenth century.
42. Haberman, *Acting as a Way of Salvation*, p. 13.
43. *Yajña*.
44. *Mokṣa*.
45. Vatsyayan, 'Drama: Indian Dance and Dance Drama', p. 452.
46. Rangacharya (trs), *Nāṭyaśāstra*, ch. 1, p. 2.
47. Haberman, *Acting as a Way of Salvation*, p. 14.
48. The 33 secondary emotions are called *vyabhicārins*. The full list is given on p. 52.
49. Or *madhūrya*.

50. Delmonico, *Sacred Rapture*, p. 51.
51. Ibid.
52. Ibid., pp. 355–6.
53. Or depression.
54. Masson and Pathwardan, *Aesthetic Rapture*, p. 45.
55. Rangacharya (trs), *Nāṭyaśāstra*, ch. 7, pp. 46–51.
56. Bharata, *Nāṭya-śāstra*, p. 272: *vibhāvānubhāva-vyabhicāri-saṁyogād rasa-niṣpattiḥ*. The interpretation of this statement has been debated for centuries, the main points under discussion being the meaning of the word *niṣpatti* (produced), the nature of the term *saṁyoga* (union) and the absence of the most central term in the *rasa* theory, which is *sthāyibhāva* (primary emotion).
57. Rangacharya (trs), *Nāṭyaśāstra*, 7.6, p. 44.
58. Ibid., 6.31–2, p. 38.
59. Ibid., p. 288.
60. *Sumanas*.
61. Bharata, *Nāṭya-śāstra*, p. 271: *na hi rasād ṛte kaścid arthaḥ pravartate*.
62. Delmonico, *Sacred Rapture*, p. 46.
63. *Āsvāda*.
64. *Sthāyin*.
65. *Bhāva*.
66. Delmonico, *Sacred Rapture*, p. 62.
67. Haberman, *Acting as a Way of Salvation*, p. 17.
68. Cited by Haberman, *Acting as a Way of Salvation*, p. 17.
69. Ibid., p. 18.
70. Suggestion.
71. Stating that *rasa* is produced from the combination of the *vibhāva*, *anubhāva* and *vyabhicāribhāva*.
72. Haberman, *Acting as a Way of Salvation*, p. 20.
73. *Sahṛdaya*.
74. Abhinavagupta cited by Haberman, *Acting as a Way of Salvation*, pp. 20–1. Translation by Masson and Patwardhan.
75. *Śabda*.
76. Ānandavardhana, *Dhvanyāloka*, 2nd edn, p. 14 – cited by Delmonico, *Sacred Rapture*, p. 67.
77. Delmonico, *Sacred Rapture*, p. 68.
78. Ānandavardhana, *Dhvanyāloka*, p. 23, cited by Delmonico, *Sacred Rapture*, p. 69.
79. *Vāsanās*.
80. *Hṛdaya-samvāda*.
81. *Tanmayībhāvanā*.
82. Delmonico, *Sacred Rapture*, p. 70.
83. Abhinavagupta, *Abhinava-bharati*, pp. 266–7, cited by Delmonico, *Sacred Rapture*, p. 72.
84. Haberman, *Acting as a Way of Salvation*, p. 27.
85. *Tattva-jñāna*.

86. *Ātma-jñāna.*
87. Ibid., pp. 27–8.
88. *Tattva-jñāna.*
89. *Ātma-jñāna.*
90. *Yogaś cittavṛtti nirodha – yoga sūtra of patañjali*, 1.2.
91. Singh, *Bhoja Paramāra and His Times*, p. 22.
92. Raghavan, *Bhoja*'s *Śṛṅgrāra Prakāśa*, p. 6.
93. Ibid. p. 9.
94. Ibid., pp. 453–4.
95. Pollock, 'Bhoja's *Śṛṅgāraprakāśa*', p. 126.
96. *Sarasvatī-kaṇṭhābharaṇa and śṛṅgāra-prakāśa.*
97. Chapters 337–47.
98. See Delmonico, *Sacred Rapture*, p. 40.
99. Raghavan, *Bhoja*'s *Śṛṅgāra Prakāśa*, p. 8.
100. *Yo bhāvanāpatham atītya vivartamānaḥ svāhaṅkṛtau hṛdi paraṁ svadate raso* 'sau, *śṛṅgāra-prakāśa* 2.436, cited by Delmonico, *Sacred Rapture*, p. 42.
101. *S-ka* V 1–3. Raghavan, *Bhoja*'s *Śṛṅgāra Prakāśa*, p. 399.
102. Raghavan, *Bhoja*'s *Śṛṅgāra Prakāśa*, p. 8.
103. Pollock, 'The Social Aesthetic and Sanskrit Literary Theory', p. 216.
104. Raghavan, *Bhoja*'s *Śṛṅgāra Prakāśa*, p. 423.
105. *Bg* 7.19, my translation.
106. Raghavan, *Bhoja*'s *Śṛṅgāra Prakāśa*, p. 442.
107. See *Bg* 7.3.
108. Raghavan, *Bhoja*'s *Śṛṅgāra Prakāśa*, pp. 466–7.
109. See *Bg* 14.6.
110. Raghavan, *Bhoja*'s *Śṛṅgāra Prakāśa*, p. 440.
111. Ibid., pp. 454–5.
112. Ibid., p. 639.
113. Ibid., p. 423.
114. Ibid., p. 443.
115. Ibid., p. 458.
116. Forty nine: eight *sthāyi-bhāvas*, eight *sāttvika-bhāvas*, and 33 *vyabhicāri-bhāvas.*
117. *Ahaṅkāra.*
118. Haberman, *Acting as a Way of Salvation*, pp. 28–9.
119. Raghavan, *Bhoja*'s *Śṛṅgāra Prakāśa*, p. 743.
120. *Śṛṅgāra rasa.*
121. Haberman, *Acting as a Way of Salvation*, p. 29.
122. Raghavan, *Bhoja*'s *Śṛṅgāra Prakāśa*, p. 431.
123. Ibid., p. 450.
124. Ibid., p. 439.
125. Ibid., p. 440.
126. Here Raghavan quotes *Śṛṅgāra Prakāśa*, vol. II, pp. 366–7. The verse starts with *aho aho namo Mahyaṁ.*
127. Raghavan, *Bhoja*'s *Śṛṅgāra Prakāśa*, p. 441.

128. The four questions under discussion are: 1. What is *rasa*? 2. How is *rasa* aroused? 3. What is the relationship between *rasa* and *bhāva*? 4. Who experiences *rasa*?
129. Delmonico, *Sacred Rapture*, p. 7.
130. *BhP* 1.1.3. The readers are addressed as *aho rasikā*. Translation for the second half of the verse is: 'Oh connoisseurs of *rasa*, always relish this treatise of the Supreme Person, which is full of *rasa* – on this earth and in the final state.'
131. Primary emotion.
132. Haberman, *Acting as a Way of Salvation*, p. 26.
133. Ibid. p. 27.
134. Quoted by Haberman, *Acting as a Way of Salvation*, p. 28.
135. Ibid. pp. 28–9.
136. Ibid., p. 29.
137. Probably it was not finished until 1615 CE. See Dimock, *Caitanya Caritāmṛta of Kṛṣṇadāsa Kavirāja*, p. 31.
138. Flood, *An Introduction to Hinduism*, p. 138.
139. Ibid., p. 140.
140. 1486–1533.
141. Dimock, *The Caitanya Caritāmṛta of Kṛṣṇadāsa Kavirāja*, pp. 621–2, CC, *Mad.*, 19.133–46.
142. Hearing and speaking of, or singing.
143. Love of Kṛṣṇa.
144. Dimock, *The Caitanya Caritāmṛta of Kṛṣṇadāsa Kavirāja*, p. 622, CC, *Mad.*, 19.144–5.
145. Ibid., p. 622.
146. The *BhP* section quoted is 3.29.11–14.
147. *BhP* 3.29.12; see Dimock, *The Caitanya Caritāmṛta of Kṛṣṇadāsa Kavirāja*, p. 623.
148. Dimock, *The Caitanya Caritāmṛta of Kṛṣṇadāsa Kavirāja*, p. 624.
149. Ibid., pp. 625–6. CC, *Mad.* 19, 159–64.
150. *BhP* book 3, chs 15–16. Sanaka and the others are the four *Kumāras*.
151. *BhP* book 11, chs 2–5.
152. *BhP* book 1, ch. 7.
153. Vasudeva and Nanda.
154. *BhP* book 10, chs 3–11.
155. *BhP* book 10, chs 29–33.
156. Dimock, *The Caitanya Caritāmṛta of Kṛṣṇadāsa kavirāja*, pp. 628–9. CC, *Mad.* 19, 173–4. The verse quoted is from Rūpa Goswāmin's *Bhaktirasāmṛtasindhu*, 3.1.47. I have omitted the next quotation from *BhP* 11.19.36 which is quoted by Kavirāja.
157. Ibid., p. 629. CC, *Mad.* 19, 177.
158. I take the term *Paramātman* to indicate the *Upaniṣadic antaryāmin*, a representation of the divine situated in the heart, being the object of contemplation for *yogīs*.

159. Dimock, *The Caitanya Caritāmṛta of Kṛṣṇadāsa kavirāja*, p. 629. CC, *Mad.* 19, 178–80.
160. Ibid., pp. 629–30. CC, *Mad.* 19, 181–4.
161. Bhaktivedanta Swami, for example, translates it in the latter way, see Bhaktivedanta Swami, *Śrī Caitanya Caritāmṛta*, p. 401, CC, Mad. 19, 225 (verses are numbered differently).
162. Dimock, *The Caitanya Caritāmṛta of Kṛṣṇadāsa kavirāja*, p. 630. CC, *Mad.* 19, 185–8.
163. Maintenance is Bhaktivedanta Swami's translation of the term *pālana*. See Bhaktivedanta Swami, *Śrī Caitanya Caritāmṛta*, p. 402, verse 226.
164. Dimock, *The Caitanya Caritāmṛta of Kṛṣṇadāsa Kavirāja*, pp. 630–1. CC, *Mad.* 19, 189–92.
165. *BhP* Book 10, chs 29–33.

Chapter 3 Notions of Personal Divinity in the *Bhāgavata Purāṇa*

1. *BhP* Book 10, chs 29–33.
2. See for example, Matchett, '*Bhakti* in the Bhāgavata Purāṇa', p. 113.
3. *BhP* 1.1.16–18.
4. E.g. pp. 68–9.
5. An example of a traditional commentator is *Kṛṣṇadāsa kavirāja*, who follows Rūpa Goswami in analysing Kṛṣṇaite theology according to five sequential *rasas*. See pp. 97–104.
6. Delmonico, *Sacred Rapture*, p. 260.
7. Ibid., p. 260, n. 40.
8. *Praśānta*.
9. *BhP* 2.6.39–40a.
10. *BhP* 2.1.23–38.
11. *BhP* 2.2.6–20.
12. Only a few *avatāras* in the *dāsya* category are presented, although the *BhP* mentions numerous examples.
13. *BhP* 3.13.16–33.
14. *BhP* 7.8.16–23.
15. *BhP* 8.20.21–8.
16. *BhP* 4.9.6–17.
17. *BhP* 10.12.1–12.
18. *BhP* 10.9.1–5.
19. *BhP* Book 10, chs 29–33.
20. Haberman (trs), *The Bhaktirasāmṛtasindhu of Rūpa Gosvāmin*, p. lx.
21. Ibid., pp. lx–lxi.
22. See quote no. 67 in ch. 3. pp. 172–3.
23. Haberman (trs), *The Bhaktirasāmṛtasindhu of Rūpa Gosvāmin*, 3.1.9, p. 399.
24. *BhP* 1.3.31–32.

25. *BhP* 8.12.5; Śiva addresses Viśṇu.
26. *BhP* 1.7.9–10.
27. *BhP* 2.1.9.
28. The phrase *polymorphic monotheism* may be applied here, as both systems refer to the same supreme truth although articulating themselves differently.
29. *BhP* 1.2.11.
30. The verse quoted presents three notions. It may well be that the intermediate notion, i.e. *Paramātman*, refers to the Person in the heart or *antaryāmin*, which is a divine notion more personalized than *Brahman*, but less personalized than *Bhagavān*. A discussion of the *antaryāmin* ensues later in this chapter.
31. Schweig, *Dance of Divine Love*, p. 100.
32. *BhP* 2.1.23–38.
33. *Ṛg Veda* 10.90.
34. *BhP* Book 2, ch. 6.
35. *BhP* 1.19.37–8.
36. *BhP* 2.1.24–8.
37. *BhP* 2.1.29–32.
38. Time.
39. Existence.
40. *Mahat*.
41. *Pradhāna*.
42. The *Sāṅkhya* principle of intelligence.
43. Made up of *manas*, *citta*, *ahaṁkāra* and *buddhi*.
44. *BhP* 2.1.33–5.
45. *BhP* 2.1.36–8.
46. Lit. 'hymn to the *puruṣa*'.
47. Doniger O'Flaherty, *The Rig Veda*, p. 30.
48. See 'Vedic association with poetry and transcendental vision', pp. 26–8.
49. Witzel, 'Vedas and Upaniṣads', p. 69.
50. Shulman, *Lectures on Indian Poetry*, p. 10 (my translation from Hebrew).
51. Ibid., p. 11.
52. Peterson, *Poems To Śiva*, p. 115. The note refers to the following section: The Cosmic Person, 27. Appar IV.4.8 Tiruvārūr (Ārūr): 'The god who has / A thousand feet like a thousand red lotuses, / A thousand shoulders like a thousand golden hills, / A thousand long strands of hair like a thousand suns, / And has taken for himself a thousand names, / Is our Lord who lives in Ārūr.'
53. Lipner, *Hindus*, p. 355.
54. Haberman (trs), *The Bhaktirasāmṛtasindhu of Rūpa Gosvāmin*, p. lx.
55. *BhP* 2.1.23.
56. There are two parallel descriptions of the cosmic man in the *BhP*'s Second book, the first comprising vv. 24–38 of ch. 1, and the second comprising the entire sixth chapter.
57. See *BhP* 2.6.27–8.
58. Referring to *BhP* 2.1.33 quoted above.

59. See *Bhagavad Gītā* 9.9 and 13.20–2.
60. *Bg*. 18.45–7.
61. *BhP* 2.9.32.
62. V. 37, which establishes the four *varṇas* as being of a divine origin, furthers *dāsya* indirectly, as it follows that adhering to one's duty in practical service is sacred.
63. The *antaryāmin* section appears in *BhP*, Second book, ch. 2.
64. For another textual example relating the *antaryāmin* with *śānta rasa* see 1.6.16–26, where Nārada is granted a vision of the Lord in the Heart through meditation.
65. Klostermaier, *A Concise Encyclopedia of Hinduism*, p. 23.
66. Venkatesachar, 'The Concept of the Finite Self in the *Tattvavāda* of Śrī Madhva', p. 23.
67. *BhP* 2.2.4–5.
68. Tagare adds here (p. 161) the following verse: 'As long as the mind remains steady in concentration, one should gaze fixedly on this Supreme Lord who manifests himself in meditation.' However, it does not appear in Śrīdhara's *Bhāvārthabhodinī*, and Tagare numbers both this verse and the following one with the same number, i.e. 9. It may well be that this verse appears in some version but not others.
69. *BhP* 2.2.6–9.
70. *BhP* 2.2.10–12.
71. *BhP* 2.2.13–14.
72. Haberman (trs), *The Bhaktirasāmṛtasindhu of Rūpa Gosvāmin*, p. lxi.
73. Śrīnivasachāri, *The Philosophy Of Viśiṣṭādvaita*, p. 143.
74. Olivelle, *Upaniṣads*, p. 242.
75. 'Ruling over the light', a somewhat obscure phrase, presumably meaning 'ruling over the creation'.
76. Olivelle, *Upaniṣads*, p. 258.
77. See p. 87 of this chapter for the full translation.
78. Olivelle, *Upaniṣads*, p. 259.
79. *Śvetāśvatara Upaniṣad*, 4.1–10.
80. Doniger O'Flaherty (ed), *Textual Sources for the Study of Hinduism*, p. 34.
81. See the *BhP*'s version in 11.11.4–10, where Kṛṣṇa represents the *paramātman*.
82. *Muṇḍaka Upaniṣad*, 3.1.1. Swami Gambhirānanda (trs), *Eight Upaniṣads*, vol. II, p. 137.
83. Commentary on *Muṇḍaka Upaniṣad*, 3.1.1: Swami Gambhirānanda (trs), *Eight Upaniṣads*, vol. II, p. 138.
84. Lipner describes the *antaryāmin* in Rāmānuja's thought as having unmeasured qualities, and as desirous of guiding the soul to his true and final end. He even goes as far as mentioning the *antaryāmin* along with the *avatāras* as saving agents, the *avatāras* offering protection and the *antaryāmin* not only controlling but offering guidance as well. See Lipner, *The Face of Truth*: '*Brahman* as inner Controller or Mover [. . .], essentially of a "flood" of unmeasured (noble)

qualities' (p. 88). 'The Lord himself indwells man as his inner controller and support, desirous of guiding him to his true and final end' (p. 100). 'But Rāmānuja would answer the charge against the benevolence of his creator God not only by reference to primal *karma*, but also by pointing to the Lord's *avatāras* into this world for the protection of the righteous and the confounding of the evil-doers, and by stressing that the Lord indwells this world and each person individually as Controller and Guide (*antaryāmin*) unto fulfillment' (p. 94).

85. Śrīnivasachāri, *The Philosophy of Viśiṣṭādvaita*, p. 235.
86. Ibid., p. 420.
87. Ibid., p. 156.
88. Ibid., pp. 205–6.
89. Sheridan, *The Advaitic Theism of The Bhāgavata Purāṇa*, p. 59, quoting *BhP* 12.12.45.
90. For an example of an *avatāra* narration see appendix, p. 167.
91. Haberman (trs), *The Bhaktirasāmṛtasindhu of Rūpa Gosvāmin*, pp. lxi–lxii.
92. Ibid., p. lxi, and the corresponding n. 112, p. lxxiv.
93. For a deeper analysis of this *rasa* see Haberman (trs), *The Bhaktirasāmṛtasindhu of Rūpa Gosvāmin*, vv. 3.2.16–18, pp. 415–17 – the four types of servant, 3.2.76, p. 433 – the foundational emotion, and 3.2.139–43, p. 453 – how this emotion comprises a *rasa* in the *BhP*.
94. *BhP* 1.3.1–5.
95. *Puruṣa*.
96. Parrinder considers this *puruṣa* to be the first *āvatāra*; see Parrinder, *Avatar and Incarnation*, p. 75.
97. The full list of *avatārs* and their deeds follows: see *BhP* 1.3.6–26. Tagare, pp. 24–9.
98. *BhP* 1.3.6–13.
99. *BhP* 1.3.6–26. Tagare, pp. 24–9.
100. The text (*BhP* 1.3.24) speaks in the future tense.
101. *BhP* 1.3.26, Tagare, p. 29.
102. Parrinder, *Avatar and Incarnation*, p. 48.
103. Ibid., pp. 48–9.
104. Ibid., p. 50.
105. Klostermaier, *A Survey of Hinduism*, p. 419.
106. Sheridan, *The Advaitic Theism of The Bhāgavata Purāṇa*, p. 61.
107. Ibid., p. 148.
108. Ibid., pp. 23–4.
109. *Paramātman*.
110. Chadwick, *Boethius*, pp. 192–3.
111. Parrinder, *Avatar and Incarnation*, pp. 120–6.
112. Ibid., p. 124.
113. Ibid., p. 123.
114. Although there are some traces of *rasa* in the *Bg*, too, conveyed, for example, by the usage of various epithets for both Kṛṣṇa and Arjuna.

115. Ward, *Religion and Human Nature*, p. 44.
116. See ch. 3, pp. 180–2.
117. For a description of *Vaikuṇṭha* and the fall from there, see *BhP*, Book 3, chs 15–16. A certain traditional view considers the fall of Jaya and Vijaya to represent the soul's falling from the spiritual world into *saṁsāra*. See Bhaktivedanta Swami, *Śrīmad Bhāgavatam, Third Canto – Part One*, p. 752.
118. See for example *BhP* 1.3.45.
119. Matchett, *Kṛṣṇa: Lord Or Avatāra?*, p. 4.
120. Apparently by their mothers.
121. *BhP*. 10.12.1–12.
122. Schweig, *Dance of Divine Love*, p. 100.
123. Haberman (trs), *The Bhaktirasāmṛtasindhu of Rūpa Gosvāmin*, p. lxii.
124. For an analysis of Arjuna's encounter with Kṛṣṇa which involves a transfer from awe to friendship see Haberman (trs), *The Bhaktirasāmṛtasindhu of Rūpa Gosvāmin*, p. lx.
125. *BRS* 3.3.105–6b, in Haberman (trs), *The Bhaktirasāmṛtasindhu of Rūpa Gosvāmin*, p. 497.
126. Haberman (trs), *The Bhaktirasāmṛtasindhu of Rūpa Gosvāmin*, p. 506, n. 5, referring to 3.3.106.
127. *Suhṛt*.
128. *Sakha*.
129. *Priya sakha*.
130. *Priya narma vayasyāḥ*.
131. *BRS* 3.3.18, in Haberman (trs), *The Bhaktirasāmṛtasindhu of Rūpa Gosvāmin*, p. 473.
132. *BRS* 3.3.54–56, in Haberman (trs), *The Bhaktirasāmṛtasindhu of Rūpa Gosvāmin*, p. 483.
133. Haberman (trs), *The Bhaktirasāmṛtasindhu of Rūpa Gosvāmin*, 3.3.6–8, pp. 469–71.
134. *BRS* 3.3.106b, in Haberman (trs), *The Bhaktirasāmṛtasindhu of Rūpa Gosvāmin*, p. 497.
135. *BhP* 10.9. 1–14.
136. Schweig, *Dance of Divine Love*, p. 100.
137. *BRS* 3.4.52, in Haberman (trs), *The Bhaktirasāmṛtasindhu of Rūpa Gosvāmin*, p. 523.
138. Haberman (trs), *The Bhaktirasāmṛtasindhu of Rūpa Gosvāmin*, p. lxiii.
139. Ibid.
140. Ibid.
141. *BRS* 3.4.58–74, in Haberman (trs), *The Bhaktirasāmṛtasindhu of Rūpa Gosvāmin*, pp. 525–9.
142. *BRS* 3.4.62, in ibid., p. 525, quoting *BhP* 10.46.28.
143. Book 10, chs 29–33.
144. Schweig, *Dance of Divine Love*, p. 1.
145. On the sandy bank of the *Yamunā*.

146. A certain metrical pattern.
147. *BhP* 10.33.1–10.
148. Schweig, *Dance of Divine Love*, p. 100.
149. See also the concluding paragraph of ibid., ch. 3, p. 201.
150. *BRS* 3.5.19, in Haberman (trs), *The Bhaktirasāmṛtasindhu of Rūpa Gosvāmin*, p. 541.
151. *BRS* 2.5.36, in ibid., p. 363.
152. *BRS* 3.5.24, in ibid., p. 543.
153. *BRS* 3.5.21, in ibid., p. 541.
154. Haberman (trs), *The Bhaktirasāmṛtasindhu of Rūpa Gosvāmin*, pp.lxiii–lxiv.
155. Ibid., p. lxiv.
156. *BRS* 1.2.59, in Haberman (trs), *The Bhaktirasāmṛtasindhu of Rūpa Gosvāmin*, p. 33.
157. Haberman (trs), *The Bhaktirasāmṛtasindhu of Rūpa Gosvāmin*, p. 88, n. 29.
158. For a full list of the 64 qualities see *BRS* 2.1.
159. Haberman (trs), *The Bhaktirasāmṛtasindhu of Rūpa Gosvāmin*, p. lxiii.
160. Hein, 'Foreword', in Schweig, *Dance of Divine Love*, p. xiv.
161. Ibid., pp. xiv–xv.
162. I.e. Rāmānuja's *Viśiṣṭādvaita*, Madhva's *Dvaita*, Nimbārka's *Dvaitādvaita*, Vallabha's *Śuddhādvaita* and the Bengal *Gosvāmīs' Acintyadvaitādvaita*.
163. Hardy, *Viraha Bhakti*, p. 557.
164. Haberman (trs), *The Bhaktirasāmṛtasindhu of Rūpa Gosvāmin*, p. lxiv.

Chapter 4 A Textual Encounter

1. *Sākhya* will be exemplified by three examples.
2. The text (3.26.11) reads as follows: '*pañcabhiḥ pañcabhir brahma caturbhir daśabhis thatā / etac catur-viṁśatikaṁ gaṇaṁ prādhānikaṁ viduḥ*.' It specifically mentions *Brahman* and this reinforces the idea of the *BhP* presenting a theistic or at least *Vedāntic* version of *Sāṅkhya*.
3. *Manas, buddhi, ahaṁkāra* and *citta*.
4. Also called sometimes 'space' or 'ether'.
5. These are the five knowledge-gathering senses or *jñānendriyāṇi*.
6. These are the five working senses or *karmendriyāṇi*.
7. *Manas*.
8. *Buddhi*.
9. *Ahaṁkāra*.
10. *Citta*.
11. *Kāla*.
12. The term for the Supreme Person is *paraḥ pumān*; see 3.26.19.
13. *BhP* 3.26.10.
14. *BhP* 3.26.18.
15. Schweig, *Dance of Divine Love*, p. 100. For the full quote of the *śānta rasa* see ch. 3, p. 123.

16. The name used for the Supreme Person is Hari; see 1.6.16.
17. I.e. with Viṣṇu.
18. Schweig, *Dance of Divine Love*, p. 100.
19. Ch. 9.1–35.
20. Concentration.
21. The story of Dhruva appears also in the *Viṣṇu Purāṇa*, Book 1, chs 11–13. See Wilson (trs), *The Vishnu Purāṇa*, p. 95. However, although the VP follows the same epic framework, it is more simple both emotionally and aesthetically.
22. Schweig, Dance of Divine Love, p. 100. For the full quote regarding *dāsya rasa* see ch. 3, p. 142.
23. *BhP* 7.5.23–4.
24. *Siddhas*.
25. For the full story see *BhP* Book 8 chs 2–4.
26. Righteousness, piety, self-control, austerity, non-jealousy, modesty, forbearance, tolerance, performance of sacrifice, charity, courage and study of the *Veda*. See Tagare, p. 943, n. 2.
27. Schweig, *Dance of Divine Love*, p. 100.
28. Ibid. For the full quote regarding *sākhya-rasa* see ch. 3, p. 146.
29. Ibid.
30. Celestial musicians.
31. The four signs of Viṣṇu.
32. Schweig, *Dance of Divine Love*, p. 100. For the full quote regarding *vātsalya rasa* see ch. 3, p. 151.
33. Ibid. For the full quote regarding *śṛṅgāra rasa* see ch. 3, p. 155.
34. *BhP* 29.12 etc.
35. Schweig, *Dance of Divine Love*, p. 1.
36. Ibid., p. 100.

BIBLIOGRAPHY

Ādidevānanda Svāmī (translator) *Śrī Rāmānuja Gītā Bhāṣya*, Śrī Rāmakṛṣṇa Math, Madras.

Baker, L.R., *Persons and Bodies – A Constitution View*, Cambridge University Press, New York, 2000.

Balaban, O. and Erev, A., *The Bounds of Freedom*, Peter Lang, American University Studies, New York, 1995.

Bhaktivedanta Swami, *Śrīmad Bhāgavatam*, Bhaktivedanta Book Trust, Botany, 1987 (1993).

——— *Śrīmad Bhāgavatam, Second Canto*, Bhaktivedanta Book Trust, Botany, 1987 (1993).

——— *Śrī Caitanya Caritāmṛta*, Bhaktivedanta Book Trust, Botany, 1996.

Bharata, *Nāṭya-śāstra*, Banaras Hindu University, Varanasi, 1971.

Brockington, J.L., *The Sacred Thread*, Edinburgh University Press, Edinburgh, 1981 (1996).

Bryant, E.F. 'The Date and Provenance of the *Bhāgavata Purāṇa* and the Vaikuṇṭha Perumāl Temple', *Journal of Vaiṣṇava Studies*, 11.1, Fall 2002, pp. 51–80.

——— (trs), *Krishna: The Beautiful Legend of God (Śrīmad Bhāgavata Purāṇa Book X)*, Penguin Books, London, 2003.

——— 'Kṛṣṇa in the Tenth Book of the *Bhāgavta Purāṇa*', in Bryant, E.F. (ed.), *Kṛṣṇa – A Sourcebook*, Oxford University Press, New York, 2007.

Carman, J.B., *The Theology Of Rāmānuja*, Yale University Press, New Haven and London, 1974.

——— 'Rāmānuja', in Eliade, M. (ed.), *Encyclopedia of Religion*, vol. 12, Macmillan, New York, 1986.

Chadwick, H., *Boethius: The Consolations of Music, Logic, Theology and Philosophy*, Oxford University Press, Oxford, 1990.

Clifford, G.H., 'Līlā in the Bhāgavata Purāṇa', *Purāṇa*, 22.1, 1980.

——— 'Bhāgavata Purāṇa', in Rosen, S. (ed.), *Vaiṣṇavism*, Folk Books, New York, 1992.

Clooney, F.X., S.J., *Seeing through Texts*, SUNY Press, Albany, 1996.

——— 'Rāmānuja and the Meaning of Kṛṣṇa's Descent', in Bryant, E. (ed.), *Kṛṣṇa – A Sourcebook*, Oxford University Press, New York, 2007.

Dandekar, R.N., 'Vedānta', in Eliade, M. (ed.), *Encyclopedia of Religion*, vol. 15, Macmillan, New York, 1986.

Dasgupta, S., *A History of Indian Philosophy*, vols 1–5, Motilal Banarsidas, Cambridge, 1932, Rep. Delhi, 2000.

De S.K., *History of Sanskrit Poetics*, Firma KLM Private Limited, Calcutta, 2nd edn, 1960 (1976).

——— *Early History of the Vaisnava Faith and Movement in Bengal*, Firma K.L. Mukhopadhyay, Calcutta, 1961.

Delmonico, N.G., 'Sacred Rapture: A Study of the Religious Aesthetics of Rūpa Gosvāmin', PhD Thesis, University of Chicago, 1990.

De Smet, R., 'Towards an Indian View of the Person', in Chatterjee, M. (ed.), *Contemporary Indian Philosophy*, George Allen & Unwin, London, 1974.

Deutsch, E., *Advaita Vedānta – A Philosophical Reconstruction*, University of Hawaii Press, Honolulu, 1969.

——— 'Reflections on Some Aspects of the Theory of Rasa', in Van M. Baumer, R., and Brandon, J.R. (eds), *Sanskrit Drama In Performance*, University Hawaii Press, Honolulu, 1981.

Dimock, E.C., Jr, *Caitanya Caritāmṛta of Kṛṣṇadāsa Kavirāja – A Translation and Commentary*, Harvard University Press, Cambridge, MA, 1999.

Doniger O'Flaherty, W., *The Rig Veda*, Penguin Books, London, 1981.

——— (ed.), *Textual Sources for the Study of Hinduism*, University of Chicago Press, Chicago, 1990.

Dunuwila, R.A., *Śaiva Siddhānta Theology*, Motilal Banarsidass, New Delhi, 1985.

Farquhar, J.N., *An Outline Of The Religious Literature of India*, Motilal Banarsidas, by arrangement with Oxford University Press, New Delhi, 1920 (rep. 1984).

Flood, G., *An Introduction to Hinduism*, Cambridge University Press, Cambridge, 1996.

Gerow, E., *A Glossary of Indian Figures of Speech*, Mouton, The Hague, 1971.

——— 'Rasa as a Category of Literary Criticism', in Van M. Baumer, R., and Brandon, J.R., *Sanskrit Drama in Performance*, University of Hawaii Press, Honolulu, 1981.

Gonda, J., *Aspects Of Early Viṣṇuism*, Motilal Banarsidas, Leiden, 1954 (Delhi, 1993).

——— 'Vedic Literature', in Gonda, J. (ed.), *A History of Indian Literature*, vol. I, fasc. 1, Otto Harrassowitz, Wiesbaden, 1975.

Gupta, R., *The Caitanya Vaiṣṇava Vedānta of Jīva Gosvāmī*, Routledge, London and New York, 2007.

Haberman, D.L., *Acting as a Way of Salvation*, Oxford University Press, New York, 1988.

——— (trs), *The Bhaktirasāmṛtasindhu of Rūpa Gosvāmin*, Indira Gandhi National Centre for the Arts and Motilal Banarsidas, Delhi, 2003.

Hamilton, S., *Indian Philosophy – A Very Short Introduction*, Oxford University Press, New York, 2001.

Hardy, F., *Viraha Bhakti*, Oxford University Press, New Delhi 1983 (2001).

——— *The Religious Culture of India – Power, Love and Wisdom*, Cambridge University Press, Cambridge, 1994.

Hein, N., *The Miracle Plays of Mathurā*, Oxford University Press, Delhi, 1972.

Hiriyanna, M., *The Essentials of Indian Philosophy*, Mandala Books – Unwin Paperbacks, London, 1951 (rep. 1978).

Hopkins, T.J., 'The Social Teaching of the *Bhāgavata Purāṇa*', in Singer, M. (ed.), *Krishna: Myths, Rites, and Attitudes*, University of Chicago Press, Chicago, 1966.

——— *The Hindu Religious Tradition*, Dickenson, Encino, 1971.

James, W., *The Varieties of Religious Experience*, Longmans, Green and Co., London, 1907.

Jīva Gosvāmī, *Śrī Tattva Sandarbha*, translation and commentary Satya Nārāyaṇa dāsa and Kuṇḍalī dāsa, Jīva institute for Vaiṣṇava Studies, Vṛndāvana, 1995.

Joshi, R.V., 'The First Verse of the Bhāgavata-Mahāpurāṇa', *Purāṇa*, 6.1, 1964.

——— '*Catuḥślokī* or *Saptaślokī Bhāgavata*: A Critical Study', *Purāṇa*, 16.1, 1974.

Kane, P.V., *History of Sanskrit Poetics*, Motilal Banarsidas, Delhi, 1961.

Kapoor, K., *Literary Theory – Indian Conceptual Framework*, Affiliated East–West Press Private Limited, New Delhi, 1998.

Kapoor, O.B.L., *The Philosophy and Religion of Śrī Caitanya*, Munshiram Manoharlal, New Delhi, 1976 (rep. 1994).

Keith, A.B., *The Religion and Philosophy of the Veda and Upanishads*, Harvard Oriental Series, Motilal Banarsidas 1925, Delhi (1989), parts 1 and 2.

Kinsley, D.R., *The Divine Player*, Motilal Banarsidas, Delhi, 1979.

Klostermaier, K.K., *Mythologies and Philosophies of Salvation in the Theistic Traditions of India*, Wilfrid Laurier University Press, Waterloo, ON, 1984.

——— *A Concise Encyclopedia of Hinduism*, Oneworld Publications, Oxford, 1998.

——— *A Survey of Hinduism*, SUNY, Albany, 2nd edn, 1994.

——— 'A Universe of Feelings', in Bilimoria, P. and Fenner, P. (eds), *Religions and Comparative Thought*, Delhi, Śrī Śatguru, 1999.

Kohak, E., *The Embers and the Stars*, University of Chicago Press, Chicago, 1984.

Kulke, H., and Rothermund, D., *A History of India*, Routledge, London and New York, 3rd edn, 1998.

Larson, J.G., and Bhattacharya, R.S. (eds), *Encyclopedia of Indian Philosophies: Sāṁkhya – A Dualist Tradition in Indian Philosophy*, Princeton University Press, Princeton, 1987.

Lipner, J.J., *The Face of Truth*, SUNY Press, Albany, 1986.

——— *Hindus – Their Religious Beliefs and Practices*, Routledge, London and New York, 1994.

Lorand, R., *Aesthetic Order – A Philosophy of Order, Beauty and Art*, Routledge, London, 2000.

Lott, E., *Vedantic Approaches To God*, Macmillan, London, 1980.

Masson, J.L., and Patwardhan, M.V., *Aesthetic Rapture – The Rasādhyāya of the Nāṭyaśāstra*, Deccan College, Poona, 1970.

Matchett, F., *Logical and Ethical Issues of Religious Belief*, University of Calcutta, Calcutta, 1982.

——— 'Jñāna', in Eliade, M. (ed.), *Encyclopedia of Religion*, vol. VIII, Macmillan, New York, 1986.

——— Matilal, B.K., 'Dharma and Rationality', in Biderman, S., and Scharfstein, B.A. (eds), *Rationality In Question*, Brill, Leiden, 1989.

——— '*Bhakti* in the Bhāgavata Purāṇa', in Werner, K. (ed.), *Love Divine: Studies in Bhakti and Devotional Mysticism*, Curzon Press, Richmond Surrey, 1993.

——— *Kṛṣṇa: Lord or Avatāra?*, Curzon, Richmond Surrey, 2001.

——— 'The Purāṇas', in Flood, G. (ed.), *The Blackwell Companion to Hinduism*, Blackwell, Oxford, 2003.

Mauss, M., 'A Category of the Human Mind: The Notion of Person; The Notion of Self', in Carrithers, M., Collins, S. and Lukes, S. (eds), *The Category of The Person*, Cambridge University Press, New York, 1985.

Merrill, S.B., *Defining Personhood – Towards the Ethics of Quality in Clinical Care*, Rodopi, Atlanta, 1998.

Minor, R.N., 'The Gītā's Way as the Only Way', *Philosophy East and West*, 30.3, July, 1980.

Mishra, V., *Devotional Poetics and the Indian Sublime*, SUNY Press, Albany, 1998.

Monier Williams, M., *Sanskrit–English Dictionary*, Oxford University Press, Oxford, 1899 (1998).

Narayanan, V., *The Way and the Goal*, Institute For Vaishnava Studies and Center for the Study of World Religions, Harvard University, Washington, D.C., 1987.

Nelson, L.E., 'The Ontology of *Bhakti*: Devotion as *Paramapuruṣārtha* in *Gauḍīya Vaiṣṇavism* and Madhusūdana Sarasvatī', *Journal of Indian Philosophy*, 32, 2004.

O'Connell, J.T., 'Caitanya', in Eliade, M. (ed.), *Encyclopedia of Religion*, vol. III, Macmillan, New York, 1986.

Olivelle, Patrick, *Upaniṣads*, Oxford University Press, New York, 1996.

Overzee, A.H., *The Body Divine*, Cambridge University Press, Cambridge, 1992.

Parrinder, G., *Avatar and Incarnation – A Comparison of Indian and Christian Beliefs*, Oxford University Press, New York, 1982.

Parthasarathi, J., 'The Drāvida Veda-Vedāṅga: A Revolutionary Cross-Current', *Śrī Rāmānuja Vāṇi*, April 1981.

Pearsall, J. (ed.), *The New Oxford Dictionary of English*, Oxford University Press, Oxford, 1998.

Peterson, I.V., *Poems To Śiva – The Hymns of the Tamil Saints*, Princeton University Press, 1989 (rep. Motilal Banarsidass, Delhi, 1991).

Pollock, S., 'Bhoja's *Sṛṅgāraprakāśa* and the Problem of *Rasa*: A Historical Introduction and Translation', *Asiatische Studien/Études asiatiques*, 70.1, 1998.

——— 'The Social Aesthetic and Sanskrit Literary Theory', *Journal of Indian Philosophy*, 29, 2001.

Radhakrishnan, S., and Moore, C.A. (eds), *A Sourcebook in Indian Philosophy*, Princeton University Press, Princeton, 1957 (rep. 1989).

Raghavan, A.S., 'Ālvārs', in Raghavan, V., *Devotional Poets and Mystics* (part 1), Government of India – Publications Division, New Delhi, 1978.

Raghavan, V., *Bhoja's Śṛṅgrāra Prakāśa*, Punarvasu, the Theosophical Society, Adyar, Madras, 1978.

——— *History of Viśiṣṭādvaita Literature*, Ajanta Publications, Delhi, 1979.

Raju, P.T., 'The Concept of Man in Indian Thought', in Radhakrishnan, S. and Raju, P.T. (eds), *The Concept of Man*, George Allen & Unwin, London, 1960.

Rāmānuja, *Śrī-Bhāṣya,* trs Swami Vireswarananda, Advaita Ashrama, Calcutta, 1978.

Rangacharya, A. (trs), *Nāṭyaśāstra*, IBH Prakashana, Bangalore, 1986.

Rocher, L., 'The Purāṇas', in Gonda, J. (ed.), *A History of Indian Literature*, vol. II, fasc. 3, Otto Harrassowitz, Wiesbaden, 1986.

Rukmani, T.S., *A Critical Study of the Bhāgavata Purāṇa*, the Chowkhamba Sanskrit Series Office, Varanasi, 1970.

Śaṅkara, *The Bhagavad Gītā with the Commentary of Ādi Śrī Śaṅkarācārya*, trs Śāstri, A. M., 1897, rep. Samata Books, Chennai, 1995.

Sarma, D., *An Introduction to Mādhva Vedānta*, Ashgate, Aldershot, 2003.

Sarma, D. 'Mādhva *Vedānta* and Kṛṣṇa', in Bryant, E. (ed.), *Kṛṣṇa – A Sourcebook*, Oxford University Press, New York, 2007.

Satchidananda Murti, K, *Revelation and Reason in Advaita Vedānta*, New York, Colombia University Press, 1959.

Satya Nārāyaṇa dāsa, 'The Six *Sandarbhas of* Jīva Gosvāmī', in Bryant, E. (ed.), *Kṛṣṇa – A Sourcebook*, Oxford University Press, New York, 2007.

Schweig, G.M., *Dance of Divine Love*, Princeton University Press, Princeton, 2005.

Shakespeare, William, 'Romeo and Juliet', Clark, G.C., and Wright, W.A. (eds), *The Complete Works of William Shakespeare*, Parragon, Bath, 1895 (2000).

Sharma, A., *The Hindu Gītā – Ancient and Classical Interpretations of the Bhagavadgītā*, Open Court, IL, 1986.

——— *Classical Hindu Thought*, Oxford University Press, New Delhi, 2000.

Sharma, B.N.K., *Philosophy of Śrī Madhvācārya*, Motilal Banarsidas, Delhi, 1962 (rep. 1991).

Sharma, B.R., *The Concept of Ātman in the Principal Upaniṣads*, Dinesh Publications, New Delhi, 1972.

Sharma, R.P., *Human Personality in Ancient Indian Thought*, Kanishka Publishers, New Delhi, 2001.

Sheridan, D.P., *The Advaitic Theism of The Bhāgavata Purāṇa*, Motilal Banarsidas, New Delhi, 1986.

——— 'Śrīdhara and His Commentary on the Bhāgavata Purāṇa', in Rosen, S.J. (ed.), *Journal of Vaiṣṇava Studies*, 2.3, 1994.

Sheth, N., S.J., *The Divinity of Krishna*, Munshiram Manoharlal Publishers, New Delhi, 1984.

Shulman, D.D., *Lectures on Indian Poetry*, Ministry of Defence Publications, Tel Aviv, 1986 (published in Hebrew).

——— 'Remarking a Purāṇa: The Rescue of Gajendra in Potana's Telugu Mahābhāgavatamu', in Doniger, W. (ed.), *Purāṇa Perennis: Reciprocity and Transformation in Hindu and Jaina Texts*, SUNY–Sri Satguru Publications, Delhi, 1993.

Singh, M., *Bhoja Paramāra and His Times*, Bharatiya Vidya Prakashan, Delhi and Varanasi, 1984.

Singh, S., *Vedānta Deśika: His Life, Works and Philosophy*, Chowkhamba Sanskrit Series Studies, vol. V, Varanasi, 1958.

Sinha, J., *Indian Psychology, Emotion and Will*, vol. II, Sinha Publishing House, Calcutta, 1961.

Smith, C., *Moral, Beleiving Animals – Human Personhood and Culture*, Oxford University Press, New York, 2003.

Śrīdhara Swāmin, 'Bhāvārtha Bodinī', in Śāstrī (ed.), *Śrīmadbhāgavatapurāṇam*, Motilal Banarsidas, India.

Śrīnivasachāri, P.N., *The Philosophy of Viśiṣṭādvaita*, Adyar Library, Madras, 1943.

Śrīrāma Bhārati, *The Sacred Book of Four Thousand – Nalayira Divya Prabandham*, Sri Sadagopan Tirunarayanaswami Divya Prabandha Pathasala Jaladampet, Chennai, 2000.

Suthren Hirst, J.G., '*Bhakti* in Śaṅkara's Vedānta', in Werner, K. (ed.), *Love Divine: Studies in Bhakti and Devotional Mysticism*, Curzon Press, Richmond Surrey, 1993.

——— *Śaṁkara's Advaita Vedānta – A Way of Teaching*, RoutledgeCurzon, Abingdon, 2005.

Swami Gambhirananda (trs), *Eight Upaniṣads*, vol. I, Advaita Ashrama, Calcutta, 1957 (1991).

——— (trs) *Eight Upaniṣads*, vol. II, Advaita Ashrama, Calcutta (1990).

Tagare, G.V. (trs), *The Bhāgavata-Purāṇa*, in Shastri, J.L. (ed.), *Ancient Indian Tradition and Mythology*, Motilal Banarsidas Publishers, Delhi 1976 (1999).

Thibaut, G. (trs), *The Vedānta-Sūtras with the Commentary of Rāmānuga*, in Muller, F.M. (ed.), *The Sacred Books of the East*, Clarendon Press, Oxford, 1904.

Van Buitenen, J.A.B., 'On the Archaism of the Bhāgavata Purāṇa', in Singer, M. (ed.), *Krishna: Myths, Rites, and Attitudes*, University of Chicago Press, Chicago 1966.

——— *Rāmānuja on the Bhagavadgītā*, Motilal Banarsidass, Delhi, 1968 (rep. 1974).

Vatsyayan, K., 'Drama: Indian Dance and Dance Drama', in Eliade, M. (ed.), *Encyclopedia of Religion*, vol. IV, Macmillan, New York, 1986.

Venkatesachar, B., 'The Concept of the Finite Self in the Tattvavāda of Śrī Madhva', in Swami B.H. Bon Mahāraja (ed.), *Indian Philosophy and Culture – Quarterly Magazine of the Institute of Oriental Philosophy*, 8.1, March 1963.

Ward, K. *Concepts of God*, Oneworld, Oxford, 1987 (1998).

——— *Religion and Human Nature*, Oxford University Press, Oxford, 1998.

Wilson, H.H. (trs), *The Vishnu Purāṇa*, John Murray, London 1840.

Witzel, M., 'Vedas and Upaniṣads', in Flood, G. (ed.), *The Blackwell Companion to Hinduism*, Blackwell, Oxford, 2003.

Wulff. D.M., *Drama as a Mode of Religious Realization – The Vidagdhamādhava of Rūpa Gosvāmī*, American Academy of Religion Series 43, Scholars Press, Chico, CA, 1984.

Zaehner, R.C., *Hinduism*, Oxford University Press, Oxford, 1962 (1988).

Zimmer, H., *Philosophies of India*, ed. J. Campbell, Bollingen Foundation, New York, 1951 (rep. Motilal Banarsidass, 1990).

INDEX

www.ingramcontent.com/pod-product-compliance
Lightning Source LLC
Chambersburg PA
CBHW071522110726
47908CB00003B/921

* 9 7 8 0 7 5 5 6 2 7 3 1 8 *